Tales of

A NARRATIVE COMMENTARY
ON THE BOOK OF REVELATION

David L. Barr

POLEBRIDGE PRESS

Library of Congress Cataloging-in-Publication Data

Barr, David L.
    Tales of the end : a narrative commentary on the book of revelation / David L. Barr.
        p. cm. — (The storytellers Bible ; v. 1)
    Includes bibliographical references.
    ISBN 0-944344-66-6 (pbk. : alk. paper)
    1. Bible. N.T. Revelation—Commentaries. I. Title. II. Series.
BS2825.3.B22 1998
228´.077—DC21   97-3221
                                                                  CIP
                                                                  Rev.

Printed in the United States of America

10   9   8   7   6   5   4   3   2   1

For Mary Elizabeth Kenton
LOVER OF STORIES
AND OF STORY-TELLERS

TABLE OF CONTENTS

LIST OF TABLES

PREFACE

"I would ask you to remember only this one thing," said
Badger. "The stories people tell have a way of taking care
of them. If stories come to you, care for them. And learn to
give them away where they are needed. Sometimes a person needs a story more than food to stay alive. That is why
we put these stories in each other's memory. This is how
people care for themselves."[1]

BARRY LOPEZ, *Crow and Weasel*

Another Commentary on the Apocalypse?

Literary works, no less than children, are apt to answer only the questions
we ask of them. They do not often volunteer information on their own.
They only *seem* to be repositories of information available to any reader.
Even the most cursory review of the development of literary criticism will
show that each generation of critics brings new questions, new methods,
new concerns to the texts: one generation asks about the biography of the
author and the text's relations with contemporary events; another generation asks about the inner world of the text, disclaiming any interest in the
author; another is concerned about the structure of the text. Not surprisingly, each finds only what it is looking for.

This implies two important conclusions. We can never be through writing commentaries on literary works, for each new set of questions we bring
them will produce new interpretations, new insights, new answers. When a
friend asks, only partly in jest, why I would want to write another commentary on the Apocalypse—after nearly two thousand years hasn't everything
been said?—the answer is clear: this old work has more to say, if we can just
think of the right questions to ask it. Second, this commentary will differ
significantly from most other commentaries on the Apocalypse, because it
asks a different set of questions.

When commentators asked the Apocalypse to describe the end of the world and tell them when it would occur, they got certain kinds of answers back. All too often, these answers turned out to be nonsense, for the world has stubbornly refused to end. When commentators shifted their ground and asked, rather, that the Apocalypse describe life in the first century, another kind of answer echoed back. We have learned much about the Roman Empire, persecution and tolerance, the development of city life in Asia Minor, divergent forms of Christianity, and much else, by asking these questions. When we moved on to ask about the symbolic forms employed, the feelings expressed, the psychological states addressed, the social situation involved, we learned much about the deep human longings manifested here.

While informed by these earlier questions and answers, this commentary has other concerns. We ask the Apocalypse to answer our questions about stories, how they are told, whom they are about, what they consist of, where they go. These questions, often simple, will sometimes take on a complex character as we refine them in the light of recent studies of narrative. Technical vocabulary and scholarly disputes will be kept to a minimum, for our effort is to hear the answers not to display the questions. When other points of view need to be considered, when I want to refer to further reading, or add further comments that do not directly affect the argument, I have used endnotes. These notes are never necessary for following the main argument.

My hope is that this work will not be used simply as a reference work, as is usually the case with historical-critical commentaries. I do not think one can read a verse or paragraph of the story in isolation and understand it. Such a portion must be heard in the larger context of the scene, segment, and story of which it is a part. One must consider the setting, characterization, and sequence of action that leads to (and from) the incident. Thus the comments on each section begin first with these broader concerns and only then do we consider the details of smaller textual units. Ideally, one would read a section of the story in Revelation, read the comments on this section, and then reread the story. To avoid repetition and to direct the reader to broader issues, I have made frequent use of cross references.

The Book of Revelation has been subjected to much abuse by interpreters and I could offer no better preliminary advice than to forget whatever you have heard about its meaning and to read the book afresh. It was only when I began to listen to John's story without the prejudicial readings of my culture (particularly those readings by people who fancy themselves prophets) that I discovered what a wonderful story this is. You will find my understanding of that story in the pages that follow, but that is not my purpose. Rather, the purpose of this commentary is to provide the knowledge and resources needed for you to make your own fresh reading of John's Revelation as a story.

Of course Revelation is a strange book and one cannot expect to just pick it up and read it without some preliminary knowledge. The Prologue is designed to consider these necessary preliminaries. It is, in very general terms, the road map that will guide our whole journey. Then follow three further chapters, one on each major narrative unit in Revelation. Each provides a general overview of the unit and then detailed discussion of the structure, plot, characters, settings and other relevant details. The goal in each case is to assist you to make a viable interpretation of the story. The Epilogue reflects further on some of the underlying issues, such as the way this story has been used in America, the significance of this kind of literature, and the implications of this story for understanding its original audience.

The commentary is based on the Greek text of Revelation but the remarks are always oriented to the New Revised Standard Version. The Greek text is cited (in transliteration) and translated when necessary to see some interesting use of language.

Acknowledgments

While the writing of this book has been a solitary exercise it has never been an isolated one, and I am deeply grateful to all those who have aided me. First thanks must go to my colleagues in the Seminar on Reading the Apocalypse in the Society of Biblical Literature, from whom I have learned much about the Apocalypse, about literary theory, about social and ethical issues, and about differing ways of reading. While each member of the Seminar has in turn been my teacher, I learned special lessons from a few. From Michael Harris I learned more subtle literary analysis; from Elisabeth Schüssler Fiorenza I learned lessons in ethical responsibility; from Leonard Thompson I learned how to synthesize divergent views; from Tina Pippin I learned a playful seriousness with interpretation; from David Aune I learned the power of details. I will leave to them to judge whether the lessons they taught have been sufficiently assimilated to this manuscript.

Thanks are also offered to the many students, adult learners, colleagues, and friends who have discussed this material with me along the way. Of the many students who have thought their way through these preliminaries with me, many making valuable suggestions, I especially want to thank David Day and Kristi Grasse, who read and offered substantive comments on an early version of this material, and Marc Smith, who provided a close reading of the (near) final manuscript.

I am also deeply grateful to Wright State University and especially the College of Liberal Arts and its dean, Perry Moore, for on-going support of my research and, particularly, for the professional development leave that provided me sufficient extended time to finish this manuscript.

Finally, the vision, nurture, and balance of support and freedom provided by Alan Culpepper and Robert Funk in bringing this book—and the series it launches—to birth has been invaluable. The editorial work of Geneviève Duboscq of Polebridge Press has been thorough, intelligent, and genuinely helpful, for which I am most grateful.

Prologue
THE APOCALYPSE AS STORY

It is hard to follow one great vision in this world of darkness and of many changing shadows.[1]

BLACK ELK

Because it is part of the Bible, because it is used in our culture to advocate political agendas both of the left and right, because it utilizes an obscure set of images and ideas, because it is all divided up into neat chapters and discrete verses, because we are so familiar with a few of its symbols (such as the four horsemen or 666), it is easy to miss the most important thing for understanding the Apocalypse: it is a narrative. This commentary is an attempt to read the Apocalypse consistently as a narrative, ignoring for the moment its chapters and verses, its political application, its status as scripture, its use in theology. Rather than seeking its relation to history or its presumed views of the end-time, we seek its story.

The notion of story is both obvious and intuitive and incredibly difficult to define.[2] For our purposes it is sufficient to say that generally stories result from the telling of a sequentially related series of actions that make some reasonably unified impact on the hearer. Many things mitigate against our hearing the Book of Revelation (known also as the Apocalypse, the only New Testament writing known by two separate names) in this way: its complexity, its strange symbols, its foreign view of the world, its seeming incoherence at places, its ambiguous setting in place and time, and much else. The purpose of this section is to prepare for reading and hearing that story. The underlying principle of what's included here is: what is necessary for a modern American reader to enable her or him to hear the story of the Apocalypse?

Minimal preliminaries include having some sense of what the story is about (content), some clues as to how this content is being communicated (form), a general notion of how this material is arranged (structure and plot), an orientation to the characters in the story—including its audience

1

(characterization), some sense of the meaning of the strange creatures and mystical numbers we encounter (symbolization), and a placing of the story in time and geography (setting). Let us consider each of these.

The Content of the Story

The story it tells is complex, convoluted, fantastic, yet based on well-known historical events surrounding the life and death of Jesus of Nazareth. At this constitutional level the Apocalypse is like a gospel—it is a story about Jesus. But it is a different *kind* of story, one that projects its action on a cosmic screen, as a fundamental battle between good and evil. The audience knew this story well, just as the audiences of Greek drama knew the stories there told. Unlike modern stories, a part of whose pleasure is often the suspense about what is going to happen next, most ancient stories derive their pleasure from the ways they were told, the emotional and intellectual effects they had on the audience, and the convincing vision of life they could elicit.[3] We will give considerable attention to the *way* the Apocalypse tells its story—what modern literary critics call the *discourse* of the narrative.[4] But a more basic point needs to be explored first: the story underlying the Apocalypse is the story of Jesus.

This is suggested by the very beginning of the narrative, which in Greek is an incomplete sentence—a little irony in a work that seems to be about the completion of all things. A fairly literal English rendition of that sentence is as follows (try to imagine it said aloud in a proclaiming voice, rather like someone making an announcement):

A revelation of Jesus Christ
　　which God gave him
　　　　　to show to his servants what must occur speedily
　　and he signified
　　　　sending through his messenger to his servant John
　　　　　who witnessed to the word of God
　　　　　and the witness of Jesus Christ,
　whatever he saw.

This is our first clue to the nature and content of this enigmatic work, and it does in fact provide a lot of guidance. For the ancient reader/hearer it functioned somewhat like a book's title and preface function for us, orienting us to the work that follows. It was not uncommon for ancient writings to begin with a titular statement: both the gospels of Matthew and Mark do, as do most of the prophetic writings. This sentence fragment provides valuable signals for us about the meaning of what follows.

Most importantly, this declaration orients us to the content of this work: Jesus Christ. This is the revelation *of* Jesus Christ. Now the "of" construction is ambiguous in both English and Greek. Grammarians have technical names for such things; in this case they make a distinction between the objective genitive and subjective genitive. But since I can never remember which is which, I find it easier to distinguish between the case of ownership (a book of David Barr) and the case of subject or content (the Book of Job). In each case the "of"construction uses one noun to modify the meaning of another and so, in this case, to distinguish that book from other books. In the case of ownership it distinguishes one book from others by claiming it is mine; in the case of subject it distinguishes one book from others by saying that it is the one about Job. Using the "of"construction to indicate meaning or content is fairly common, for example in expressions like the message of the cross, the gospel of the kingdom, the life of freedom.

So the question is: does Jesus own the revelation or is Jesus the subject of the revelation? Jesus might own it insofar as it is a thing (this vision-book) or Jesus might define the significance of it insofar as it is a message— or could it be both? For the revelation is both this vision-writing and its significance. Each is "of Jesus." The story belongs to Jesus because he performs the central role in it: it is his story.

The recognition that the narrative of Revelation is about Jesus (not about the future or about the United States and Russia or about puzzles to solve) is for me the crucial insight for understanding this work. Much of its seeming ambiguity and cruelty takes on new meaning when seen in the light of the Jesus story. It is this insight that reveals Revelation to be a Christian work, and not the gory and vindictive story that so offended D. H. Lawrence.[5] To understand the Apocalypse we must always keep clearly in mind the struggle of Jesus with the evil powers of this world, their unremitting destruction of him, and his ultimate vindication—a vindication expressed by early believers as his resurrection from the dead and/or being raised to share the throne of God. The Apocalypse is in its most basic sense a retelling of this story of Jesus in a new way and with new images.

If we fail to recognize that this is the gospel story, it is because it does not come in a gospel form. It is a different kind of literature. It is Revelation Literature, the genre taking its name from the opening word of this writing. Scholars generally use the underlying Greek term, *apocalypsis*, and thus call a writing like this an *apocalypse* or, more generally, the kind of writing is called apocalyptic literature. A more technical discussion of the genre can be found in the Epilogue to this volume, but some general understanding of its aims and techniques is needed as we begin to read.

The Worldview and Genre of Revelation

The opening declaration provides a second important clue to the meaning of what follows, giving some insight into the worldview of this writing, for it is far different from the worldview of modern Americans. Whereas the American worldview is egalitarian with each individual having direct access to power, John's worldview is hierarchical and power is brokered through intermediaries. In theory (which is all that concerns this illustration) any American can call or write the President and express an opinion; John lived in a world where access to power was always through some intermediary—even in theory. The theory is sometimes called patronage.6 In the opening declaration the audience stands at the end of a chain of transmission that goes back through John, through an angel (messenger), through Jesus, to God. This gulf between John's world and ours (and this is only a hint of its extent) must be accounted for if we are to avoid the most serious sort of misreading.7

The worldview of Revelation is not only hierarchical, it imagines a certain corresponding relationship between the world above and the world below. This correspondence can be seen in the opening declaration in the use of the terms *signified* and *witness*. The usual English translation ("He made it known . . . " in RSV, NRSV, NIV, NEB, and JBP) of the clause I translate "he signified" obscures its meaning, for the Greek term, *sēmainō*, means to show by a sign, to give signs or signals. Now signs communicate because there is some sort of correspondence between the sign and the thing signified. This relationship can be either arbitrary (red means stop) or intrinsic (blood means life). The world we encounter in Revelation is a world permeated with significance; things mean things. This has two important implications.

We must never stop at the surface meaning of the text. What we see and hear are signs whose significance lies on some other level. The simple notion that a text means what it says is always inadequate, but with Revelation is always wrong. Revelation does not mean what it says, it means what it means. It is a book of signs. Further, signs are the only appropriate means of communication because the world imagined here exists on two levels: heaven and earth, above and below. And these two worlds are dynamically interconnected so that things done on one level affect things on the other level. This worldview of correspondence, though not unknown in America,8 is foreign to the dominant Protestant sensibility of our culture. A reader of Revelation must be prepared to enter this two-storied world, seeing and hearing things that mean more than meets the eye.

The multilayered reality can be glimpsed in John's description of his work as a witness to the witness of Jesus. Now witness is itself a two-faced word; it can mean both what one sees and what one says about what one sees. One is a witness both when one sees the accident and when one tells about it in court. But one's witness is not limited to one's words. In fact one's witness would ring hollow if contradicted by one's actions, like the person who advocates integration but lives in an isolated community, attends schools that have only one race enrolled, and belongs to clubs and groups that do not admit those of other races.

But of course the witness of Jesus is just the opposite of this. The witness of Jesus is first his action in life and death and then the report of that action. And notice that we have again that ambiguous of-construction: the witness *of* Jesus is both the witness that belongs to Jesus and the witness which is Jesus. Just so, John's witness mirrors that of Jesus, expressing his witness in both word and life.9 The chain of witness is not just words but deeds:

Jesus' Deeds ➡ Witness ➡ John's Witness ➡ Deeds of John

This mirroring of Jesus adds a horizontal complexity to the vertical layers, resulting in a narrative that is richly textured. Of course, looking in mirrors that reflect other mirrors can be very disorienting, but it is the very stuff of the world of Revelation.

The image of a mirror is not quite adequate for Revelation, however, for it is really a double or even triple mirror. On one side it is reflecting the life of Jesus, on another it is reflecting the contemporary experience of John and his communities, on yet another it is reflecting some notion of the world above, which is also construed temporally as the world of the future. It is a trait of the Apocalypse to do all three at once.

Many apocalypses are built on the narrative device of a dream, a vision, or a transportation to heaven. While in heaven, the seer is alternately baffled and instructed (often by an angelic guide) as to the real meaning of what is seen.10 Instructions and explanations are necessary because the things seen are often incomprehensible: strange animals, arcane actions, stylized numbers. We will see in the commentary that these symbolic elements began to form an idiom of their own, often retaining significant meaning as they were utilized in various apocalypses. Prominent among these are symbolic animals, colors, and numbers. Seven, for example, is always a symbol for perfection or completion (pp. 6–10). Familiarity with these other apocalypses will often help us decipher John's meaning.11 In addition, John will often tell us what his symbols mean. Thus at the end of the very first vision, he consciously interprets the two dominant symbols: the stars and the lampstands (1:20). The meaning of other symbols requires only a general knowledge of early Christianity; thus we know that the lamb on the heavenly throne is Jesus (chapter 5) as is the child born of the woman (chapter 12). We will look more closely at John's symbols in the next section, but the most important point to remember is: we are reading an *apocalypse,* which is a highly symbolic visionary form.

The Apocalypse of John is an even more complex form, including as it does the form of a letter and forms of prophetic speech. These will become clear as we read it, and these preliminary words about the nature of a symbolic vision are sufficient to allow us to read.

The Symbols of Sound and Sight

Not only is John's world multileveled and the experience multifaceted, looking to past, present, and future, but the vision itself is multimedia—both seen and heard. John witnesses to "whatever he saw" (1:2) and the whole of Revelation is presented under the guise of one vast vision. Hence the usual title give to the work is the Book of Revelation not the plural Revelations as one often hears in popular speech. But this vision itself contains both seeing and hearing, and often what is heard will interpret what is seen—giving the inner spiritual reality of the outward appearance.[12] But it will also work the other way, what is seen will reinterpret what was heard, for example in 5:1–10, where the vision of Jesus as lamb transforms the word about Jesus as lion. It is this unstable dynamic of word and sight that must be accounted for in our own appropriation of Revelation.

Because the ancient world comes to us silently, in mute monuments and in texts whose accents we no longer know how to sound out, we have often failed to grasp how noisy a world it was. This was true on every level from the everyday to the poetic. Listen to the curmudgeon Dio Chrysostom (ca. 40–120 CE) as he recalls a scene from a visit to Corinth at the time of the Isthmian Games (second only to the Olympics in the ancient world).

> That was the time when one could hear crowds of wretched sophists [rhetoric teachers] around Poseidon's temple shouting and reviling one another, and their disciples, as they were called, fighting with one another, many writers reading aloud their stupid works, and many poets reciting their poems, while others applauded them, many jugglers showing their tricks, many fortune tellers interpreting fortunes, lawyers innumerable perverting judgement, and peddlers not a few peddling whatever they happened to have.
>
> *Discourses* 8:9

He doesn't include the philosophers, like himself, proclaiming their wisdom from temple porches and city squares. It could be a noisy world, because everybody did things out loud.

More basically, all reading was done aloud, even private reading. Revelation itself clearly shows itself to be an oral experience, mentioning the public reader (1:3) and repeatedly urging the audience to listen: "the one who has an ear should hear what the Spirit says to the churches" (2:7, 2:11, 2:17, 2:29, etc.). It will thus be a good idea to do your reading of the Apocalypse out loud whenever possible. Train your ear to hear.

Many of the symbols of the story are better heard than seen—like the beast with seven heads. Artists have never convincingly drawn such a critter; one just runs out of places to attach that many heads. But one can easily hear what it meant, for seven heads represents perfect or complete authority. Just so the seven eyes of the lamb are better heard as perfect insight and not pictured (5:6). Again we are reminded that Revelation does not mean what it says. It means what it means. But how does one know what these symbols mean?

As suggested above, one source of information is the author's own interpretation. Table 1 lists at least a dozen instances when John explicitly labels the meaning of symbols. This helps, even if it doesn't resolve all our questions (just who the angels of the churches might be still presents a problem, for example). Nevertheless, what is intriguing about all John's own interpretations is how ordinary they are. God, churches, prayers, prophesying, the death of Jesus, and so on. This should caution us to keep our heads among all the bizarre symbols we will encounter (dragons, beasts, earthquakes, whores, battles) and remember we are probably talking about common elements of Christian tradition and experience.

A second source of symbol interpretation is to look to other literature of the period, especially other apocalypses and prophetic writings. We will discover an extensive web of interconnections between John's story and those of earlier prophets. Although John never quotes an earlier work, never cites scripture ("it is written"), never utilizes the fulfillment paradigm (this happened to fulfill what the prophet said),[13] the Apocalypse is replete with images and actions drawn from earlier works. I will follow the common literary terminology and refer to this as *intertextuality*, though that is

TABLE 1 *Symbols in Revelation*

Ref.	Symbol	John's Interpretation
1:8	Alpha and Omega	The One who was, who is, and who is coming
1:20	Seven stars and lamps	Angels and churches
8:3	Angel with censer	Prayers of the saints
10:1–11	Little open book	Must prophesy again
11:7	Great city, Sodom	Where the Lord was crucified
13:6	God's tabernacle	Those dwelling on earth
13:18	Six-sixty-six	Number of (a) human
14:14–20	Winepress	Wrath of God
17:9–15	Seven heads	Seven mountains and kings
17:12	Ten horns	Ten kings
18:21	Angel with millstone	Babylon cast down
19:8	The fine linen of the bride	The righteous deeds of the saints
19:11–16	One on a white horse	Word of God

TABLE 2 *John's Use of Numbers*

Three	The spiritual order
Four	The created order
Seven	Perfection (contrast six)
Ten	Totality
Twelve	Israel (God's People)
Three & one-half	The number of evil
Multiples & repetitions	Intensification

not entirely appropriate. John is not referencing a text as much as alluding to an oral tradition. Memory, not papyrus, seems to be the agency of appropriation.

In addition to works that John directly borrows from, we must consider other works similar to the Apocalypse with which his audience would be familiar. Audiences of apocalypses would expect certain images and symbols to have certain meanings. As a somewhat oversimplified beginning, we can say there are three standard categories of symbols widely used in apocalypses: numbers, animals, and colors. All of them possess fairly standard meanings.

For example, Earth was widely thought to have four corners, four winds, four directions—thus things in fours generally symbolize earthly realities. (Notice that the four horse riders in Revelation 6 represent our destruction of the earth.) Three, by contrast, is a heavenly number, associated with the divine in both Plato and Pythagoras. Aristotle associated it with the worship of the Gods.[14] Three and four together would thus represent fulfillment, perfection, wholeness and such—all traits of the number seven. That there were said to be twelve tribes of Israel, and twelve being the product of three and four, would have been felt to be significant. In short, the symbolism in Table 2 seems to undergird John's use of numbers. These are virtually all the numbers John uses, though there appear to be more because these basic numbers are manipulated in various ways. The two basic manipulations are squaring the number and multiplying by ten (or a hundred or a thousand); thus 144,000 redeemed mentioned in Rev 7:4 should be understood as (12 x 12) and (10 x 10 x 10) with the basic meaning of 12 and 10 (the totality of Israel or all God's people). And the blood from the grape harvest covers 1,600 stadia: 4 and 10—the whole earth. (One has to be careful with some modern translations that transform John's measures into modern terms. These 1,600 stadia become about 200 miles, which completely obscures John's number symbolism.) A less obvious manipulation involves taking the three and a half as years, then using either the number of months (42) or the number of days (1,260). But they are all three and a half, a broken seven, the time of evil.[15]

Colors too have relatively constant meaning, and they are not the meanings usually attached to them in our culture. White signifies victory (not necessarily purity), black represents suffering (not evil), red stands for strife and war, and pale (a kind of yellowish grey) signals death.

The basic meaning of animal symbolism is the contrast between the human and the bestial, good and evil, divine and demonic. But specific animals also take on special meanings. The horse generally refers to conquest; the lamb is the animal of sacrifice; the eagle, lion, and ox stand at the heads of their respective orders: the air, the wilderness, and the cultivated land. Multiple heads signify multiple rulers; multiple horns represent either a measure of power or multiple rulers.

Much of John's narrative becomes easily understood when we have recourse to such minimal decoding. Series of seven events no longer need to be read as a literal sequence, for we know that seven represents completion. Thus any sequence of any length will be a sequence of seven in John's system. If John says there are ten rulers, we don't need to try to count them or identify them. There will always be ten whenever John talks about the powers of this age. Grasping the significance of John's elemental symbolism will prevent the most naive kind of misreading and will prepare us to encounter the more dynamic symbolism of the narrative.

I do not want to give the impression, however, that John's symbolic narrative can be treated like a code book. The ciphers in a code have a one-to-one correspondence with meaning. Dot-dot-dot dash-dash-dash dot-dot-dot is universal Morse code for distress. That's what it always means; that's all that it means. Such is not the case with John's symbols. Symbols are, in modern literary terms, polyvalent: capable of multiple interactions, or as the medievals said, polysemous: many-seeded. A symbol does not so much *mean* something as it docs *imply,* so deciphering symbols is less a rational act than an imaginative act. It is thus of the utmost importance that we read the Apocalypse with our imaginations engaged.

There are many reasons why one might choose to communicate in symbols rather than in straightforward speech, but two seem paramount. First, symbols allow us to express what cannot be expressed in ordinary words. Thus our most cherished convictions—be they religious, political, national, or existential—find their expression in symbols: the cross, the yin-yang, Gettysburg, the flag, a bouquet of flowers. When the Chinese government sent in the armed forces to crush the pro-democracy demonstrations in 1990, one image was burned into the consciences of all who saw the lone man holding his ground in front of a tank, refusing to allow it to maneuver around him. This symbolic action communicated something more than a statement such as "we ought to resist tyranny."

Second, and related, symbols communicate on a different level than ordinary speech. They affect us deep down (by which language we suggest there is a depth to us beyond intellectual understanding). Symbols do not simply carry information; they reach out and take hold of us, demand our attention. John's book has that power once we prepare ourselves to receive its symbolic speech.

The Structure and Plot

The complexity of Revelation can be seen in the fact that there is no consensus on how we should organize or outline the material in the book. There are almost as many outlines as there are commentators doing the organizing. Scholars who look for additional sets of seven beyond those John explicitly numbered find them.[16] Those who look for parallels with the apocalyptic discourses in the gospels find them.[17] Those who look for chiastic structures* find them.[18] One point clearly emerges: how you arrange the material depends on what you are looking for. (For further discussion of the structure of Revelation, see pp. 148–49.) What we are looking for is the story told. If we look at the Apocalypse in terms of its action (understood as a series of causally connected events) a reasonably clear pattern emerges.

First, there is a strong correlation between the beginning and the ending—as we expect in a good story. Consider Table 3. There are at least eleven points of correspondence here, summarized in Table 4 (p. 12). But the parallels are more than just verbal and thematic, there is also a parallel of action. Set within the context of a letter that begins "John to the seven churches" (1:4) and ends with the letter formula so familiar from Paul's letters, "the grace of the Lord Jesus Christ be with all" (22:21), the action starts with John directly addressing the audience and describing his sojourn on Patmos where he has a vision (1:9–10). It ends with John again directly addressing the audience, saying this is what he heard and saw (22:8). It is the classic technique of the storyteller: I was off alone one day and I saw something very interesting. . . . This double envelope of letter and vision-report frames all the action of the story.

Thus the action portrayed at the beginning and end of the Apocalypse is continuous: John addressing the audience. In between, much else happens. Is this material also connected? Does it form a sequence? Or, in other words, does the Apocalypse have a plot?

At the heart of the notion of plot is the idea of a causal connection between events in a sequence. Aristotle defined plot as the relationship

---

*A chiasm takes its name from Greek letter Chi, which looks like an English X. In a chiasm the first and last items correspond, the second and next to last, and so on. Emphasis fall on the middle term, where the lines of the X cross.

between the incidents, the cause-and-effect logic that binds the incidents together and mandates that one follow the other.[19] E. M. Forster illustrates plot with the little story.

The king died and then the queen died.

This is a story, but it lacks a plot, for there is no cause-and-effect logic between the incidents. He suggests another story, one with a plot:

The king died and then the queen died of grief.[20]

TABLE 3 *Parallels in the Opening and Closing*

Opening	Closing
Revelation 1:1–4 The revelation of Jesus Christ, which God gave him to show his servants what must soon take place; he made it known by sending his angel to his servant John, 2who testified to the word of God and to the testimony of Jesus Christ, even to all that he saw. 3Blessed is the one who reads aloud the words of the prophecy, and blessed are those who hear and who keep what is written in it; for the time is near. 4John to the seven churches that are in Asia: Grace to you and peace from him who is and who was and who is to come, and from the seven spirits who are before his throne,	*Revelation 22:6–10* And he said to me, "These words are trustworthy and true, for the Lord, the God of the spirits of the prophets, has sent his angel to show his servants what must soon take place." 7"See , I am coming soon! Blessed is the one who keeps the words of the prophecy of this book." 8I, John, am the one who heard and saw these things. And when I heard and saw them, I fell down to worship at the feet of the angel who showed them to me; 9but he said to me, "You must not do that! I am a fellow servant with you and your comrades the prophets, and with those who keep the words of this book. Worship God!" 10And he said to me, "Do not seal up the words of the prophecy of this book, for the time is near.
Revelation 1:8 "I am the Alpha and the Omega," says the Lord God, who is and who was and who is to come, the Almighty.	*Revelation 22:13* "I am the Alpha and the Omega, the first and the last, the beginning and the end."
Revelation 1:10 I was in the spirit on the Lord's day, and I heard behind me a loud voice like a trumpet	*Revelation 22:17* The Spirit and the bride say, "Come." And let everyone who hears say, "Come." And let everyone who is thirsty come. Let anyone who wishes take the water of life as a gift.
Revelation 1:16–17 In his right hand he held seven stars, and from his mouth came a sharp, two-edged sword, and his face was like the sun shining with full force. 17When I saw him, I fell at his feet as though dead. But he placed his right hand on me, saying, "Do not be afraid; I am the first and the last, . . . " (See 1:4 above.)	*Revelation 22:16* "It is I, Jesus, who sent my angel to you with this testimony for the churches. I am the root and the descendant of David, the bright morning star." (See 22:8 above.) *Revelation 22:21* The grace of the Lord Jesus be with all the saints. Amen.

TABLE 4 *Points of Correspondence between the Opening and Closing*

Opening	Points of Correspondence	Closing
1:1, 4, 9	John names himself	22:8
1:1	An angel sent	22:6
1:1	Will soon take place	22:6
1:1	The servants	22:6
1:3	Reader blessed	22:7
1:3	The time is near	22:10
1:4	Grace to you	22:21
1:8	The Alpha and Omega	22:13
1:10	The Spirit	22:17
1:16, 20	Stars and angels	22:16
1:17	John falls at feet	22:8

Now a causal relationship exists—or can be imagined—between the incidents. Forster's point is a useful one, helping us see more clearly what is meant by causal connection. But I wonder if he gives the reader enough credit, for even in the first sequence one tries to imagine a connection between the events and may well have made a plotted story of them even before the writer supplied the explicit connection. Plotting—creating causal connections between events in a sequence—is a cooperative venture involving both author and audience. One should not assume that there is only one possible plot, except in the simplest of stories.

In fact, stories range over a spectrum from simple, unilinear, tightly plotted sequences (a joke) to complex, multilinear, sequences wherein any number of possible connections between events may be inferred (an epic). The Apocalypse is a complex story and no single reading will ever imagine all the possible connections between incidents. What follows is one reading of one set of interconnections.

One way critics simplify complex stories is by classifying incidents into two separate categories: kernels (incidents that are directly linked and determinative of the future course of the action) and satellites (incidents that orbit around these kernels adding nuance and complexity).[21] This is a useful tool, as long as we recognize that the selection of kernels is an interpretive act; different readers may see different relationships. Nor should we think kernel incidents are more important than satellite incidents. They are more significant for plot, but plot is only one aspect of story. Other incidents may be more important for other aspects. In fact, the satellites carry experiences and information crucial to the reading experience.

My own reading of the dominant line of action in the Apocalypse sees the story of the Apocalypse unfolding in three distinct and interrelated movements set in a common frame. Let me elaborate.

Within the frame account of John addressing the audience, John tells three stories. He begins with an autobiographical tale:

> I, John, your brother who share with you in Jesus the persecution and the kingdom and the patient endurance, was on the island called Patmos because of the word of God and the testimony of Jesus. I was in the spirit on the Lord's day, and I heard behind me a loud voice like a trumpet saying, "Write in a book what you see. . . . " REV 1:9–11

This first story segment details what happened to John on Patmos (a majestic human being appears to him and dictates seven messages to the angels of seven churches). Having finished this task, John is called up to heaven, where he observes a scene at the divine court. This second story segment concerns the process by which a slaughtered-yet-standing lamb opens a divine scroll and reveals its contents. John next looks into the heavenly temple and sees strange new signs. In this third story segment a cosmic dragon pursues a cosmic woman but is eventually defeated by a cosmic warrior, resulting in the establishment of a wholly new cosmic order.

I make two preliminary observations about these stories. First, they are ever more fantastic. The audience is led into ever stranger territory and witnesses ever more bizarre actions. From John standing on Patmos (a real world event), to the vision experience, to a trip to heaven, to a cosmic battle. Then back to earth again in the closing address to the reader. It is a fantastic journey—rather like a shaman's journey.22 In literary terms we find three different literary types sandwiched between realistic narratives of John on Patmos: the first vision is a revelation of a divine figure (a theophany), the second is a vision of the throne of God (a throne vision type highly developed in a kind of Jewish mysticism known as *Merkavah*), and the third is the story of cosmic war (a holy war).

Second, while these three stories are themselves sequences of causally connected action, there is very little connection between the incidents in the separate stories. Each sequence has its own logic, its own set of characters, its own base locale, and John plays a somewhat different role in each. These stories may be set forth schematically as in Table 5 (p. 14).

If I briefly sketch the action of each segment, two points will become clear: they each can be viewed as a unified action, but they do not form a causal sequence between them. I would characterize the kernel incidents of these stories as follows. One: A majestic human being appears to John on Patmos and commands him to write a scroll and send it to the seven churches of Asia. After a detailed description of this divine figure, the figure comforts John, explains particular symbols to him, and then dictates seven

TABLE 5 *Story Segments in Revelation*

	Movement One	Movement Two	Movement Three
Place	Patmos	Heaven	Earth
Characters	Jesus as majestic human John Churches	Jesus as Lamb-slain Elders and heavenly beings	Jesus as heavenly warrior Dragon and beasts Woman and her children
Action	Letter writing	Worship	War
John Presented as	Secretary	Heavenly traveler	Seer/prophet
Mythic Paradigm	Theophany	Throne vision	Holy war
Chapters	1–3	4–11	12–22

Note: Movement Three's new action begins with the heavenly temple's opening, 11:19.

messages to the angels of the seven churches. Two: John ascends to heaven at divine initiative, sees God on the throne surrounded by the heavenly court, and hears the heavenly liturgy. A scroll is presented that is sealed and that no one can open, causing John to weep. Then a character, announced as a lion but revealed as a slain-yet-standing lamb, proceeds to open the scroll in seven stages. In the silence of the seventh seal, seven trumpets sound, followed by the announcement: God's kingdom has come. Three: A majestic heavenly woman about to give birth is pursued by a heavenly dragon who seeks to consume her child. The woman is saved and the child preserved, but the dragon turns to make war on her other children. Two great beasts are conjured from the sea and the earth; the lamb gathers 144,000 on Mount Zion. Scenes of heavenly harvest predict earthly judgment, then enacted in seven plague events, leading to the great announcement: it is done. Just what is done is now related in two sets of scenes, one grouped around the great prostitute (war against heaven, heavenly warrior, destruction, a thousand years of peace, final battle, final judgment, new creation) and the bride/wife of the lamb (restoration of the city).

A third point can perhaps be added to these two: each of these story segments represents a different revelatory type: The first story is clearly a theophany; and the third is just as surely a holy war. I am not so clear how to characterize the second, except to say it is neither theophany nor holy war. While our knowledge of *Merkavah* mysticism is limited, there does seem to have been a throne vision genre, perhaps built on the famous vision in Isaiah 6. Some would also connect the throne scene with the rituals of the imperial court.[23]

Thus each of these three units can be viewed as a unified action, but what becomes obvious is that there is no real connection between the three actions. While one can point to strong thematic continuity between these

sections, there is not a continuity of action. The action of the first movement does not lead to that of the second or the third. They do not form a
causal sequence, yet within each movement there is a reasonably clear causal
sequence. How should we understand their relationship? Is Revelation one
story or three?

There is an O. Henry short story called "Roads of Destiny" that offers
some analogy to John's narrative strategy. In O. Henry's story a young man
leaves his native village to explore the world and write poetry. But when he
comes to a fork in the road, he cannot decide which way to proceed. So the
story is told showing him taking all three options: first he takes one branch;
then the second; and finally he returns to his village. For each path taken a
different series of events ensues, but each leads inexorably to the same end:
the young man is shot and killed—each time with the very same pistol. Now
clearly all three events belong in the same narrative, for the narrative could
not make its point without all of them. Yet just as clearly the actions within
each event can have no causal connection with actions in the other two; for
the initial act of choosing one road excludes the acts that lie down another
path. It would be to miss the point were we to ask whether our young man
went down path two *before* or *after* going down path one. The connection
is not one of before and after. What then are the connections between the
three?

These connections have to do with theme (destiny) and characters rather
than with continuous sequential actions. Yet they gain their meaning only
by being seen in comparison within the same narrative.24 When one finishes
O. Henry's story one understands the seductive/destructive allure of poetry
in a new way, a way that takes destiny beyond accidental encounters. One
also understands that action within a story is not necessarily sequential.

In a similar way, John's three dramatic actions do not constitute a
sequential, unified action. One does not happen before or after the other.
They represent alternative tellings of the story of Jesus with a common
theme and overlapping characters. The dragon does not attack the woman's
children (chapter 12) after Jesus dictates the letters (chapters 2–3) or after
the triumphant consummation of heavenly worship (chapter 11); that attack
is contemporaneous with the life of the church and is as old as Eve. Scene
three is a retelling of the story of redemption with a new focus. It is as if the
narrator finished the triumphant heavenly announcement that the kingdoms
of this world have become the kingdom of God and of the Christ (11:15)
and then turned to the audience and said, "Do you wonder how that came
about? Well, let me tell you. . . . " The focus now is on the attack of the
dragon and the ensuing cosmic war, with Jesus being presented in the guise
of the divine warrior.

Rather than one unfolding event, Revelation presents three interrelated
tellings of the story of Jesus.25 One does not lead to the other, yet they gain
their meaning by appearing together within the common frame of John's

vision and letter. The commentary that follows will explore their individual stories and their many points of connection, as well as the ways in which the audience's understanding is shaped by experiencing them.

The Audience and Characters

Modern literary studies have shown that the notion of the audience of a work of literature can be a very complex topic.26 Usually these studies are cast in terms of a "reader" since modern literature most commonly addresses its audience as a reader. But since the ancient audience consisted largely of listeners rather than readers, I prefer the neutral term audience. For our purposes we must distinguish at least two things we can mean by audience: the actual audience to whom this writing was read in first-century Asia Minor and the literary representation of those people in the writing itself. This latter group is often called the "implied audience" or the fictional audience or the authorial audience. It is the audience the author allows us to imply from the reading of the narrative. It will in some degree corre- spond to the actual audience, but it is certainly not the same. For example, the audience implied in the Apocalypse is intimately familiar with several writings from the Hebrew Scriptures, especially Ezekiel and Daniel, but whether all the actual hearers of the story really knew these writings may be doubted. The audience we meet in a text is the audience the author intends for us to meet, or more precisely, it is the audience the author wishes the real audience to imagine themselves to be.

In fact, in some ways this implied audience is very like one of the charac- ters in the story. It would be naive to assume that the audience implied in the narrative is the same as the real men and women to whom this story was told. It will be important for us to see that there might well be other ways of understanding the real audience besides the one the narrative presents us.

On the other hand, the real audience will be pulled toward this imagined audience. The real audience will have to become familiar with Ezekiel, for example, if they wish to understand the story told. And so will we. One value of delineating the implied audience is to be able to enter into the world the author creates for us. Reading literature demands nearly as much imagination from the audience as creating it demands of the author.

We meet this audience directly only in the frame narrative (1:1–11 and 22:6–20), but of course they are always listening to the story even when we cannot see or hear them. We will gradually build a more complete picture of them as we work our way through the narrative. For now it is sufficient if we understand that the audience we meet in the story is not simply the his- torical audience and that by paying attention to this implied audience we can discover strategies to assist our hearing of the story. We will consider the audience more fully in the Epilogue. Now let us briefly consider the other characters in the story.

Quite a lengthy list of characters appear in John's story, though many of them have only cameo roles. You can find a list in narrative order in the appendix. Here I venture three generalizations: two quite different types of characters are included (realistic and fantastic); certain characters belong properly to one of the three story segments but also turn up in segments where they aren't expected; and many characters travel under more than one name.

CHARACTERS FROM DIFFERENT WORLDS: EARTH AND BEYOND

While it is obvious that John's two worlds, the above and the below, will produce two different types of characters, we might not be prepared for all the sorts of folk we will meet in this story. In addition to the various earth dwellers we might expect (including John, the seven churches, the reader, the hearers, Antipas, Jezebel, kings and ordinary people), and in addition to the heaven dwellers we might expect (God, Jesus, Spirit, angels of various types, the dead), John includes an entourage of extraordinary others. These include the slain-yet-standing lamb, the woman clothed with the sun, a great red dragon, beasts (from the pit, from the sea, from the land), a heavenly warrior, a spectacular whore, and a heavenly bride. Where do such characters come from and what do they reveal about the nature of this story?

We might ask the question this way: in what sort of story might one find a dragon, a woman in danger, and a rider on a white horse? I know of only two types (if we discount computer games): legends and myths. Legends are hero tales from the distant past in which uncanny events occur and often involve journeys into other worlds. The medieval romance was built on such legends. Myths are stories of divine figures, often recounting what happened "in the beginning," and always revealing basic aspects of what the world is really like. In this regard, John is closer to myth; at least he derives his characters from a standard stock of ancient mythology.

The oldest version of the myth of the battle between the divine young warrior and the chaos dragon stretches back to ancient Babylon—as long before John's time as John is before ours. In that story Tiamat, portrayed as a sea dragon, decides to eliminate all the Gods for they have become too noisy. The Gods of course regret this but none of them is powerful enough to stop her. After deliberation, they decide to each invest one of their number, the young warrior Marduk, with their special powers. Thus endowed, Marduk battles and slays the dragon, creating humans from her shed blood.[27] Then, after judging the deeds of the others, Marduk marries and reigns over all. Clearly John has heard the story; just as clearly he thinks the true version applies to the true ruler, the resurrected Christ.[28]

This identification of Christ with the warrior God is, of course, in some tension with the gospel tradition of Jesus as the one who turns the other

cheek, even to the point of his unjust death. This is one of the major problems any consistent interpretation of Revelation must work out. But John is
not afraid to present the story of Jesus in daring new forms.

WHICH CHARACTERS IN WHICH STORY?

Of course this characterization of Jesus as the heavenly warrior occurs
only in the third movement of John's story, although the motif is alluded to
already in the first movement (2:16). But this is to misstate the case somewhat. What we actually find in the three movements is three separate sets of
characters, which we identify with continuing persons underlying the narrative. Thus, in the first movement we are presented with a majestic figure
designated in the story as "one like a son of humanity." This is a literal
translation of the Greek *huion anthropou*, which has come into English as
son of man. The origin of the phrase is much disputed but certainly owes
something to the vision in Daniel 7 where the son of humanity is contrasted
with the beasts, thus contrasting Israel's humanity with the bestial nature of
her enemies. This emphasis on the humanity of the person is thus one basic
aspect of its meaning.[29] Now it will be obvious that this character is "really"
Jesus, but we ought not let that identification obscure the fact that *in the
story* we encounter a heavenly human being whose narrative role is to carry
the action of the first movement.

In the second movement we encounter the figure of the slain-yet-standing lamb—again clearly referring to Jesus. In the story the lamb character
sits on the throne with God and opens a sealed scroll—tasks we might have
trouble attributing to a lamb. We will need to ask why this characterization
was used in this story.

In the third movement, Jesus first appears as the newborn son of the
heavenly woman, thus echoing the characterization in the first movement.
This figure later appears as a rider on a white horse, descending from
heaven. It is easy to see how this character fits the story of the battle with
the dragon. But John obscures the issues by inserting the lamb figure into
this third movement as well, both as the leader of the gathered army of
God's people (14:1) and—more surprising still—as the husband of the
heavenly woman who descends at the end of the story. Even more distress-
ing, she is portrayed as a city! An odd marriage indeed.[30] The son of
humanity also appears briefly (14:14).

Other characters too seem to wander onto the wrong set. The beast, for
example, belongs in the third movement of cosmic war, but already makes a
cameo appearance within the second movement (11:7). The army of
144,000 gathered to resist the beast in the third movement were introduced
in the second movement (7:4)—and they are led by the lamb of the second
movement (14:1).

What we find, then, are three sets of characters in three scenarios, with some overlap—John, for example, appears in all three as a character—and some migration. Characters from one scenario appear in another scenario without introduction and without commentary or explanation. This raises two questions: what does John gain by this technique? And why do readers generally accept it?

ALIASES AND DISGUISES

Audiences do seem to accept this mixing of characters without much protest. Few commentators even bother to comment on it. I suspect that the reason for this is that each of these characters is really a pseudonym. Consider John's late introduction of the dragon in chapter 12:

> The great dragon was thrown down, that ancient serpent, who is called the Devil and Satan, the deceiver of the whole world—he was thrown down to the earth, and his angels were thrown down with him.   REV 12:9 (also 20:2)

A name and four aliases! Or is it five aliases? In any case the audience understands that the characters in the story are also characters beyond the story, so that the story functions as a kind of allegory on life. Again we are confronted with a two-plane system. Wandering characters do not bother us because we know that on some higher plane the son of humanity, the lamb, and the heavenly warrior are the same person. Thus when the lamb shows up in the war scene as head of an army (!), we accept it because we know who the lamb is.

Then what is gained by this shifting of names and characters? Precisely a new perspective on this higher plane. By choosing to show Jesus, or Satan, or the community of believers as one character or another the writer highlights one aspect of their identity. An army headed by a slain lamb implies a rather unusual conception of warfare. It will pay to keep close track of how each is being characterized at each point in the story.

The Time and Place

From within the perspective of the story, everything in Revelation happens in one day—the Lord's day (1:10). This is what we will call the fictional setting of the first narrative level. At this level, all the action takes place on the island of Patmos on the Lord's day. If we move deeper into the story, we find other times and other places. After transcribing the letters to the seven churches, for example, John moves from Patmos to heaven. Although the time frame remains indeterminate, the action seems to be a heavenly worship scene and thus not unsuited to the time frame of the Lord's day.

Beginning with the vision of the heavenly woman (chapter 12), however, both the time and place within the story become very vague. John seems suspended somewhere between heaven and earth, able to participate in both. Time too seems suspended. Everything happens in quick succession. There are no markers of days or weeks or seasons. More can be said about the story time and we will give detailed attention to it in the commentary that follows; for now it suffices to be aware of the difference between story time and historical time. We must take seriously the fact that we are reading a narrative work and not naively assume that the times and places we read of in the story are the actual times and places of the audience of the work. Thus, John is not necessarily on Patmos when this story is being presented to the seven churches. His Patmos location in the first segment of the story is no different from his location in heaven in the second segment. Nor, given the nature of John's symbolism, should the seven churches be taken literally. There would be *seven* churches whether John intended his work to be read by one or a dozen congregations.

This realization significantly complicates our attempt to delineate the actual historical time and place of the writing of the Apocalypse. There are some ameliorating circumstances. The seven churches are named and they correspond to known cities located in a rough circle in the Roman province of Asia. In addition, things said to each church often correspond to some known local condition.[31] This gives us some confidence that the writing should be located in this general area.

We know a good bit about the area from archaeological and literary sources. It was a fairly well-to-do region and these cities were leading cities of the area—six of them being the capitals of their region.[32] Nor were these hard times; this region was at the height of its prosperity.[33] The number of new public buildings undertaken in the first and second centuries is quite astonishing: my own rough count showed twenty-two at Ephesus and eleven at Pergamum, the only two sites for which we have a sufficiently large number of datable structures to hazard a count.[34] The first and second centuries were a time of increasing prosperity for the region. Prosperity, of course, is never evenly distributed and, as in all the provinces, there was an elite minority strongly attached to Rome and a much larger majority tired of high taxes and foreign domination. The area was prone to rebellion.

The situation of Christians in the area is subject to considerable debate. There are two basic positions: those who think that there was some rather deliberate and intense persecution of Christians and those who think there was little, if any, persecution. While the former is the standard view, I am more persuaded by the latter. If we take the Apocalypse itself as evidence only for what is happening in the story rather than as historical evidence, there is little to support the thesis of persecution.[35] For the time being it will be sufficient to keep an open mind on the issue.

A precise dating of the book is impossible. Again there are two major views: the time of Nero (late sixties) and the time of Domitian (late nineties). In favor of the Neronian date is the fact that some of the material in the book seems to fit Nero precisely (such as the decoding of the numerical puzzle 666; see the commentary on 13:18). In favor of the Domitian date is the clear statement by the late second century author Irenaeus (ca. 180), who says that the Revelation "was seen no long time ago, but almost in our own day, towards the end of Domitian's reign" (*Against the Heretics* 5.30.3).

My own view is that the question is wrongly put. We give too much credence to the story incident that John received this entire revelation in one day on Patmos. More likely, the work contains the visions of a lifetime, together with John's reflections on them. They were perhaps "written" over the course of decades, perhaps beginning in or shortly after the time of Nero and achieving their final form near the end of the first century. That at least is a hypothesis against which we can test our actual reading of the work.

Making an Interpretation

Every literary critic faces a great problem. We believe on the one hand that we have read a literary work with sufficient attention to know what it is about, to understand it, even to be able to explain it to others. On the other hand, we are convinced that a literary work is untranslatable; what it says cannot be said in some other way and still be the same thing. It is to this paradox that Archibald MacLeish pointed in his poem, "Ars Poetica":[36]

A poem should be palpable and mute
As a globed fruit
Dumb
As old medallions to the thumb
Silent as the sleeve-worn stone
Of casement ledges where the moss has grown—
A poem should be wordless
As the flight of birds
A poem should be motionless in time
As the moon climbs
Leaving, as the moon releases
Twig by twig the night-entangled trees,
Leaving, as the moon behind the winter leaves,
Memory by memory the mind—
A poem should be motionless in time
As the moon climbs
A poem should be equal to:
Not true

For all the history of grief
An empty doorway and a maple leaf
For love
The leaning grasses and two lights above the sea—
A poem should not mean
But be.

In addition, most of us are convinced that literary works are capable of
more than one interpretation. In fact, it is nearly impossible to write a document that is not capable of more than one interpretation; witness how difficult it is to write a contract with a determinate meaning—and notice that
the closer one comes to this goal the less readable the document becomes,
until only lawyers can understand it. And of course the great number of
commentaries written on the New Testament writings is ample testimony to
their indeterminate nature. This, of course, raises the question of the relationship between these interpretations. Are they all valid? Are some valid
and others wrong? Are they all wrong?

If this were a multiple choice test, I would have to choose "all of the
above." All interpretations that are grounded in what a text actually says are
to some degree valid. All interpretations are partial and fragmentary, however, and thus to some degree wrong. But some are more partial, more
faulty, more wrong, than others. Or to be positive, some interpretations are
more authentic than others. Why is this so?

It is important to raise the question of how we make an interpretation.
This is an enormously complicated subject, but let's make it as simple as
possible. Let's say that I make an interpretation when I read something and
then tell someone what it means. What is hidden in such a simple sentence?
We can note three important ambiguities. First, we must ask what we mean
by *read*. Reading is not simply decoding a string of letters. When we read,
the words elicit a scenario in our minds, an image or a hypothesis of what
meaning is intended. As we read on, the scenario shifts—as it is confirmed,
modified, or contradicted by further reading. The effect of a joke, for example, depends on its ability to take us in, deceive us into thinking along one
scenario and then surprising us with a new meaning that incorporates all the
data of the former into a different scenario.

> A rather gruff-looking fellow walked into a bar in Ireland with a huge alliga-
> tor under his arm and brusquely demanded of the bartender, "Do you serve
> protestants here?" Somewhat intimidated the bartender replied, "Yes, of
> course." To which the fellow responded, "Fine, a double Scotch for me and a
> protestant for my 'gator."

Most stories do not contradict the early scenarios, but all interesting stories
will evolve and challenge a reader to adopt varying perspectives on the

action. Reading is not a straightforward experience that simply adds up the meanings of the words on the page. It is a creative endeavor.

Second, hidden between the two verbs of my sentence (read . . . tell) is a presumed third action: understand. Here we enter murky waters indeed. Attempts to teach computers to understand even simple speech demonstrate how little we know about this process. I once saw a demonstration of a sentence we would all be able to interpret:

Time flies like an arrow.

But how do we know *flies* is the verb? What if *like* is the verb and time flies are analogous to time bombs? Or what if *time* is the verb and flies the object of our imperative to compare their speed with that of an arrow? We know, I suspect, because we have a general experience of the world that makes these alternatives unacceptable even if grammatically possible. But this appeal to the reader's experience raises a whole new issue, for no two readers will have the same experience.

This leads us then, third and most importantly, to the subject of my sentence: the "I" who "reads, understands, tells." Just what is the role of the reader in interpretation? On one extreme are those who claim everything for the reader. Without the reader a text means nothing; we might even say it does not even exist until someone reads it. Without a reader a text is only marks on a page, at most a potentiality. Meaning then becomes a function of the reader, so all interpretations are valid because each is determined by the individual reader.[37]

At the other extreme are those who say the reader is only actualizing the potential of the text. Thus meaning resides in the text. If a reader does not have the "right" experience, one misreads the text and has only a faulty interpretation.[38]

There is a third alternative, of course, that gives authority *both* to the reader and to the text. While a given text might not determine our reading it does constrain it. A reading that can be shown to violate the ordinary reading of a text will be recognized as wrong, perhaps even humorous. A former student tells of playing tennis with a friend at a neighboring private school. The sign on the court plainly stated:

Faculty Only No Students Allowed

Uneasy about this, my student protested only to be told that the sign clearly permitted their playing tennis, for it should be read: Faculty Only? No! Students Allowed.

This creative misreading confirms our suspicion that there is a point at which a reading of a text loses credibility. Texts permit more than one reading; literary texts permit various readings; no text permits just any reading. Texts control readings, but so do readers.

Literary texts especially invite a variety of readings, for they leave much to the imagination. We must imagine scenes, characters, connections; we must infer motives, values, character; we must reconstruct past events, relationships, sequence. As one critic illustrated:

> Two people gazing at the night sky may both be looking at the same collection of stars, but one will see the image of a plough, and the other will make out a dipper. The "stars" in a literary text are fixed; the lines that join them are variable.[39]

Given this understanding of text and interpretation, it is clearly not my task as a commentator to tell you what Revelation means. Not only is it impossible to extract a meaning from a text, it is also impossible to provide a reading that is relevant to other readers. A reading of Revelation for blacks living under apartheid in South Africa may be moving, but it will lack a certain relevance for those of us living in a representative democracy.[40] And our reading may seem trivial or unimportant to those living under tyranny. So my reading is mine; you must make your own.

Rather than providing a meaning or even a reading, this commentary will provide the literary and cultural tools that will open Revelation to your reading.[41] Or perhaps I should say open the story to your hearing, for we must always remember that this was primarily a story heard not a text studied. Revelation stands on the boundary between the oral story that was unique each time it was repeated and the fixed text to be studied and compared with itself and with earlier texts. It was a text meant to be read aloud. Such an aural appropriation of the story would not fixate on small details and would not demand exact consistency. Hearing the Revelation was an experience meant to transform the listener. Learn to listen.[42]

The Letter Scroll

REVELATION 1:1–3:22

Every short story is essentially a story of revelation, either
the hero's or the audience's.[1]

THOMAS M. LEITCH, *What Stories Are*

Overview of the Unit

The section contains a short preface (1:1–3), a letter opening with a doxology (1:4–8), an inaugural vision (1:9–20), and messages to seven churches (2:1–3:22). The inaugural vision and the messages comprise the first major movement of the story which we might summarize as: The risen Christ appears to John and dictates individual communications to the seven churches, though this hardly captures the rich texture of image and action found here.

Orienting the Reader: The Author's Preface

The shift from scrolls to bound pages as the medium of writing was just beginning when Revelation was written, but our author clearly maintained the older technology. He uses the term for scroll at 1:11, 5:1; and 10:2. Thus the original reader would have been presented with a roll of papyrus, a sort of stiff paper, perhaps about twenty feet long, rolled from one end.[2] It would be read by unrolling a portion, revealing a narrow column of writing, and then rerolling the front portion as you progress through the writing. The writing would have been in all capital letters with no spaces between words and few indicators of how it was to be read—what we call punctuation. Reading a new document at first sight was so difficult that it was considered a remarkable feat.[3] Someone intending to read in public would spend hours practicing, perhaps even being trained by the original writer. In part because of this difficulty in grasping the sense of the writing, all reading was done out loud, even if one were reading by oneself.* More commonly, one heard a writing read aloud to a group.4

Writers developed a great variety of techniques to assist the reader and to enable the listening audience to understand. We will discover many such devices in Revelation: repetition, parallelism, chiasm, formulas, numbering. Two devices are found in this opening: titling and framing. Obviously a scroll could not have a title page, nor did handwritten manuscripts or even the first printed books.5 How then would an author title a writing? Either such information was lacking altogether (as in the beginning of John's gospel) or it was incorporated into the opening sentence (as in the beginning of Mark, Matthew, and Luke). This opening could vary from a bare title (Mark) to an elaborate preface (Luke). Revelation occupies a middle ground, with a clear title and enough additional information to orient the reader.

THE OUTSIDE FRAME: THE SPEAKING VOICE

Apocalypsis Iēsou Christou—Revelation of Jesus Christ—is the opening declaration and it functions as the title for the work. It also gives this work its two common English titles: the Apocalypse (deriving from the opening Greek word) and the Book of Revelation (deriving from the meaning of the word by way of the Latin, *revelatio*). Ironically, Roman Catholics, who traditionally relied on the Latin *Vulgate*, prefer the title Apocalypse; Protestants, who traditionally insisted on returning to the Greek original, tend to use the Latin derivative: Book of Revelation. I will use the two titles interchangeably. The title actually extends through verse two, a lengthy sentence fragment whose clarity of meaning helps us overlook the fact that it has no main verb. (For a translation and additional discussion see the Prologue, pp. 2–3.) We are told at the very beginning that we will hear a story about Jesus Christ, one mediated to John by a messenger from God in words and visions. What more can we learn from this voice?

First, it raises the question of *point of view*, a term with both a literal and a figurative meaning. Literally, point of view means through whose eyes does our perception of events come? Figuratively, it means through whose values, interest, or ideology. Even when we were children we understood enough about stories to recognize that it is important to know whose point of view a story is told from, and we were careful that our parents always

---

*This situation is nicely illustrated in a story recorded in Acts, when Philip *hears* a fellow reading as he travels in his chariot. He asks him, "Do you understand what you are reading?" Rather than being offended, the fellow responds, "How can I unless someone guides me?" Reading was a difficult skill for which people did not mind admitting they needed help. The closest modern analogy would be to see someone studying a campus map; they would not be offended if you offered them assistance, for "map reading" is not a highly developed modern skill.

heard *our* version of the events, rather than that of our sibling, a version focused through our experience and values. The heart of the literary notion of point of view is this sense of *focalization:* whose experience and values focus this story? Where does this person stand: in space? in time? in convictions? in relation to the author? in relation to other characters in the story? in relation to the audience?

Whose voice is this anyway? The voice of God? of Jesus? of John? of someone else? The reader cannot be sure at this point—an important ambiguity that colors much of the following story. Whatever its source, the voice boldly declares, in this the outermost frame of the narrative, the nature and origin of our story: it is a revelation of Jesus Christ . . . given by God. Thus the implicit point of view is divine; God is the ultimate source of this story. Or so our author would have the audience believe.

Second, the voice introduces us to some of the main characters of the story: God, Jesus, the messenger (in Greek: *angelos*, angel), servants, John (who, the voice implies, is the author of what follows). There is no description of these characters, though a certain affinity between them is clear; the implication is that the audience already knows who they are. Both the nature of these characters and the identity of the implied audience will come more clearly into focus as our story proceeds.

Third, the voice names what follows a "revelation." The Greek word is *apokalypsis,* from the root *kalupto* (to cover, hide) and the preposition *apo* (off, from), thus meaning: to unveil, remove the covering, make naked. The word could be used literally of uncovering one's head, for example, or metaphorically of uncovering one's mind, to reveal what one is thinking. Metaphorically, then, the word has the sense of a discovery, the making of a revelation. There is some evidence that the bringing of such revelations was a common component of early Christian worship. At least Paul described the worship practice of the Corinthians as a mutual sharing of gifts: "When you come together, each one has a hymn, a lesson, a revelation [apokalypsis], a tongue, or an interpretation" (1 Cor 14:26). We cannot be certain that the communities to which this work is addressed constructed their worship out of these same elements. Corinth is on the Greek mainland across the bay from the Asian cities addressed in Revelation, and Paul wrote decades earlier. Nevertheless, it is a reasonable hypothesis that they had a good deal of experience with "revelations."

Another factor supporting this hypothesis is the existence of a large number of works of "revelation" in the surrounding cultures—both Jewish and Greek. Jewish writers had been constructing apocalypses for more than two centuries by the time John wrote.[6] Already the Book of Daniel, in the Hebrew Scriptures, has many of the characteristics of an apocalypse. Symbolic dreams and visions are given to a prophetic figure who, with the aid of a divine messenger, interprets their meaning (see especially Daniel

7–12). In addition there were numerous compositions written in the names of Enoch, Ezra, Isaiah, Baruch, Abraham, and other ancient worthies. And analogous revelatory writings can be traced in Greek, Persian, and Egyptian contexts.[7] There are numerous other Christian apocalypses and several traces of such literature within the New Testament: Jude, 2 Peter, Mark 13, Matthew 24–25, 2 Thessalonians 2, for example.[8] Thus such revelations were a well-known literary type. John's book would not have sounded nearly so strange to its original audience as it does to us.

Fourth, the voice makes certain assumptions about the world that will orient us to the story that follows. John does not get this revelation directly from God, for example, or even from Jesus; rather, it proceeds through a complex chain of transmission: God to Jesus to messenger to John to servants. The spiritual world envisioned here mirrors the political world of the Roman era, where a remote emperor ruled through a series of representatives. The story world, like the life world of the audience, is hierarchical, with all power and action flowing from above.

This world above has been opened to John; he has seen something; and now he is bearing testimony to it. This is the overarching frame on which our story is woven. Its warp and woof is the subtle interplay between the verbs: show, see, hear, tell—verbs that will recur throughout the story. Its fabric is further defined as "the word of God and the testimony of Jesus Christ." Both are complex phenomena. The *word of God* is both what John hears in the story, a present speaking, but also what John hears as he reads the scrolls of scripture. John will never cite scripture in his story, but the allusions to it, paraphrases of it, and creative recasting of scriptural scenes and words pervade this story. The *testimony of Jesus* also exhibits two sides: it is both the testimony *about* Jesus (that is, the gospel story) and the testimony *belonging to* Jesus (that is, what he testified). His ultimate testimony is his death, so the two are not in any real tension. The Greek word for testimony is *martys*, which already here seems to be on its way to meaning the ultimate testimony of laying down one's life: martyr. For a discussion of the ambiguity of the "of" construction and the meaning of the title (Revelation of Jesus Christ) see the Prologue, pp. 2–3.

The ancient audience is thus oriented by this opening voice to receive a story: the owner and subject of this story is Jesus; its content the word of God. The author is John, who received it from the heavenly world via a messenger of Jesus. The story itself is called an apocalypse, a revelation.

The voice now continues for one more sentence, boldly setting the stage on which the following story is performed:

> Supremely happy the one reading aloud and the ones hearing the words of this prophecy and keeping the things written in it; for the opportune-time is near . . .   REV 1:3 (author's translation)

This sentence both reveals and hides the identity of the speaker. On the one hand, we can now see clearly the implied setting of the story: a group of people have gathered together and an individual reads these words to them. So the manifest identity of the speaking voice is that rhetor—the public reader who also functions as the narrator.* It was the one reading aloud who announced that this is the Revelation of Jesus Christ. But this leads to a difficulty which immediately revokes this obvious identification: the point of view of this sentence is clearly not that of the rhetor; someone else pronounces the blessing. Whose voice is the rhetor reading? On one level, at least, the rhetor is reproducing the voice of John, the author implied in the opening statement.

This would not be an unusual experience for someone in the ancient world, where reading was always done aloud and usually in groups. Silent reading was virtually unknown in the Greco-Roman world, and written documents were so expensive (and libraries rare) that public readings were fairly common. So most people could be expected to be familiar with the scene set by this opening: a rhetor enacts these words in front of an audience already familiar with the major characters. But the rhetor does not speak only for John.

For the form of this statement, a beatitude, implies that John speaks for the divine. Certain people in that world were felt to have special powers with words; they were inspired by some divine being and spoke blessings or curses with divine force. Such figures were seen as prophets, magicians, or sorcerers. By speaking John's words out loud, the reader once again empowered them. (The Greek word translated "to read" is *anaginosko*, from roots that mean to come into being once again. A reader was someone who caused words to live again.) So at a second level, this voice speaks for the divine.

We have, thus, a telescoping point of view: rhetor < John < Divine. In this case, the divine includes not only God, but Jesus and the messengers who serve as intermediaries. This ultimate, complex point of view, in which each lower-level voice embodies and includes the voice of those above, pervades all that follows; but the immediate point of view, as witnessed by the characters in the story, shifts as the narrative shifts from one level to another. Sometimes they hear the rhetor, sometimes John, sometimes the Divine.

---

*Whether this setting is to be understood as the actual setting of the work or only as the fictional setting need not yet concern us, though it is a question that will demand to be answered before we finish with our reading. What we encounter here is a strikingly complex situation in which the literary work appears in the literary work we are reading: the effect can be rather like looking in a mirror at yourself looking in a mirror. I am reminded of an absurd scene in the movie *Spaceballs:* when the villains cannot locate their escaped foes, they get the videotape of their own movie and fast-forward to the point of the escape and so discover where their prey have fled. Needless to say, the time distortion is disorienting. But we shall see that the time distortion of the Apocalypse is also great.

THE INNER FRAME: THE WRITTEN LETTER

Such a shift of narrative level and point of view occurs in the second preliminary section: 1:4–8. Here we encounter all the trappings of an apostolic letter and the direct voice of John:

John to the seven churches, the ones in Asia,
grace to you and peace
    from the one who is, who was, and who is coming and
    from the seven spirits, the ones before the throne, and
    from Jesus Christ,
        the witness,
        the faithful,
        the firstborn from among the dead, and
        the ruler of the kings of the earth.

To the one loving us and having freed us from our sins by his blood,
    And he made us a kingdom,
    priests to God and his father;
to him be glory and power unto the ages, amen.
    Behold he comes with the clouds,
and every eye will see him, and whoever pierced him,
and all the tribes of the earth will wail on account of him.
Yes, amen.

I am the Alpha and the Omega, says the lord God,
the one who is, who was and who is coming, the ruler over all.

                                      (author's translation)

These words would have been immediately recognized as a letter by the original audience. The form of the letter was well established, both in general and in specifically Christian circles.[9] In its most basic formulation, a letter consisted of: the names of the sender and the receiver, followed by a wish/blessing and a thanksgiving, leading to the body of the letter (often finishing with exhortations to moral behavior), and closing with a blessing on the readers. So important did the letter-form become to early Christians that eventually only gospels and letters were accepted for reading aloud in church.[10]

The expectations aroused by the letter-form would have included such things as learning about the situation of an absent friend, anticipating a request of some sort, hearing someone else speak for the absent one—embodying their voice, so to speak. It seems likely also that Christians in Asia Minor would have associated such letters with services of worship, due to the enormous influence of Paul in this region. John satisfies these initial expectations: his opening, including the "Grace and Peace," is standard. Instead of a thanksgiving, we find a series of liturgical sentences in a proto-trinitarian configuration: God, spirit, and Jesus. This is the first mention of the spirit, strangely absent from the opening declaration.

Aside from the spirit, these other characters were already introduced in the opening statement: God, Jesus, John, and the servants—now further characterized as the seven churches in Asia. At least the churches and the servants are functional equivalents as the implied recipients of the communication. The messenger of the opening is not mentioned, perhaps substituted for by the spirit.

Each of these characters receives initial development in the liturgical sentences attached to this letter opening. *God* is characterized by relation to time: the one who is, who was, and who is coming (Greek: *ho ōn, ho ēn, kai ho erchomenos*).[11] *The one who is* reaches back to the ancient self disclosure of the God of Israel to Moses in the prelude to the Exodus story. When asked for a name, God is said to have replied, "I am that I am" and added, "Say that I Am has sent me to you" (Exod 3:14). It became quite common among Jews of the Greco-Roman era to refer to God as *ho ōn*, literally the being or as I have translated it here: the one who is. This was the preferred expression of Jews trying to relate their tradition to Greek philosophical speculation which conceived of God as "being itself" rather than as a human-like person. Some, like Philo of Alexandria, even went so far as to refer to God as *to ōn*, the neuter form ("that which is"). All such references to God as Being are grounded in the Exodus story; this is the first of many echoes of the Exodus we will hear in this story.

To hear that God is and was naturally leads the hearer to expect that God "will be,"[12] but John studiously avoids positing a future for God, using instead the expression *the one coming*. We must resist the temptation to transform it into "the one who will come;" it is a present, not a future, participle. It is important for understanding the temporal point of view of this story to understand that one of its characters knows no future. Instead, God is said to be the One Coming; such coming will be a major motif of the story.[13] Thus the human characters, including the implied audience, may approach a future, but only to find God already there, coming to meet them.

In strict parallelism, grace and peace are also said to be from "the seven spirits who are before his throne." That the one who is should sit on a throne will not surprise us, though this is the first such political reference. Throne imagery will dominate the vision in chapter four. That there are *seven* spirits would be puzzling, if we were not familiar with the conventions of visionary, symbolic writing in John's time, which used numbers to signify qualities not quantities. The quality of the number seven is a divine quality, signifying fulfillment, perfection, and completion. (For a preliminary overview of such number symbolism see "The Symbols of Sound and Sight," pp. 6–10.) John signifies the quality of the spirit as seven/perfect not a quantity of spirit by this symbol.

We will have to return to this understanding of numbers repeatedly in what follows, but we can catch a small glimpse of the way ancient peoples grasped the meaning of numbers in this excerpt from a Jewish writer in Alexandria near the beginning of the first century:

> So august is the dignity inherent by nature in the number seven, that it has a unique relation distinguishing it from all the other numbers within the decade [the first ten numbers]: for of these some beget without being begotten, some are begotten but do not beget, some do both of these, both beget and are begotten: seven alone is found in no such category. *On the Creation* 99

By "beget" here Philo means a number generates another number from one to ten by being doubled or tripled; being "begotten" is to be produced in such a manner. So one through five all beget; six, eight, nine, and ten are all begotten. Seven alone remains ungenerated and ungenerating. In this way it is a fit symbol for God, understood by Greeks as the unmoved mover—the first cause, itself uncaused. This is admittedly a strange way to look at numbers; but it was widely felt to be true in the world in which the Apocalypse was produced. With this background, we can see that "seven spirits" is a symbolic way to point to the spirit of God.

The same may be said for the *seven churches*. While John does name seven actual cities in 1:11, the number is chosen for its qualitative not its quantitative significance. There were many more than seven churches in the province of Asia (western Turkey, today). To write to seven is to write to the divine entirety, the whole church. It is interesting to speculate why these seven were named and not others. Perhaps they were the most important centers, perhaps they were where John's influence was strongest; perhaps they each typified situations John wished to address. We will see that each of the seven is also symbolic of larger realities.

Even so, setting the scene with seven spirits has a certain dramatic effect, recalling both an ancient cosmology and a biblical scene. A cosmology is a picture of how the world is put together (cosmos=world), and these seven spirits are also found in a picture of the world deriving from Babylonian astrology, which taught that the cosmos consists of seven spheres or seven heavens, presided over by seven spirits of God and visible in the five planets, the moon, and the sun.[14] Jewish tradition seems to have picked up and modified this system, imagining seven archangels before God (see Tob 12:15). John's conception has perhaps moved further into symbolism, but the fact that the "reality" echoes this astrological worldview would present a convincing case to those listening. The biblical scene which John may also be echoing is found in Zechariah 4, which we will discuss in connection with the lampstands in the inaugural vision.

Finally, John adds *Jesus Christ* into the parallel construction with God and the spirit, carefully attributing characteristics that are important in the story that follows. Jesus is *the witness* because he bore testimony to God's truth. In the Apocalypse such witness is closely associated with sacrificing one's life, and in this case it points to Jesus' death. The *faithful* highlights Jesus' devotion to the divine mission; it is a trait that John will return to repeatedly. *The first born among the dead* is clearly a reference to Jesus' resurrection, but understood as a preliminary to a general resurrection. Such a general resurrection was widely expected by many Jews, and seems to have been especially keenly anticipated by many early Christians. *The ruler of the kings of the earth* completes the sequence: vindicated by the resurrection, Jesus has been exalted to heaven where he now rules. (These attributes of Jesus may stem from a meditation on Psalm 89 where witness, faithfulness, firstborn, and ruling are combined in a lament for the fallen king.) The lack of a future tense verb here is quite shocking, for we might expect John to say that Jesus will rule.

The majesty of this conception seems to prompt John to utter three liturgical sentences, praising Jesus and God. Such liturgical language is appropriate both to the letter form (which itself had become a liturgical performance) and to the implied setting of the opening voice: a community gathered to hear the reading, with the implication that they have gathered for worship.

These sentences also provide more insight into the *point of view* from which the story is to be told. Every story is told from some perspective, which we call the point of view of the narrator. Thus a story that began, "I remember a long time ago, when I was but a lad. . . . " is being told from the viewpoint of an old man. Most narrators stand at the end-time of the story, else they could not tell it. Only when a narrative is told through the limited perceptions of one involved in the story do we have a sense of a limited temporal point of view. Such is the case here.

Consider John's declaration, noticing especially the tenses, "He is coming with the clouds; every eye will see him, even those who pierced him; and on his account all the tribes of the earth will wail. So it is to be. Amen" (1:7). We encounter here our first future tense, combined with a present tense and a past tense. The implication is that the speaker stands *after* the time Jesus was "pierced" (past tense) *at the time* when Jesus "comes with the clouds" (present tense) but *before* "every eye will see him" (future tense). This rather unusual temporal point of view, placing the story at the time of Jesus' coming, should be marked well for it will greatly assist in hearing the rest of the story.

The base vision itself occurs "on the Lord's day" (1:10)—a day of present experience that also looks to the past (the day of Jesus' resurrection) and the future (the day of Jesus' coming). This ambiguity creates a shifting temporal point of view that may simultaneously speak from the past, the present, or the future.

In addition, these liturgical sentences imply a certain conviction, revealing another aspect of point of view, a figurative aspect often called the ideological or conceptual point of view. By this is meant the norms and general worldview through which the characters and actions are evaluated. Thus the audience is instructed to hear the story that follows as those who worship and anticipate the complete revelation of the one whose blood has freed them from their sins. They see this one as already having begun the resurrection of the just and as, even now, ruler of the kings of the earth.

We find, then, that attention to the narrative elements of this opening section leads us to expect a story quite different from the interpretation of Revelation most common in American culture. There is little emphasis on the future; the content and owner of the story is Jesus; the scope of the story extends from his witness to his rule. This story has devolved in hierarchical stages from God to John who shares it with those who serve God (the church) in a setting best understood as itself a service of worship. Before we turn to the story itself, let us take a brief look at the way elements from this opening frame are echoed in the closing.

THE BACKSIDE OF THE FRAME: PARALLELS IN THE CLOSING

We saw in the Prologue (pp. 10–16) that there are a significant number of verbal and thematic parallels between the opening and closing sections of Revelation. Here we want to pursue a bit more the continuity of action in these two sections. The exact limits of these two sections are subject to some debate, but setting such limits is not of much concern to a narrative approach, especially when we recognize the oral mode of the work. Thus the opening initiates the letter form (1:4) and the closing concludes like a letter (22:21). In both sections we have what appears to be a kind of liturgical dialogue that could involve audience response (1:6 and 7; 22:20).[15] And in both cases there is a direct address to the implied audiences, in fact, the implied author appears on stage:

I John, your brother . . . heard. (1:9–10)

I John am he who heard and saw these things. (22:8)

The opening and closing then provide a frame around the narrative, so that the main story does not begin until after the first address, and it ends before the second.

From a literary perspective we have a story within a story; the outer frame is the narrative of the telling of the central story. In fact, the outer frame is bipartite: the oral voice and the written letter, both of which envelop and contain the story that follows.

From a social perspective these frames provide an example of boundary crossing. There are numerous times in our lives when we cross over the boundary of ordinary reality into some special enclave, where the rules and procedures of everyday life no longer pertain: a ball game, a theatrical performance, a movie, a trip. In each case there are transitional events to guide us over the boundary and back: the little rituals at the beginning and end of the game; the curtain rising and falling; the lights dimming and brightening and the credits written on the screen; the steward welcoming you on board and wishing you a good trip as you leave. Within these enclaves we experience another world—an altered state of consciousness, so to speak. It is no longer three o'clock; it is the seventh inning.[16]

Just so the Apocalypse imagines that it conducts its audience into an altered state of consciousness, a new reality. In this new reality Jesus stands in the midst of the churches and instructs them (1:17–2:1). In this new reality one witnesses the ceremonies of the throne room of God in heaven and sees the results of what happens there (4:1–2). In this new reality one observes the futile attack of the powers of darkness and experiences their ultimate defeat (12:1–4). It is a story that becomes progressively esoteric, moving from earth to heaven to realms of spiritual warfare, until finally the author draws us back to our senses, back to our ordinary world (22:8). Only at that point, the world will never again appear ordinary.

Having provided us with an implied audience (people of the Greek cities of Asia Minor who are familiar with John, Jesus, God, etc.), an implied setting (a worship assembly), an implied author (John), a narrator (the public reader), some generic indicators (the letter form and the form of the symbolic vision), as well as some indication of the temporal, spatial, and ideological points of view, our story begins.

The Story of Jesus' Letters to the Churches[17]

The first major section of the Apocalypse stretches from 1:9 through 3:22, a scene in which the risen Jesus appears to John on a deserted Aegean island and dictates seven messages to be sent to the messengers of the seven churches mentioned in the frame letter. (For a view of the relation of this event to the rest of the story of Revelation see pp. 10–16, including Table 5.) We will first trace the point of view expressed in the scene, then examine the plot significance of the action portrayed, explore the characters involved, and finally develop a portrait of the implied audience.

THE SHIFTING POINT OF VIEW

While the ultimate point of view remains that of the rhetor-narrator of the frame, that rhetor takes on several masks in this scene. Notice how within a couple of minutes of time, the audience would hear the rhetor declare, "I am the Alpha and the Omega," "I John," and "I am the first and the last" (1:8, 9, 17), alternately enacting the voice of God, the voice of

John, and the voice of Jesus. First the rhetor addresses us as John (1:9), then in the persona of John-in-the-spirit speaks as Jesus (1:10–11), the voice which eventually dominates the scene (all of 2:1–3:22), but a voice which is also attributed to the spirit (2:7, 11, etc.).

Thus when we ask the traditional questions about the psychology of the narrator, namely, is the narrator limited or omniscient in perspective and is the narrator a character in the story or a voice beyond the story, we must answer like the logic teacher who responds to an either/or-question: yes. While the rhetor is a character in the frame story, he or she is not a character in the central story. To the extent the rhetor remains the narrator of the central story, he or she remains the voice of the implied author—a voice from the outside. Yet this voice never breaks into the telling of this scene; there are no comments, inner views of characters, or other evidence of this narrator's presence. This ultimate narrator remains entirely covert in the printed story, though, of course, in the oral situation the audience would be hearing his or her voice.

The overt narrators, John and Jesus, each speak in an appropriate way. John narrates from only a limited point of view, having no extra knowledge of either events or of the inner life of other characters. He is portrayed as confused and fearful (1:17) and needs to have things explained to him (1:20). He reports only what he heard and saw. Not so with Jesus. He claims to surpass temporal limits (1:17) and says he will reveal both "what is and what is about to occur" (1:19). He repeatedly claims to know the inner life of the seven churches (2:23),[18] to know the future (2:10), to know them better than others do (3:1), better even than they know themselves (3:17). His words can be equated with the voice of the Spirit (2:7, 11, etc). This character-narrator is unlimited either by time, by knowledge, or by space. Needless to say, he is completely reliable and closely allied with John who, in the frame narrative, becomes his voice. It would be hard to imagine a device that would give more weight to the messages narrated.

In fact John has obscured both ends of this communication. Rather than an address from John to the churches, these are messages from Jesus to the angels of the churches. Such a device allows John to maintain his position as "brother" and still offer the most authoritative praise and blame.

FOLLOWING THE PLOT

The narrative of Revelation is very confusing partly because the narrative repeatedly shifts from one level to another; already we have experienced the level of the rhetor narrating the letter of John to the churches; John narrating his experience on the island; and Jesus narrating his letters to the churches. Only the middle one of the three is told *as* a story; we begin by looking at the level of John telling his story.

The Plot of the Inaugural Vision, 1:9–20

John's experience on the island of Patmos is the glue that holds the entire narrative of the Apocalypse together. The work is explicitly a telling of what happened to him on a certain day in a certain place. This is the primary level of story beyond the frame. John's recounting of his experience will extend throughout each section of the book, but within this first section, this story is rather simple. In synopsis:

> I John your brother and partner . . . happened to be on the island called Patmos. . . . And it happened that I was in the spirit on the Lord's day and I heard behind me a great voice—like the voice of a trumpet—saying: what you see write in a scroll and send to the seven churches. . . . And I turned to see the voice which spoke with me. When I turned I saw seven golden lampstands and among the lampstands one like a human being. . . . And when I saw him, I fell at his feet like one dead. And he placed his right hand on me saying: Fear not. . . . Write what you saw. . . .   (author's translation)

A specific dictation to each of the seven churches follows.

We find here a tightly plotted explanation for the existence of the seven letters: John writes them because he has been comforted and commanded to write; he is comforted because of a terrifying sight; he saw this sight because he happened to be in the right place and time. It is a not unlikely story. It shows John's method of gradually enchanting the reader/hearer, leading us into ever more fantastic territory.

The story becomes even more plausible when we consider its relations to other stories that were known to its earliest audience, for aspects of this brief scene echo scenes in other Jewish literature. This practice of cross-referencing other stories, alluding to other literature, is usually called *intertextuality* today. While the name is certainly not appropriate for the largely oral culture of the Apocalypse, the phenomenon is nonetheless real. Even with this caveat, I will use the notion of intertextuality both because it has become a standard literary term and because we experience both the Apocalypse and its intertexts as texts. Briefly, intertextuality refers to "the relation(s) obtaining between a given text and other texts which it cites, rewrites, absorbs, prolongs, or generally transforms and in terms of which it is intelligible."[19] In fact, intertextuality works two ways: the older writing influences how one hears the newer; but the newer writing now also shapes how one understands the older.

Revelation reverberates with echoes of earlier, usually prophetic, literature. Table 6 (over) displays the echoes an attentive hearer might have detected in the Patmos scene. Such echoing not only adds to the verisimilitude of the story (such stories have been known to occur before), it also enhances the credibility of the visionary. The audience is perhaps supposed to think that since this vision is not unlike those of old, this too must be a

TABLE 6 *Intertextual Echoes in the Opening Scene*

Ref.	Other Literature	Echo
1:9	Dan 8:15; 1 Enoch 12:3; 4 Ezra 3:1	Prophet names self in vision scene
1:10	Ezek 3:12, 2:2	Hears loud sound behind him while in the spirit
1:12	Zech 4:2	Lampstand, seven lamps
1:13	Dan 7:13, 10:5	One like a human being Clothed, girded with gold belt
1:14–16	Dan 7–10	Elements of the description: white hair, fiery eyes, brasslike feet
1:15	Ezek 43:2	Voice like many waters
1:16	Isa 11:4; 49:2	Sword (rod) of mouth
1:17	Dan 10:7–9	Vision causes prophet to fall to the ground
1:18	Dan 10:10–11	Seer touched by visionary visitor, comforted and addressed

true prophet. The critic must also raise the question of whether such extensive echoing of earlier writings does not indicate that, in part at least, John's visions are a carefully crafted composition.

The following notes are designed to help you read this scene and understand its symbolism and allusions.

REV 1:9–20 *Readers' Notes on the Inaugural Vision*

Rev 1:9

BROTHER Metaphor deriving from an understanding of the community as a new family, thus implying a rejection of traditional family relationships. Where leaders are brothers rather than fathers or elders, the community is more egalitarian than hierarchical.

PERSECUTION Though in some ways a key concern of Revelation, this actual term occurs only five times: 1:9; 2:9; 2:10; 2:22; and 7:14.

KINGDOM A very old, complex, and multiform idea.[20] The underlying idea goes back to the time centuries before John when Israel was ruled by kings who were thought to be reigning for God or in God's stead (see Psalms 2 and 72). Gradually the idea was variously interpreted to include any sense in which God could be said to rule on earth.

PATIENT ENDURANCE A key concept for this work, best defined by its contexts, which are 1:9, 2:2, 2:19, 3:10, 13:10, 14:12. This latter verse sets it in parallel with keeping the commandments of God and holding fast the faith of Jesus. Elisabeth Schüssler Fiorenza suggests that it be understood as "consistent resistance" to the powers of evil which seek to undermine God's rule.[21] This more active sense seems to fit John's message better than the passive sense of endurance.

PATMOS An island off the coast of Asia Minor, probably inhabited in John's day, but only sparsely. There is no evidence that it was ever used as a Roman penal colony in spite of many assertions to the contrary. John's allusive reason for being there ("because of the word of God and the testimony of Jesus") could be understood in three ways: he is there for retreat (perhaps to edit his visions for publication); he is there to spread the gospel of Jesus; he is there as punishment (banished, or more technically, relegated there by Roman authority). How the reader chooses to construe this will have a major impact on how one reads the rest of the story.22

Rev 1:10

IN THE SPIRIT Indicates either a trance-like state in which visions were received or a state of spiritual awareness. Notice that the English, like the Greek, could shift meanings by simply re-punctuating: "I . . . was on the island called Patmos. Because of the word of God and testimony of Jesus, I was in the spirit." Of course John wrote without any punctuation. The text is open to both readings.

THE LORD'S DAY An unusual expression which could be understood as either the Lord's day (Sunday) or the Imperial day. The implied contrast between Jesus and emperor will become increasingly important as the story progresses. The expression could also be understood in three temporal senses; the Lord's day as Sunday (present), as Easter (past), and as judgment day (future; compare the expression "day of the Lord"—Isaiah 13, Joel 2, etc).

Rev 1:11–12

SEVEN CHURCHES The symbolic use of the number seven should be emphasized: the whole church is addressed. At the same time seven specific cities are mentioned: Ephesus, Smyrna, Pergamum, Thyatira, Sardis, Philadelphia, and Laodicea. Geographically, the list represents the cities one would come to if one left from Patmos and sailed to the coast of Asia Minor and then proceeded in a rough circle of about sixty miles in diameter, going first north then east. These are major centers, generally the dominant city of their regions. For comments on each city see the next section.

SEVEN GOLDEN LAMPSTANDS The first echo is probably to the seven-branched lamp of the Temple in Jerusalem, representing the presence of God. There is also a sense of the lamp as witness, and seven for perfection. See also the analogy with the seven stars noted below.

Rev 1:13-16

THE SON OF MAN Literally, son of humanity, this phrase is rich in contextual meanings. In Ezekiel it refers to the prophet; in Daniel it refers to a heavenly archetype of Israel; in early Christianity it refers to Jesus. It is difficult to translate the sense into English, for it is built on a Semitic notion that "son of" indicates likeness to (as the "sons of thunder" in Mark 3:17). Thus in the Daniel vision the contrast is between the beastly figures of the previous visions with the one like "a son of humanity" (i.e., a human being). The significance, then, is an exalted figure who is truly human.

ROBE Such a long robe would be a sign of status, perhaps royal or priestly; see Isa 6:1.

GIRT BENEATH THE ARMS Again a sign of status, ordinary folk girded their robes at the waist or hips to facilitate movement.

EYES . . . FIRE Certainly penetrating, discerning, perhaps also with a suggestion of judgment or even anger. The enraged Agamemnon is described as having "two eyes that showed like fire in their blazing" (*Iliad* 1.104).

SEVEN STARS The connection of lamps and stars would be natural for people who thought in terms of a two-leveled reality, with a correspondence between the above and the below. Stars above and lamps below both give light. In a Jewish interpretive work, called the Targum on Exodus, the seven branched lamp in the tabernacle is equated with the seven planets and also with "the just that shine unto eternity in their righteousness."[23]

TWO-EDGED SWORD Outside Revelation this peculiar word for sword occurs only at Luke 2:35, of the sword that will pierce Mary's heart. Within Revelation it is used of the sword of Jesus' mouth at 1:16; 2:12; 2:16; 19:15; and 19:21; and once of the sword of Death (6:8). "Two-edged" is literally "two-mouthed," apparently from an ancient metaphor for the biting power of the weapon. The symbolism here suggests that it be understood as the word of Jesus, but this is capable of several constructions. Jesus may be thought to pronounce the Word of God (see Heb 4:12, which however uses the more common word for sword) or to speak his own testimony (see the two paired in 1:2, 9). Jesus' testimony is itself two-edged, both what he said and what he did, which in Revelation focuses on his death.

Rev 1:17–20

THE FIRST AND THE LAST Compare the Alpha and Omega of 1:8. The one pictured here may be *like* a human being (1:13), but these are divine attributes. See Isa 41:4; 44:6; and 48:12 where this sentence is attributed to Yahweh, God of Israel.

LIVING ONE The middle term between the First and the Last; compare "the one who is" in 1:8.

I WAS DEAD, AND SEE, I AM ALIVE FOREVER AND EVER Literally: I became dead . . . I am living. The wording makes it more surprising that the living one should have become dead than that such a one should be living.

KEYS OF DEATH AND OF HADES The key is a natural symbol of authority. Revelation will mention two other keys: that of David (3:7) and that of the bottomless pit (9:1; 20:1).

MYSTERY The primary sense is that of a secret or hidden knowledge, often something known only to God (see 10:7). In Revelation it carries the sense of a symbolic significance to some physical sign (see also 17:5–7).

ANGELS Messengers of any kind, but by John's day there had developed a rather elaborate set of beliefs about the messengers/angels of the divine court.[24] Many people believed that there were guardian angels, not only for individuals but also for corporate groups. Also, many people identified the angels with the Greco-Roman deities and with the rulers of the stars and planets known from astrology.

(See the excerpt from Theodotus cited in the discussion of the characterization of Jesus, p. 46.) In John's two-tiered world angels probably represent a heavenly reality corresponding to the messengers of God on earth.

The Stories of the Letters

The inaugural vision actually contains the seven letters to the churches, although this is somewhat obscured by the division of the work into chapters. The earliest division of the biblical text into chapters was done in the fourth century, and the present division into chapters and verses was done in the Middle Ages to facilitate finding passages. They are best ignored when reading.25 What we see as 2:1 is really the continuation of the speech of the risen Jesus: "The seven lampstands are the seven churches. To the messenger of the church at Ephesus, write . . . " (1:20–2:1). Thus the letters are completely embedded in the vision narrative. What is the effect of embedding such letters in a narrative and how should we understand their narrative significance? What does the author gain by embedding them in the narrative?

The most obvious narrative significance is that the letters represent the "revelation of Jesus" promised by the opening voice (1:1), a revelation that John receives to deliver to the servants. Viewed this way, they represent the culmination of the action, fulfilling the expectations raised in the opening. On first hearing, one might expect no more than to learn the content of these letters. This could have been the end of the story, for it achieves an appropriate closure. So the first thing our author gains by embedding the letters in a narrative is an attentive listening to the content of those letters.

But more, finding them within a larger narrative forces us to imagine that they have some connection to that larger narrative, forces us to consider their contribution to the narrative as narrative. This constraint is increased by the careful way in which John opens each letter with an aspect of the description of Jesus from the inaugural vision, thus binding the two into a unified package. Letters, especially the early Christian letters, have so long been treated as simply messages or, worse yet, as theology to be communicated that we seldom reflect on the narrative qualities they manifest. Two distinctions developed in modern narrative theory help us to redress this imbalance: the distinction between the real world and the fictional world of the story and the distinction between story and discourse.26

Stories refer to and imply the real world, but they contain only the fictional world created by their authors. If stories did not refer to the real world, if they were wholly fictional, they would be incomprehensible. It is this dual aspect of stories, creating a world and referring to a world, that allows us to explore the narrative potential of letters. For letters too refer to and create worlds. "Dear Dad" the letter begins, and so refers to a real-world situation, but immediately it conjures up other, imaginative scenarios:

a child is separated from a father, something has happened that there is a need to communicate. . . . This other, imaginative world lies implicit in every letter. Whereas narratives imagine a world and we must reconstruct their real world situations, letters point directly to the real world and we must imagine their story.

The other set of categories grows out of the possibility of talking about both the actual story and about the *way* it is told, about content and expression, about story and discourse. The discourse is the statement of the story.27 Because the story is thus stated it communicates a meaning to its audience. Once again the relationship is reversed, but the process is analogous with letters. As Norman Petersen epitomized, "In narratives, the message is in the story. In letters, the story is in the message."28

Thus we can see that the story implied in the frame-letter, that John has found it necessary to write to the seven churches in Asia, is the same story that the narrative enacts in the opening scene of John's experience on Patmos. In this way the frame and the first scene reinforce each other and emphasize to the audience the divine compulsion behind this revelation. Now we must look at the individual letters and try to uncover their stories.

There are seven letters, one to each of the cities named at the beginning of the vision report (1:11). The letters differ in length, in content, and in tone, but are remarkably alike in structure. The pattern each follows is:

1. The addressee is named as: the messenger (angel) of the church at (city).
2. The sender is described with characteristics drawn from the inaugural vision of Jesus.
3. Their present situation is described and their character diagnosed.
4. Statements of praise and or warning follow.
5. A refrain: "The one having ears should hear what the Spirit is saying to the churches."
6. A promise is made to those who overcome.

The only variation on this pattern is that points five and six are reversed in the last four letters, so that in three letters the promise comes last and in four the refrain comes last. This dividing of seven into three and four is consistent with John's highly symbolic use of numbers. Seven as it represents the intended whole is always the sum of three (heavenly) and four (earthly) realities. (See the discussion of number symbolism, pp. 6–10.)

In addition, each letter maintains a unity of image, theme and action. Thus characteristics of each individual city are echoed in the description of their situation and the resulting diagnosis corresponds both to the description of the sender and the promise for victory.29 *Ephesus,* for example, was a city renowned for its industry and prosperity. Located on the sea coast, it lacked natural defenses and was dominated by stronger neighbors until Rome imposed peace on the area. With peace, trade flourished and the city grew. Twice the city had been forced to move in order to maintain its harbor, for the river there was notorious for silting the harbor—a problem so bad that the harbor site was abandoned by the sixth century. But in John's time the city was nearing the zenith of its prosperity.

The great temple to Artemis that Ephesus built was called one of the wonders of the ancient world. A monumental, marble structure (largest in the Hellenic world) built on swampy ground, it was an engineering wonder. And it housed the worship of a very important deity: the Ephesian Artemis (whom the Romans called Diana). As was common in the Hellenistic world, the Ephesian Artemis was a blend of local goddess traditions with those of the dominant Greek culture. Whereas the Greek Artemis was a virgin hunter, portrayed in rustic garb, the Ephesian Artemis was a fertility figure, portrayed in richly embroidered robes with animal figures. The image was hung with ripe fruit, so that she was sometimes called "many-breasted" or the "tree of life."

Ephesus also had a temple to the emperor Augustus, a mark of distinction for a city, as well as a major temple to the Egyptian God Sarapis.[30] Nero had built a sports stadium there (which also doubled as an arena for gladiatorial contests), and successive emperors continued to enhance the public works. A very large, platformed temple to the emperor Domitian was built, perhaps during John's time. The harbor was dominated by a huge gymnasium complex, including public baths. From the harbor, one would first see the theater, the most impressive building in Ephesus with seating for 24,000 patrons. The central marketplace was more than a hundred yards square, surrounded by a two-tiered colonnade. In the center of the market was a large water clock and sundial, surrounded by hundreds of statues of rhetoricians, philosophers, athletes, and government officials. It was a magnificent city with close ties to Rome.[31]

Similar conditions persisted in the other cities, for these were the leading cities of the region. *Smyrna* was then a city of great wealth, though it had been destroyed in 600 BCE and rebuilt in 290. The geographer Strabo (d. 21 CE) called it the finest city in the region. One of the great finds there is a large marble scene with statues of Demeter (Goddess of grain) and Poseidon (God of the sea) standing side by side, a tribute to Smyrna's dual heritage in agriculture and sea trade. *Pergamum* was an immense, mountaintop city, strongly fortified. It dominated the whole region until Rome imposed its own order. A major Asklepion, a temple-health complex dedicated to Asclepias, God of healing, was located there. An Asklepion was the closest thing to a hospital or sanatorium known in the ancient world. Asclepias' symbol, the snake, is still visible today in the physician's staff. Pergamum was also famous for its extensive library, said to contain 200,000 volumes and second only to that of Alexandria in Egypt.

Thyatira was an inland, mercantile city, located in the Lycus River valley. Numerous inscriptions attest to its manufacturing trades, each with its associated trade guild: copper workers, tanners, leather workers, dyers, wool workers, linen workers. The native deity, Tyrimnaios had become identified with Helios (the Sun) and Apollo. The city was also a center for an oracle of the Sibyl, a female prophetic figure who gave ecstatic prophecies. *Sardis,* too, was an inland city, prosperous in John's time but famous as a city of lost wealth. Originally built on a mountainous peak, the city was theoretically impregnable but it had been twice devastated through surprise night-time attacks. The Roman peace had led the population down from the mountain into the surrounding river valley, where it prospered. An enormous temple to Artemis, which took over four centuries to complete, was nearing completion in John's time. Archeological remains from the next century attest to a remarkably close relation between Jews and Greeks in the city, with the synagogue actually physically attached to a bath complex and a hall dedicated to the emperors.

Philadelphia, unlike these other cities, was built as a Greek city about 150 BCE. Because of extensive assistance by Tiberius in the aftermath of an earthquake, its name had been changed first to Neocaesarea (New City of Caesar) and then to Flavia (the emperor's family name), but it soon reverted to Philadelphia. It was the farthest from the coast and a gateway to the less civilized interior; it stood at the border of Greek culture. It was the least prosperous of the cities, dependent largely on its surrounding vineyards. *Laodicea* was built as a military colony to protect the trade routes. Ruins of two theaters and an athletic stadium dedicated to the Emperor Vespasian (79 CE) are still visible. Though it had to pipe in all its water, it prospered as a trading city, famous for its black wool, and as a health center, famous for its eye salve. The city enjoyed such prosperity that it rejected imperial aid for rebuilding after the earthquake in 17 CE. They could do it themselves.

Given the literary context within the inaugural vision and social context of these cities, we can begin to imagine the stories of the letters. For details on the puns and implications of the terms, see the Readers' Notes on pp. 54–60.

The Ephesian story is dominated by themes from astrology and from the Eden story in Genesis. The one who walks among the lamps and holds the stars reveals the meaning of the Ephesian community. While praiseworthy in their hard work, their rejection of false apostles and their patience, they are now confronted with a choice: will they have defeat or victory? They have fallen (is there an echo of the Lucifer myth of the fallen star?) from their first love; they must repent and return to their former position, else Jesus will come to them and remove their lamp. Victory, however, will result in eating from the tree of life in the garden of God.

Smyrna, from whose name we get the burial spice myrrh, hears a story of death and life. The city itself had once died and lain in ruins for four hundred years, but it now lived and prospered. The one who was dead and now lives warns them of their impending struggle. Those faithful unto death will receive a crown of life, and the victor will not taste a second death.

Pergamum, the great imperial power, is called to battle. They may either battle Satan or the one who holds the sharp, two-edged sword. While one of their number has already been faithful to death, the rest are—like Israel as it approached the promised land—listening to Balaam. They must repent and fight. The victor will receive manna—like Israel in the wilderness—and a white stone with a new name.

Thyatira must rule. Addressed by the son of God whose bronze feet and flaming eyes contrast with their own iron staff and broken pottery, they are charged—like the kings of Israel—with being seduced by Jezebel. They must repent or face great affliction. Those who avoid this idolatry must hold fast "till I come." The victor will receive kingly power to rule over the nations and the morning star—sign of victory.

Sardis is called to wakefulness and observance. They must remember their task or else "like a thief in the night" Christ will come to them. Those who have not soiled their clothes will be remembered by the one who holds the seven stars and the seven spirits. Sardis is like a plant in dry ground, dying and badly in need of tending. The holder of the spirit addresses them and offers refreshment. The victorious will receive white robes and will not have their names obliterated from the book of life.

Philadelphia stands with metaphors of open doors and temple pillars. The one who holds the key sets before them an open door, even as Philadelphia itself was a gateway to the interior. Both crown and pillar are theirs, along with the name of God and the name of God's city, the new Jerusalem. All this in a context of hostility with other Jews over who can truly claim the title Jew.

The Laodicean letter emphasizes true and false perception, with the one who is the faithful and true witness giving an analysis of their situation that is wholly at odds with their own analysis. They think themselves to be rich and without need; the witness says they are poor, blind, naked, and wretched. They are advised to buy gold, white clothes, and eye salve. The letter closes with a poignant scene of the human one standing outside a closed door and promising anyone who would open the door that they will dine together. The victor is promised a heavenly enthronement, just as Jesus was victorious and received such a heavenly throne.

For all their commonality of form and their derivation from the inaugural vision, these letters show remarkable variety. They are neither repetitious nor boring. Each of the seven is unique and each advances the story a bit further. Let us now consider the seven together, for their symbolic number implies that they are each addressed to the whole church.

I am intrigued by an apparent echo of biblical themes in the order: creation (Ephesus), exodus (Smyrna), wilderness-conquest (Pergamum), kingship (Thyatira), temple (Philadelphia), and exile (Laodicea). Only Sardis does not seem to fit the sequence of Israel's history, and it is a general exhortation to wakefulness and observance—conceivably echoing the

Wisdom tradition. Whether or not such a sequence is conscious, the under-lying paradigm holds: creation and struggle, followed by kingly rule or ruin. These basic themes—creation, struggle, rule, and ruin—run throughout the story of Revelation. In this way, the story of the letters is really the story of the whole work. The other stories are variations on the theme.

DIFFERENTIATING THE CHARACTERS

We have already given some attention to characterization (pp. 30–34); we will now consider three characters important for understanding the action of the letters: Jesus, the churches, and the opponents

Jesus

Clearly the Apocalypse has lived up to its title: the Revelation of Jesus Christ. Jesus towers over this section and dominates its action. He is "like a human being" (1:13) yet speaks as if he were God (1:17). He is at the same time the Jesus who died and rose (1:18) and the heavenly revealer portrayed in Daniel (1:13–15). This descriptive passage culminates in two important images: Jesus holds seven stars in his right hand and a sword in his mouth. Both are images of power and control.

The image of the seven stars may operate on several levels. At bottom, it is an image drawn from astrology, which nearly everyone in the first century believed in to some degree. We even find synagogue floor mosaics featuring the twelve signs of the zodiac. In astrological thinking, the stars controlled our destiny, but in John's image Jesus holds the stars. He controls their des-tiny. Here is how a second-century Christian reconciled belief in astrology with Christian faith:

> The stars, spiritual bodies, that have communications with the angels set over them, and are governed by them, are not the cause of the production of things, but are signs of what is taking place, and will take place, and has taken place. . . .   *Excerpts of Theodotus* 55

This Christian clearly still believes in astrology, but confesses that there is a power over the stars (the angels) so that the stars merely indicate. They do not control history, but one who understands may read in them the past, the present, and the future. I am reminded of the prayer of Lucius, the comi-tragic hero of the popular second-century novel *The Golden Ass.* Lucius had been rescued by the Goddess Isis from a fate worse than death (spending his life as a donkey) and, as he is initiated into her secret rites, he prays:

> Most holy and everlasting Redeemer of the human race, you munificently cherish our lives and bestow the consoling smiles of a Mother upon our tribu-lations. There is no day or night, not so much as a minutest fraction of time,

that is not stuffed with the eternity of your mercy. You protect men on land and sea. You chase the storms of life and stretch out the hand of succour to the dejected. You can untwine the hopelessly tangled threads of the Fates. You can mitigate the tempests of Fortune and check the stars in the courses of their malice. . . .

O my spirit is not able to give you sufficient praises, nor have I the means to make acceptable sacrifices. . . .

Howbeit, poor as I am, I shall do all that a truly religious man may do. I shall conjure up your divine countenance in my breast, and there in the secret depths I shall keep divinity forever guarded.[32]

Such a longing to be free from the oppressive powers of fate marked the time of John, and he portrays Jesus as one who holds the stars in his hand, thus possessing power over destiny.

A second context for this image of one holding the stars is provided by a coin that the emperor Domitian minted in 83 CE, commemorating his son's death. The coin shows a naked infant seated on a globe with his hands extended into a field of seven stars, with an inscription beginning "The Divine Caesar. . . . " There may thus be an implicit challenge to the imperial claims in this image of Jesus. In addition, the coin suggests the notion that the deceased infant has not gone to the underworld, where dead humans go, but rather has ascended to the stars, as befits a God. Suetonius wrote that a leading city official "actually swore that he had seen Augustus's spirit soaring up to Heaven through the flames" of his funeral pyre.[33] Such claims were necessary for the eventual deification of the emperor. In this context, the picture of Jesus among the stars reinforces the declaration that death could not hold him.

Coin minted by the
emperor Domitian in 83 CE
Copyright © The British Museum

The other image, the sword from his mouth, both reinforces and under-mines this image of power. The sword is an obvious image of power; in fact, having the "power of the sword" was understood to mean the right to inflict capital punishment. Clearly Jesus has such power. And yet, it is a sword proceeding from his mouth, not in his hand or even in its case at his side. It is the testimony of Jesus that is his power. For many rulers it is their power to hurt that makes their words important. For Jesus it is his words that make his power real. This device of using and subverting images of power will be common in the story that follows.

Finally, we must consider the characteristics of Jesus in relation to the action of the letters. In each letter we see the author skillfully revealing an appropriate characterization of Jesus. To the loveless and endangered Ephesians, he is the holder of the stars; to the Smyrnans facing death, he is the one who died and lives; to the belligerent Pergamenes he is the bearer of the sword, and so on. Now this is remarkable. This Jesus, like the ancient Proteus, seems to change his shape for every new situation. Even more remarkable, John presented all these characteristics in a unified vision of Jesus in chapter one, as Table 7 shows. This is no small literary achievement.[34]

The Churches

If we forget for a moment that the seven churches are distinct entities and take the larger view that seven is symbolic of the whole church, what does that church look like? It is a mixed group to be sure, containing rich and poor, Jews and Gentiles (who want to think they are Jews), male and female leaders, and significant disagreement over some basic social customs. So deep is this disagreement that our author resorts to name-calling, having abandoned any hope of reconciliation. They have experienced very little external opposition, though there have been some hostilities between these groups and the other Jewish synagogues in some of the cities. The main focus of their disagreement concerns how they should relate to Greek cul-ture.

It is crucial for us to understand the essential difference between modern and ancient cultures in order to comprehend what is at issue here. In mod-ern culture our various activities have been differentiated in separate spheres: politics, religion, education, labor, economics, family. We under-stand these spheres to be autonomous, although possibly interacting. The classic American expression of "the separation of church and state" is a use-ful example. Sure one's religion might influence one's politics, but they are two separate things. This was not the case in the ancient world.

In John's time there were only two primary social institutions: politics and the family, all other activities were embedded in these institutions—usually in both. Thus religion was sometimes a family obligation and sometimes a political obligation. Some aspects of education derived from the family, others from the state; and so on. Because of this interpenetration, each of these activities pervaded the others. For our purposes, we can see that religion permeates all other spheres of life. (For more details on the entanglements of religion and other aspects of life, see the discussion of the implied audience in the Epilogue, pp. 160–64 and the discussion of the mark of the beast on pp. 106–9 and 126–28.) Thus any cultural question was also a religious question, whether going to the theater, participating in sports, buying and selling in the marketplace, manufacturing, holding public office—every activity has also a religious dimension.

If one lives in a culture where every facet of society is permeated by what we call religion, and then one changes religion, how does one continue to

TABLE 7 *Parallel Characterizations of Jesus*

Opening Vision	Seven Letters
1:13 and in the *midst of the lampstands* I saw one like the Son of Man, clothed with a long robe and with a golden sash across his chest.	2:1 Ephesus . . . him who holds the seven stars in his right hand, who walks *among the seven golden lampstands:*
1:14 His head and his hair were white as white wool, white as snow; his *eyes were like a flame of fire, his feet were like burnished bronze,* refined as in a furnace, and his voice was like the sound of many waters.	2:18 Thyatira write: . . . the Son of God, who has *eyes like a flame of fire, and whose feet are like burnished bronze:*
1:16 *In his right hand he held seven stars,*	2:1 Ephesus . . . him who *holds the seven stars in his right hand,* who walks among the seven golden lampstands: 3:1 Sardis write: . . . him who *has* the seven spirits of God and *the seven stars:*
and from his mouth came *a sharp, two-edged sword,* and his face was like the sun shining with full force. 1:17 When I saw him, I fell at his feet as though dead. But he placed his right hand on me, saying, "Do not be afraid; *I am the first and the last,* and the living one. I *was dead,* and see, I *am alive* forever and ever;	2:12 Pergamum . . . him who has *the sharp two-edged sword:* 2:8 Smyrna . . . *the first and the last, who was dead and came to life:*
and I have the *keys* of Death and of Hades.	3:7 Philadelphia . . . the holy one, the true one, who has the *key* of David, who opens and no one will shut, who shuts and no one opens:
(And from the opening address) 1:5 and from Jesus Christ, *the faithful witness,* the **firstborn of the dead,** and the ruler of the kings of the earth.	3:14 Laodicea . . . the Amen, *the faithful and true witness,* the **origin of God's creation.** . . .

Note: Exact matches are printed in italic type; parallels in bold.

relate to these other cultural arenas (such as the family, politics, economics, education, entertainment)? These churches are characterized as not yet having made up their minds about these important relationships, though from John's perspective the issues are clear: faithfulness versus idolatry. Others saw things differently.

The Opponents

The letters characterize two groups as opponents, one group within the churches and one outside. Those within are first characterized as the *Nicolaitans,* a Greek word combining the word for victory (Nike) and people (laos), thus conquerors of people, those who win over people, or some such. Nothing is said about the specific error of these Nicolaitans, but perhaps John is playing a word game. For the next opponent is named *Balaam,* which can be derived from Hebrew words (Baal + am) meaning Lord or ruler and people. Now the errors of Balaam are manifest and well known in Jewish tradition: he led Israel to idolatry by advocating a mixing of cultures. The third opponent is guilty of much the same, for she is identified as *Jezebel,* the pagan queen of Israel and patron of the prophets of Baal. Just so John's Jezebel would accommodate to Greco-Roman culture, participating in trade, education, and cultural activities. But each of these activities is permeated with religious rites associated with the Gods of Greece and Rome.

It is instructive here to compare Paul's approach a generation earlier. Paul permitted the eating of meat sacrificed to idols (1 Corinthians 8–10) and did not believe that one could isolate oneself from general culture (1 Cor 5:9–11). If the people in John's story correspond in some way to real people in Asia Minor, as we suspect they do, it may be that they believed they were following Paul's advice.[35] But John did not see it that way. To him they are Balaam and Jezebel. Now these are not real people; these names were not used in this period. They are John's attempt to characterize one segment of the church, portraying it in the most sinister manner. John is telling a story, and within that story his rules apply. The reader must either take a stand against these opponents or reject the teller of this tale.

The other opponents are rejected in even more definite terms. Here too we must be aware that we are dealing not with real people but with John's characterization within this story. In the story they are "a synagogue of Satan" and those who "say they are Jews but are not" (2:9; 3:9). These are the only two references to Jews in the work and even here no specific charges are leveled. However, the name calling occurs within contexts devoted to affliction, blasphemy, and lying. We are to imagine, I think, a story in which there is considerable mutual recrimination, with each side claiming to be truly Jews.

Again, if there is any correlation with real people in Asia Minor, we should set this within the historical context of the late first century when

Jews everywhere were struggling for identity. Their homeland had been devastated by the Romans in 70 CE and their central institution, the Temple, completely destroyed. The synagogue was emerging as their new center and the study of the scriptures as their central rite. But some of them offered a radically new interpretation of those scriptures, centering on the life and death of Jesus whom they called Christ (Messiah). Many synagogues moved to exclude this minority viewpoint as they sought to form a common community.36 But again, that is not the case in John's story. Within that story they are allies of Satan who must be taught a lesson. Here we come to the focus of John's story world, for in that world there is only one ultimate opponent.

Satan will be richly characterized in this story, will in fact become the leading character for much of the third movement. In chapter two, we learn only that he has a synagogue, a throne, and mystery rites devoted to him.37 We should feel, probably, that Satan is the pervading force behind the world, its ultimate controller. Within such a world there can be no accommodation. One is either faithful, manifesting a consistent resistance, or one fails, joining the ranks of the enemy. That at least seems to be the construction our storyteller would have us put on life.

WHO ARE THE HEARERS?

One who would interpret the narrative of Revelation as a narrative is faced with a difficult problem. Everyone within this story is fictional—that is the nature of stories—but they also correspond in some way to people in the actual world of Roman Asia Minor. It is probably wiser to treat the story as entirely self-contained and not try to bridge the gap to actual people, but the story itself encourages such bridging. For within the story we glimpse the listening audience, gathered to hear the rhetor make the words live again in the spoken voice (1:3). This is one of the few biblical stories with an explicit narratee—the counterpart of the narrator, the one to whom the narrator tells the story.38 Now this narratee within the story is not quite the same entity as the implied audience who hears it, but they are strongly correlated. And so the question is: does this implied audience/narratee also correspond to any real audience?

Let us first consider whether the characteristics attributed to the churches as characters in the story of Jesus' letters also apply to the audience of the frame letter, the hearers who were blessed by the initial voice. One strong tie between them is just this notion of hearing, for each of the letters to the churches includes the challenge: the one having ears should hear what the spirit is saying to the churches. But they are also different, for the narrative device of seven separate letters allows each group hearing the work read to differentiate itself from some others. Thus the narratee, the group to which the whole story is told (1:3), is a less encompassing group than the implied audience of the work. This sense of separateness allows them a position of superiority, much like one gets in reading another person's mail.

This leads then to a more difficult question, namely, how do these two characters relate to the actual audiences available in first-century Asia Minor? Nearly all historical commentaries assume we can make a direct correlation between the folk addressed in the letters and actual people in Asia Minor. But a study of literature teaches us to be very leery of such equations. At the very least we are seeing first-century folk in the way John wants us to see them. His opponents are "Balaam" and "Jezebel," even though one could find no such people in Asia Minor. These are John's creation (perhaps based on real people). But so is everything else in the story, including John. (We will consider the issues of audience and author more fully in the Epilogue, pp. 159–64.)

Now obviously there is a real author to this work, and most likely he is named John. But the point of narrative criticism is that one never meets this author except in the fiction. We might say we encounter only a fictionalized portrait of the author. This way of thinking is merely an extension of an idea most of us learned in high school: the narrator is not the author. Rather the narrator is a fictional device invented by the author to tell the story. But we often assumed that the person we could detect behind the narrator was the real author. But a moment's reflection will show that this is not so. The person we see behind the narrator is the author whom the real author intends us to see. In modern narrative theory this person is called the *implied author*.

Just so, the persons we deduce to be the recipients of the story are not the actual audience, but the audience the author intends us to see (the implied audience). In our case, the churches of Asia Minor constitute the implied audience of this story. We can describe them in some detail because they are consciously characterized in the story. But this tells us nothing necessarily about the real audience. At the very least the implied audience is the real audience as the author wishes us to see them; at the most the implied audience could be a complete fiction with no relation to anyone in the real world. If Revelation were simply a work of fiction we could go no further. But Revelation is also a work of rhetoric, a work designed to persuade its audience of a certain view of reality. This allows us to infer something about the actual audience, for a rhetorical work will only be persuasive if its fictional audience has some analogy to the actual audience.[39]

Much like modern narrative theory, ancient rhetoric understood that all three aspects of the communications process must be included in the work itself: message, speaker, and audience. All three are thus what the author intends to convey. Nevertheless, in order to be persuasive all three must correspond in some basic way to what the intended audience already knows—

else they will think the author unreliable. Thus if they know the author, the author's self-presentation must be compatible with what they already know. And so too must the author's presentation of the audience be compatible with their self-understanding.

Some would argue in a similar manner for the historical setting of the work, extrapolating from the message to the setting. Since the text is a response to some definite situation, and since it is a "fitting" response, we need only imagine the situation that would call forth this response. This is the so-called "rhetorical situation." But this is not as easily done as it sounds. It is a little like having the answer and then trying to imagine the question which this answer implies. But with a work like the Apocalypse a good deal of what we take to be its message will depend on what we imagine it to be answering. The results will be far from certain.

SUMMARY OF THE FIRST SCROLL

"What you see write in a scroll and send it to the seven churches" is the instruction of the great voice of the opening vision (1:11). While the whole of Revelation may be intended here, the specific listing of the seven followed immediately by the seven messages suggests at least a strong analogy between this scroll and this first section of John's story. This is the scroll of the letters. Its surface action is simple: the one like a human appears to John on Patmos and dictates seven messages to the seven churches. Below this surface is a wonderful texture of images, symbols, actions, and patterns. Strong echoes of earlier prophetic literature, especially Daniel and Ezekiel, but also Zechariah and Isaiah, pervade the story. The one like a human is revealed in a particular way each of the seven churches, so that this revelation, the situation of the church, and the promise of victory correspond and imply a certain story. Aspects of this story seem to recall the experience of God's people from the Exodus to the Exile, with the constant theme being watchfulness and perseverance in anticipation of victory. The victory call entails a battle, and the present battle of these seven churches is portrayed as another manifestation of the cosmic and age-old battle between Satan and God—fought through surrogates. But it is not quite as simple as imagining the churches as God's agents and their enemies as agents of Satan, for there are satanic forces even within the churches. As the story continues we will see that the rewards for victory promised here are largely granted by the end. The correlations are not perfect, but enough to give the sense that things are working out as expected, as Table 8 shows (over).

The story of the first scroll is the story of conflict and victory in the ongoing life of the church. While it is set within an apocalyptic context and speaks of the "coming" of Jesus, this coming can be portrayed as a present experience (see especially 3:20 and 2:5). This movement of the story is the

TABLE 8 *The Promises of the Letters*

Promises to Those Who Conquer . . .	Parallels
Letter to Ephesus 2:7 . . . I will give permission to eat from the tree of life that is in the paradise of God.	22:2 through the middle of the street of the city. On either side of the river is the tree of life with its twelve kinds of fruit, producing its fruit each month; and the leaves of the tree are for the healing of the nations. 22:14 Blessed are those who wash their robes, so that they will have the right to the tree of life.
Letter to Smyrna 2:11 . . . will not be harmed by the second death.	20:6 Blessed and holy are those who share in the first resurrection. Over these the second death has no power, but they will be priests of God and of Christ, and they will reign with him a thousand years.
Letter to Pergamum 2:17. . . . I will give some of the hidden manna, and I will give a white stone, and on the white stone is written a new name that no one knows except the one who receives it.	*Not said but see:* 19:12 His eyes are like a flame of fire, and on his head are many diadems; and he has a name inscribed that no one knows but himself. *With 22:4* they will see his face, and his name will be on their foreheads.
Letter to Thyatira 2:26-28 . . . I will give authority over the nations; to rule them with an iron rod, as when clay pots are shattered—even as I also received authority from my Father.	20:4 Then I saw thrones, and those seated on them were given authority to judge. I also saw the souls of those who had been beheaded for their testimony to Jesus and for the word of God. They had not worshiped the beast or its image and had not received its mark on their foreheads or their hands. They came to life and reigned with Christ a thousand years. *(& see 19:15)* 22:16 It is I, Jesus, who sent my angel to you with this testimony for the churches. I

most naturalistic—so naturalistic that commentators have regularly been seduced into taking it as a sort of historical prologue to the real apocalypse. But a literary reading of this story sees this as the first movement of a three-part plot.

REV 2:1–3:22 *Readers' Notes on the Seven Letters*

Many of the symbols of this section are repeated from the inaugural vision in chapter one; see the Readers' Notes on pp. 38–41 for details.

Rev 2:1–7

ANGEL A surprising addressee of the revelation letter, since in the opening (1:1–2) John is said to receive the revelation via an angel. Now he delivers it back through an angel to the church. Some would take angel here in its basic sense of messenger and interpret it as the bishop of the church. Others see the angel as the

. . . I will also give the morning star.

Letter to Sardis
3:5 . . . you will be clothed like them in white robes, and I will not blot your name out of the book of life; I will confess your name before my Father and before his angels.

Letter to Philadelphia
3:12 . . . I will make you a pillar in the temple of my God; you will never go out of it. I will write on you the name of my God, and the name of the city of my God, the new Jerusalem that comes down from my God out of heaven, and my own new name.

Letter to Laodicea
3:21 . . . I will give a place with me on my throne, just as I myself conquered and sat down with my Father on his throne.

am the root and the descendant of David, the bright morning star.

6:11 They were each given a white robe and told to rest a little longer, until the number would be complete both of their fellow servants and of their brothers and sisters, who were soon to be killed as they themselves had been killed. *(see 7:14; 15:6)*
20:15 and anyone whose name was not found written in the book of life was thrown into the lake of fire. *(& see 21:27)*

Contrast 21:22 I saw no temple in the city, for its temple is the Lord God the Almighty and the Lamb.
19:12 His eyes are like a flame of fire, and on his head are many diadems; and he has a name inscribed that no one knows but himself.
21:2 And I saw the holy city, the new Jerusalem, coming down out of heaven from God, prepared as a bride adorned for her husband.

20:4 Then I saw thrones, and those seated on them were given authority to judge. I also saw the souls of those who had been beheaded for their testimony to Jesus and for the word of God. They had not worshiped the beast or its image and had not received its mark on their foreheads or their hands. They came to life and reigned with Christ a thousand years. *(& see 22:1)*

heavenly counterpart of the church, after the model of the lamps/stars in the inaugural vision. This latter view seems more natural to apocalyptic thought; in Daniel, for example, each nation is portrayed as headed by an angelic prince (e.g., Dan 10:20–21, "Then he said, 'Do you know why I have come to you? Now I must return to fight against the prince of Persia, and when I am through with him, the prince of Greece will come. But I am to tell you what is inscribed in the book of truth. There is no one with me who contends against these princes except Michael, your prince.'") Hearing this address to the angel, the audience knows that they are overhearing even what seems to be the most direct address of the work.

ENDURANCE See the Readers' Note on 1:9, p. 38.

APOSTLES Literally, those sent, thus Christians claiming to be emissaries or representatives of Jesus were known as apostles. Eventually the term became limited to the twelve disciples, but in John's time would have included an extensive group of men and women. Since their authority derived from spiritual experience, much like that of a prophet, the need to distinguish true and false apostles was both great and hard to meet. For an interesting attempt to distinguish them in the generation after John see *Didache* 11–13. This is our first clue that the leadership of John's communities is not all of one mind.

LOVE . . . FIRST The Greek is ambiguous, meaning either temporal priority (love you had at first) or status priority (first love, most important love).

I SHALL COME The promise of Jesus' coming permeates this writing but this warning here should caution us about understanding it too easily within the model of a "second coming" that has dominated in certain periods of history. We noted that the temporal point of view of the story is contemporaneous with this coming (see Rev 1:7); the literal expression here is "I am coming," a present tense.

LAMP The earthly counterpart of the heavenly star/angel. See the note on 1:12, p. 39.

NICOLAUS Or Nicolaitans (RSV). Neither the text nor ancient history gives us any reliable clue as to the identity of this Nicolaus or the Nicolaitans, though there are many imaginative reconstructions. Two things we know: the name means "conqueror of people" and our author is very hostile to whatever it is they stand for. Since other opponents named in the letters are symbolic (Jezebel and Balaam), this one might be also. In which case the contrast is with the need to be a conqueror (Greek: *Nikōnti;* 2:7 and end of each letter).

TO EAT At the least a sacred meal, common in Artemis' temple, but also perhaps a reference to the Eucharist.

TREE OF LIFE Multiple references: the tree in the paradise story of Genesis 2; Wisdom (Prov 3:18); the tree of Artemis; the cross of Jesus. It is the ironic contrast of the cross with the other meanings that gives John's work its bite.

GARDEN Literally, Paradise; both the temple enclosure of Artemis and Eden are called a paradise. See also Luke 22:43 "Today you shall be with me in paradise."

Rev 2:8–11

On the characterization of the speaker see the Readers' Notes on 1:17–20, pp. 40–41.

JEWS John's characterization of the Jews as claiming to be Jewish but not really being Jewish indicates that he claims that title for himself and his community. We are overhearing a bitter rivalry between two Jewish groups, with harsh words flying at least from the one side of the conversation we hear. It is most unfortunate that such language can be used for anti-Semitism once its original Jewish context is lost.

PRISON Not a punishment in the ancient world, but a holding place for those to be punished.

TEN DAYS Ten represents totality, fullness, completion; days indicates relative shortness, an endurable period. One of the rites celebrated at Smyrna was the ten days of Niobe's mourning for her slain children, followed by a feast. See the story in *Iliad* 24.602–15.

CROWN OF LIFE Crown here is not the ruler's golden diadem but the sort given to victorious athletes in the Olympian Games (also celebrated in Smyrna at the temple of Olympian Zeus); hence a garland or wreath. The double meaning of the of-construction can be read: the crown belonging to life or the crown which is life.

SECOND DEATH An idea unique to Revelation, occurring here and at 20:6; 20:14; and 21:8. It is the opposite of participating in the first resurrection and the same as the Lake of Fire in John's symbol system. I doubt if we can be more specific.

Rev 2:12–17

TWO-EDGED SWORD See the Readers' Note on 1:16, p. 40.

THRONE OF SATAN Some think the reference is to the magnificent altar to Zeus located there. Others point to this city as a center for emperor worship. But magnificent temples to deities and emperors were common in these cities and there seems no compelling reason to single Pergamum out in this fashion. It is perhaps best to say we can no longer discern the precise significance of the symbol, but we ought not to miss the political implications of a *throne*.

ANTIPAS Nothing else is known about this martyr than is said here. This is the only named martyr in Revelation, perhaps indicating that the actual social situation was not as intense as the story setting.

BALAAM The charming story of this ancient prophet can be read in Numbers 22–24, including the episode with the talking donkey. But the real significance of Balaam lies in Numbers 25, which describes an apostasy from Yahweh as the result of Jews intermarrying with their pagan neighbors. In Jewish tradition Balaam was responsible for this apostasy. Failing to earn his fee by cursing Israel, the interpretation goes, he earned it by suggesting this stratagem of accommodation. It is such cultural accommodation that John has in his sights and he uses the name of Balaam for its symbolic force.

FORNICATION To be understood in parallel with idolatry, thus a spiritual fornication. The association stems from the archaic period of Israel's history when Baal worship involved religious prostitution.

NICOLAUS See the Readers' Note at 2:6, p. 56.

I SHALL COME Literally, I am coming; present tense.

FIGHT Literally, make war.

MANNA The miraculously appearing food that preserved Israel in the wilderness; Exodus 16. Probably to be associated with the miraculous food of the Christian's sacred meal.

WHITE STONE White is always symbolic of victory in Revelation; the stone symbol remains obscure. If we think of a small stone, perhaps the jury process is in view, where not guilty/guilty votes were cast by white/dark stones. If we think larger, perhaps we should think of the practice of mounting inscriptions on white marble.

NEW NAME At bottom a metaphor for a changed person; see the classic story of Jacob's change to Israel (Gen 32:24–28). In magic it was necessary to know someone's name to have power over them, so a secret name perhaps also has connotations of invincibility.

Rev 2:18–29

For the description of the speaker, see the Readers' Notes on 1:13–16, pp. 39–40.

JEZEBEL A symbolic name derived from the ancient Phoenician queen who led Ahab, king of Israel, to combine the worship of Yahweh and Baal. A paradigmatic idolater. See 1 Kings 18–22. The use of the female name probably implies the existence of female prophets in these communities.

SACRIFICED TO IDOLS This does not necessarily imply participation in a sacrificial cult, since most meats sold in the market would have been "sacrificed" to the patron deity of the butcher's guild or of the city or of an approaching holiday. Paul had already dealt with the problem in the 50s and discussed it extensively in 1 Corinthians (8–10).[40] Paul allowed eating such food as long as it did not occur in a gentile temple and was not associated with a conscious act of consecration. John seems to take a more exclusive stance.

HER CHILDREN The disciples of the prophet with whom John disagrees.

EXAMINES THE VITALS AND THE HEARTS Literally, the kidneys and the hearts, the former seen as the seat of the emotions and feelings, the latter as the center of the will. Examining these entrails suggests a sort of divination common in the Roman world, where a priest would predict the future based on examining the organs of a sacrifice.

TO THE REST Implies a division in the community.

DEPTHS OF SATAN Another case where the meaning is lost to us, this phrase is sometimes related to the teachings of later Gnostics who did claim, according to the accounts of their opponents, to plumb the depths of Satan. Gnostics were esoteric groups who combined Greek philosophical speculation with Jewish and Christian stories to produce a version of Christianity that often reversed the traditional values, so that God and Satan might not be opposites. We have no other evidence for such teachings this early, however. Others see this as a reaction against Paul's teaching, which was based on knowing that idols are nothing (1 Cor 8:4). In this case, John's remark would be sarcastic: this is what they really know. Supporting this is the next phrase, "I shall not put another burden upon you" which is strongly reminiscent of Acts 15:28: "to impose on you no further burden than these essentials: that you abstain from what has been sacrificed to idols and from blood and from what is strangled and from fornication." In this case John would be trying to reestablish a tradition older than Paul's.

STAFF OF IRON A reference to the powers of the king of Israel which were widely viewed as referring to the coming messiah; see Ps 2:9.

MORNING STAR The planet Venus and also a symbol of victory and of Christ himself (22:16). John will be much concerned with astrological and magical practices, which he sees as a corruption of the true powers of Christ.

Rev 3:1–6

BE WAKEFUL Literally, become awake—implying that they are not now awake. Sardis had a certain fame for its failure to protect itself, its failure to stay awake. Herodotus tells how Cyrus' army conquered Sardis by secretly climbing up a cliff to the wall where the wall was unguarded because the Sardians thought it too steep to climb. They were so confident they never bothered to post guards there (*Hist.* 1.84).

LIKE A THIEF IN THE NIGHT The language is normally associated with a cosmic end-time scenario in apocalyptic writings; see Matt 25:42–43 and 1 Thess 5:2. These letters consistently use such end-time language to talk about the present.

NOT SOILED THEIR CLOTHES Soil carries the base meaning of to stain; a serious defilement. The verb is often used in a ceremonial sense: to make impure. The story sense here is that some have remained "ready" (clean/pure) for the appearance of the expected guest.

WHITE ROBES The contrast with soiled clothes might imply some sense of purity here, but the sense of white as the color of conquest prevails. Being clothed suggests an investiture ceremony, such as was common in initiation rites in various religions. See the description of Apuleius, *The Golden Ass,* Book 11.

BOOK OF LIFE Outside Revelation the expression occurs only in Phil 4:3; within Revelation it occurs at 3:5; 13:8; 17:8; 20:12; 20:15; and 21:27. The basic metaphor of God keeping track of things in a book occurs already in the Exodus story (Exod 32:32); see also Dan 12:1. Sometime in the late first century the synagogue liturgy was revised so that one of the opening prayers included the curse: "May the Nazarenes . . . be blotted out of the Book of Life and with the righteous may they not be inscribed" (Twelfth Benediction).[41]

ACKNOWLEDGE NAME "And I tell you, everyone who acknowledges me before others, the Son of Man also will acknowledge before the angels of God" (Luke 12:8).

Rev 3:7–13

Much of this scene seems to be modeled on the judgment of the King's Steward, Shebna, in Isa 22:15–25.

KEY OF DAVID See the transfer of power to Eliakim in Isa 22:20–23, which seems to be the basis for the images in this letter. Jesus is the new steward of the kingdom; the old steward has been stripped of power.

KEPT MY WORD Probably carries a double sense of keeping the teachings of the speaker and keeping the testimony of the speaker, i.e., living a similar life.

CONGREGATION OF SATAN Literally, Synagogue of Satan, a part of John's anti-Jewish rhetoric indicating strong hostility between the two communities, each claiming to be Jewish. See also the letter to Smyrna at 2:9.

HOUR OF TRIAL Hour is here used metaphorically for an indefinite, but relatively short, period of time. It was widely thought that those who were righteous would face a time of testing as the end drew near. Compare a similar idea at 2:9–10.

CROWN The victor's crown; see the Readers' Note on 2:10, p. 56.

TEMPLE This is the first reference to God's temple in Revelation. Most often the temple refers to a heavenly site, from which divine action proceeds (11:19; 14:15; 15:5; 16:1). Here and at 11:1 it more reasonably refers to the community of believers, the true dwelling place of God.[42] At 21:22 the imagery will be reversed: there will be no temple because God's presence pervades all.

NEW JERUSALEM Symbol for the new people of God. Notice that even at this early stage of the story the new Jerusalem is already spoken of in the present tense.

Rev 3:14–22

TRUE WITNESS Always in Revelation *witness* has the double-sided meaning of true knowing and true testifying. Jesus' true witness is primarily in his death, but also the testimony to that death—hence, this revelation.

ORIGIN (BEGINNING) OF CREATION An ambiguous expression that can mean the speaker was the first to be created or the source of the creation or the ruler of creation. Perhaps best understood by comparison with Col 1:15–20, where the expression is linked with the idea that the resurrection of Jesus represents the beginning of the new age.

LUKEWARM Because Laodicea was built for strategic purposes, it was not situated near a natural water supply. Located half-way between the famous hot springs of Hieropolis and the cold springs of Colossae, it was mocked for its tepid water, for by the time either was piped to Laodicea it was lukewarm.

RICH The mercantile allusions are all appropriate to Laodicea, famous both for its black wool and its eye salve. John's strong tendency to reverse cultural values is evident in this discussion of riches, and contrasts with his attitude toward the poor at Smyrna. While it is wrong to think that the Christian movement was made up of the lowest classes (in fact the chiding of the rich is good evidence that the rich were there to be chided), it is nonetheless true that John consistently sides with the poor.

DOOR . . . DINE Eating with Jesus is both a reference back to the Last Supper and forward to the marriage supper of the lamb (19:9; see also Luke 22:30, "you may eat and drink at my table in my kingdom"). The combination of the ideas of one knocking, gaining entrance, and preparing a meal is so close to a story told by Jesus that one suspects that it may be the source of this scene.

> Be dressed for action and have your lamps lit; be like those who are waiting for their master to return from the wedding banquet, so that they may open the door for him as soon as he comes and knocks. Blessed are those slaves whom the master finds alert when he comes; truly I tell you, he will fasten his belt and have them sit down to eat, and he will come and serve them.   LUKE 12:35–37

THRONE A common image in the Apocalypse, occurring 47 times beginning at 1:4. Throne imagery will dominate the next scene. The idea that the conqueror wins the throne is very common, but here the values are reversed, for one must conquer as Jesus did.

The Worship Scroll
REVELATION 4:1–11:18

> Now in this book called the Apocalypse there are, to be
> sure, many obscure statements, designed to exercise the
> mind of the reader; and there are few statements there
> whose clarity enables us to track down the meaning of the
> rest, at the price of some effort.[1]
>
> AUGUSTINE, *City of God*

Overview of the Unit: The Worship Scroll

The section opens with John being transported to heaven where he
describes the divine throne room and witnesses a liturgy of song, dance, and
reading. A crisis arises when the scroll to be read is found to be sealed with
seven seals that no one can open. John weeps, only to be comforted by one
of the participants who tells him there is one who can open the scroll: the
lion of the tribe of Judah. But instead, a lamb who had been slaughtered
appears and opens the seals one by one. As each seal is removed a dramatic
scene is witnessed, leading up to the climactic seventh. The seventh opening
is delayed by another kind of sealing wherein God's elect are sealed against
any harm. When the seventh seal opens there is a lengthy silence, followed
by the blowing of seven trumpets. Again the climactic seventh is delayed,
this time by a scene in the temple, followed by a short tale about two witnesses. These witnesses are faithful to their task and are initially protected,
then a beast from out of the pit makes war on them and kills them. But after
three and a half days they return to life and ascend to heaven. Then the seventh trumpet sounds and a loud voice (perhaps reading the scroll now
open) declares: The kingdom of the world has become the kingdom of our
Lord and of his Christ, causing the heavenly worship to resume.

The New Setting: Heaven

It is as if the closing words of the risen Christ to the Laodiceans set off
echoes in the author's mind, leading to another vision: " . . . as I myself

61

conquered and sat down with my Father on his throne." For we now visit the heavenly throne room as John is explicitly transported into heaven "in the spirit."

Such visits to heaven were relatively common in writings of this type,[2] and, in fact, visions of God and God's throne extend back into ancient traditions.[3] Even Paul claimed such a visit, though he would not repeat what he saw there:

> I know a person in Christ who fourteen years ago was caught up to the third heaven—whether in the body or out of the body I do not know; God knows. And I know that such a person—whether in the body or out of the body I do not know; God knows—was caught up into Paradise and heard things that are not to be told, that no mortal is permitted to repeat.   2 COR 12:2–4

In fact, visions of the throne of God are a mark of Jewish mystical tradition into the medieval period.[4] We have then something of a stock scene, though it will be developed in an entirely novel way, as we will see in the section on the action below.

Notice how the setting of our story has moved into ever more remote arenas. The story opens in the implied setting of a Christian assembly in Asia Minor (1:3); then shifts to the island of Patmos (1:9), a remote but realistic setting; and on through a door into heaven (4:1), a setting both remote and surreal. Story settings are rarely neutral sites.[5] Though settings may be just convenient places for the action to happen, might even be an ironic backdrop contrasting with the action, more often they symbolize the action of the plot to some degree (as Snoopy's would-be-novel opening understands: "It was a dark and stormy night. . . . "). Eerie things often happen in eerie places.

Each of these three settings provides important context for understanding Revelation. The liturgical setting of the opening and closing is of prime importance for understanding the basic theme of the work, which has to do with whom and how one worships. (This thesis will be clarified and defended in the discussion of the final scene in Revelation.) The island scene too is significant, for islands are transitional places—neither land nor sea but participating in both. So John on Patmos is in transition between the ordinary reality of everyday life and the transhistorical reality of his revelation. Entering into heaven we enter the realm of the revealed; this is the scenario behind life that an apocalypse ("unveiling") is supposed to reveal.

THE THRONE OF HEAVEN

The richness of the description should not escape us. There is this heavenly throne, established on a sea of glass, surrounded by twenty-four other thrones and flanked by four animal-like creatures and myriads of angels.

Simile tumbles over simile: the one on the throne looks like jasper and car-nelian (gems, perhaps like diamonds and rubies) and a rainbow like an emerald surrounds the throne and a sea like glass, like crystal, spreads out before the throne, where seven torches burn. What is the effect of this thick description?

Most obvious, this is a scene of heavenly worship and thus is the heavenly counterpart to what is done on earth. Now earthly worship in Roman Asia Minor could hardly be this opulent—except perhaps in the imperial cult. Almost certainly Christian worship was far more simple, done in someone's home (probably a wealthy home) or out-of-doors. The setting might seem ordinary, but it only *seems* ordinary, for the reality is what John describes here. Thus one function of this scene is to clarify and inspire worship.

Further, by setting this scene in a throne room, John invites comparison with Roman traditions. Much of what John describes here can be seen as a parody of the ceremonies of the imperial court.6 From the throne sur-rounded by courtiers to the mysterious silence of the central figure, from the circular configuration to the cosmic images, from the hymns and accla-mations of power and worth to the colors and titles used there are numer-ous echoes and parallels of the popular image of Roman court ceremonial. Thus a second function of this scene is to highlight the tensions between one's allegiances to Rome and one's allegiances to Jesus.

The throne of God is also an element of the scriptural tradition of Israel. The prophet Micaiah claimed a similar experience: "Therefore hear the word of the LORD: I saw the LORD sitting on his throne, with all the host of heaven standing beside him to the right and to the left of him" (1 Kgs 22:19). This notion that God existed in the same sort of setting as a typical king was carried over into the building of Solomon's temple, where the inmost sanctuary was a golden room wherein God sat invisibly enthroned between two angelic creatures on the ark of the covenant (see 2 Chronicles 3–5). Such notions were then carried over into synagogue and (especially) church worship. The early Christian sanctuary seems to have contained a throne (for the bishop) surrounded by elders.7

Thus this scene encompasses both liturgical (worship) and political (civic) aspects and we should not make a false dichotomy between the two. Not only do the worship elements here derive from a tradition of God-as-ruler, but they contrast with elements in John's world that think of ruler-as-God. This focus on the throne (and seventy-five percent of the references to "throne" in the New Testament writings are in Revelation) stamps this work as an important political document. In John's world the political included the religious.8

Now let us step back a bit further and consider the setting of Revelation in a larger context, for it is important to see how John's narrative world dif-fers from the ordinary world of everyday experience. We can make the point by comparing views of reality to housing styles. Our modern world is like a large ranch-style house, complex, even perhaps with many mysterious and unexplored rooms. But there is no upstairs and no basement. Oh, there are people who claim to believe in an upstairs, and some even say there is a basement, but nobody goes there anymore. John's world is like an old mansion, with an upstairs and a basement fully as complex as the ground level.

THE THREE-STORIED UNIVERSE

A common device in science fiction writings is the discovery of a time-link between the present and some other era: a secret passageway that one steps through and enters a different world. When we read science fiction we have to accept the existence of such links. So too in apocalyptic writings, only the links are not to the future or past (as in our one-story world) but to heaven and hell.[9] John's story world is one in which a person can—in the spirit at least—discover a door that allows one to enter heaven and see marvelous things (4:1).

The nature of John's three-storied world is clear in the line about the scroll that could not be opened: "And no one *in heaven* or *on earth* or *under the earth* was able to open the scroll or to look into it" (Rev 5:3). John never visits the underworld, but his perspective in heaven allows him to see things there and on earth that we could never see.

Thus John sees into the abyss (often translated the pit; Greek: *abysson*). This abyss is connected to earth by a great shaft and a locked door, which John sees unlocked (9:1–2), releasing vast smoke and surreal locusts. This abyss also holds another beast, who will come and war against the faithful (11:7). We are told that the abyss too holds a king and a kingdom (9:11) and so may anticipate trouble. For the earth is thus perched precariously between two kingdoms—antithetical in every way. And so like any small nation between two large adversaries, like Israel poised between Syria and Egypt in the centuries before Jesus, we may expect earth to be the scene of battle. But not yet, not in this phase of John's story. Here the setting anticipates the third phase of John's story (chapters 12 and following), which is devoted to the war.

This phase of the story is more concerned with heaven. The larger context of the throne room is the temple of God in heaven (7:15). Now this corresponds to the conception of the Jerusalem temple, which also contained the throne of God. On a naive level this is true of every temple; each is a sacred space that somehow corresponds to the ultimate realm of the God to whom it is dedicated. All temples presuppose a notion of sacred space and of correspondence between earthly and heavenly realities. But John, as well as others of that era, goes beyond this naive level and sees the heavenly temple as a metaphor for the whole worshiping community, which thus becomes a sort of spiritual temple.[10]

Now this facet of the setting opens a very important aspect of John's worldview to us: the notion of a spiritual link between realms above and realms below. Thus each thing in the story is both itself and something else. We will not be surprised then when John visits the altar of the heavenly temple and finds there "the souls of those who had been slaughtered for the word of God and for the testimony they had given" (6:9), for the heavenly temple and the temple of the worshiping community share a common altar. Earth and heaven correspond, but in hidden ways. Wherever the martyr dies, there is the altar of sacrifice—if one could but see. So too, the prayers of the congregation are the incense of the heavenly temple (8:3–5) and can be used by God to bring judgment on the earth. Wherever God's people offer up prayers, there is the altar of incense of the heavenly temple. The reader must become accustomed to thinking on two simultaneous levels.

John's spiritual geography imagines a clear link between realms, but we should avoid oversimplifying, for it is not a one-dimensional link. Consider, for example, the "great city" in whose streets the slain witnesses lie dead: "and their dead bodies will lie in the street of the great city that is prophetically called Sodom and Egypt, where also their Lord was crucified" (11:8). This last clause clearly demands we identify this great city with Jerusalem, now linked in John's spiritual geography with Sodom (notorious as a cesspool of immorality in the days of Abraham—Genesis 18) and Egypt (Israel's house of slavery—Exodus 1). And it will soon become evident that the great city is Rome, the city that rules over the kings of the earth (Rev 17:18). So John's unique setting allows him both to identify any given earthly place with its heavenly counterpart and to identify multiple earthly places with each other.

STORY SPACES AND THE REAL WORLD

A story is not reality, even if it is a true story. The times, places, characters, and events of a story are all developed at the discretion of the author (though there may be constraints, as when the author is working with a well-known story). A story is always another time and another place—whether that be "once upon a time in a land far away" or James Michener's *Alaska*. In a story we move from time to time and place to place and see things that no one ever saw who was simply there.

Perhaps the closest analogy to this peculiar sense of space and time is our participation in games, for a game too has a unique time and place. When one is playing baseball or softball, one doesn't mark time by saying it's 2:30 in the afternoon. Rather, it is the bottom of the seventh inning, or some analogous time. In the same way places take on their special meaning. First base and third base may simply look like points on a geometric diamond to one who doesn't understand the game, but their meaning is far different for the one who understands. They may look interchangeable, but a baseball

player would far rather be on third base than on first base. One must understand their meaning in context.

Now some stories occur in places wholly imaginary: Middle Earth or
Mudville or the Starship Enterprise. In such stories we are seldom tempted
to think of these places as somewhere we could go on a vacation. But most
stories use real places—places you could visit—like Alaska or London or the
American West. In such stories we might forget that there are crucial differ-
ences between how we experience these places in the stories and how one
might experience them in reality. The American West of fiction and film and
the London of Dickens are quite distinct from the simple experience of
these places. For it is the way an author allows the reader to experience a
place that defines the impact of that place on the reader.

Some of the locations in John's story are identifiable, such as the seven
cities of the first movement. Other locations are fabulous places that exist in
another realm and could never be located on a map. And John can blend
the two sorts together in the most ingenious way:

> And the sixth poured out its bowl upon the great river, the Euphrates, and its
> water was dried up in order to prepare the way for the kings from the rising of
> the sun. . . . And they gathered them together into the place which is called in
> Hebrew *Harmagedon*.   REV 16:12, 16

One can easily locate the Euphrates on any map of the Middle East, but
Harmagedon has never existed on any map. It is to such places that we
come in this segment of the story. These fantastic places have no obvious
relationship to the world in which one lives—and yet they appear to. For it
is the art of the writer to portray these other places in such a way that the
reader feels in relationship with them. John facilitates this relationship in
two ways.

First, he leads us from obvious places to these places in logical stages:
from the gathered assembly, to Patmos, to the seven cities, to Patmos, and
then through a door into heaven. We dutifully follow our guide. Second,
John portrays this other reality as a dimension of the reality of ordinary life.
There is a correspondence between the heavenly altars and the worship of
the community, between the abyss and the evils experienced in the world,
between the spiritual city and the cities of our experience. John sketches a
convincing spiritual geography in which we experience our world as the
middle ground between two antithetical powers.

Now this is just the meaning of an apocalypse, which literally means an
unveiling, a revelation, a showing of what is hidden. On one level this means
John allows us to see into heaven, but if that is what we take the revelation
to be, we misunderstand. Revelation does not reveal what heaven is like; it
reveals what everyday life is like by showing the everyday in relation to the
ultimate. This story enables the reader to see behind the facade of everyday

life into the world of ultimate reality. To be more precise, the Apocalypse communicates not just John's vision of the other world, it communicates his vision of what is really happening in this world by allowing the reader to identify ordinary places with the extraordinary.

OVERLAPPING SETTINGS: EMBEDDED NARRATIVES

While most of the action of this unit occurs around the heavenly throne, two complicating factors arise in considering the setting of the action. First, much of what actually is reported in this section consists of secondary narratives embedded in this throne narrative. Thus each of the seven seals and the seven trumpets produces its own narrative event, whose setting is often very vague. It is impossible to say where the four horses run, for example (6:1–8). These actions, we might say, take place nowhere; they occur in another dimension not another place. They are visions of a character in a vision. This will cause a certain amount of confusion for the reader, whose sense of reading a mysterious writing is thereby enhanced.

One example of this confusion of place is in the opening of the seventh seal: just where and at what narrative level does the silence occur? John writes: "When the Lamb opened the seventh seal, there was silence in heaven for about half an hour" (8:1). Is this silence in the heaven in the vision-window, so to speak, or in the heaven where John is watching both the throne scene and these embedded visions? Or have the two merged? Another example is in the vision of the sealing of the servants of God (chapter 7). At first the setting seems to be on earth (7:1), but then John says that the sealed are "standing before the throne" (7:9). Is this a throne in the embedded vision or the throne of the primary vision? If it is the embedded vision, that throne is surrounded by the same characters as is the throne in the primary vision (7:11).

Another sort of ambiguity occurs when John himself appears as a character in an embedded vision, so that we cannot be entirely sure which John we are hearing. Thus John reports seeing an angel descend to earth, and then tells of himself interacting with this angel—eating a scroll, measuring the temple, and hearing a story about two witnesses (chapters 10 and 11). The complexity of narrative levels here is amazing: John the letter writer (1) is telling us a story about himself on Patmos (2) where he has a vision of himself in heaven (3) where he sees an angel talking to him in the temple (4) and hears a tale of two witnesses (5). We must look at the relation between the actions that occur on these various levels below, here we only note their overlap.

Finally, we must note that there is a sense of sacred space here. The root of the idea of sacred space is the notion of a center, a fixed point which reveals and determines the meaning of all other space. It is a point of revelation and articulation between levels of reality. It is the axis of reality that connects earth and heaven (and the nether regions also).[11] Thus in Dante's *Divine Comedy* our hero ascends the various circles of hell, up Mount Purgatory, emerging at Jerusalem's temple, and there ascending into heaven. A similar set of spaces occurs in this section. We might imagine them as a set of concentric circles with the throne of God at the center, surrounded by the temple, which is surrounded by Jerusalem, which is surrounded by the whole earth. To the degree that we are dealing with a sense of sacred space, and not actual space, these places are in some measure interchangeable. Or, to speak more precisely, they symbolically permeate each other so that the center exists at the periphery and the out-most place exists at the center. It becomes a spiritual geography.

In this second section, then, John takes us beyond the ordinary to the extraordinary, setting the action in the heavenly throne room. This room echoes both the sacred reality of the temple (where the faithful believe God rules) and the secular reality of the Roman court (where devotees proclaim the ruler to be God). But this heavenly place is at the same time an earthly place, the place where God reigns and is truly worshiped: the churches of Asia. For the world above and the world below are linked by many channels, and the reader of the Apocalypse must be aware of many symbolic interchanges, where the symbols allow the audience to reflect back on the everyday world and understand it in a new way.

The New Characters

It is very easy to amalgamate the various characterizations of Jesus in the Apocalypse together; and on some level it is important that the reader do so. But this should not lead us to neglect the fact that Jesus is characterized rather differently in the various segments of the story. We can make an analogy to the situation with the four gospels. For many centuries readers simply blended the four gospels together into one harmonized "life of Jesus." But closer attention to the gospels individually reveals that each characterizes Jesus in a unique way, portraying just those aspects that are important for the story being told.[12] Only when one pays attention to these diverse characterizations can one understand the full range of the gospels. So too in the Apocalypse.

We have already discussed how Jesus is characterized in the story of the letters (see pp. 46–48). Jesus is there a figure of power and authority: holding the stars of heaven and speaking a word characterized as a sword. He is figured as one like a human being, but more like the human being of Daniel's heavenly vision than like an ordinary person. The figure in this scene contrasts sharply.

JESUS

Instead of the magnificent figure described in chapter one (whose voice we hear as this scene opens—4:1) Jesus is pictured as "a Lamb standing as if it had been slaughtered, having seven horns and seven eyes" (5:6). Every aspect of this characterization raises questions: Why a lamb? Why slaughtered yet standing? Why so many eyes and horns? Let's consider the issues in reverse order.

Why seven eyes and horns? The first thing to be said is that it is difficult to take this image pictorially. Of the artists that have attempted to illustrate the Apocalypse, few have had the temerity to put seven eyes and horns on the lamb. Nor should they. These images are not meant to be seen so much as to be understood and felt. To this we add the observation that here is an instance where John explicitly interprets one of his symbols, for he tells us that the seven eyes are "the seven spirits of God sent out into all the earth" (5:6). Now we have already met these seven spirits (1:4) and understood that they are a figure for the Holy Spirit. Thus to say that Jesus has seven eyes is to say that Jesus fully possesses the spirit of God—seven being the quality of fullness and perfection (see pp. 6–10). The seven horns, then, must also be a quality of fullness, and horns regularly signify power or rule (and by extension rulers). In this sense, a lamb with horns is an oxymoron for lambs are not powerful animals.[13]

Why slaughtered and standing? Here the reader is expected to know something of the traditions about Jesus' death and resurrection—perhaps even in the form now found in the Gospel of John. While the relationship between the Apocalypse and the Gospel of John is ambiguous at best, there are several striking correlations, for this gospel is the only one to portray Jesus as the "lamb of God" (John 1:29, 36).[14] It may not be accidental, then, that John's gospel explicitly connects the death of Jesus with the overthrow of the world's evil powers (John 12:31–33), for we will see that this is precisely the thrust of this new characterization of Jesus.

Why a lamb? To understand just how shocking this image is we should first note that the verbal characterization of Jesus is quite different. When John laments that no one has been found worthy to open the sealed scroll, he is encouraged by one of the heavenly figures: "Do not weep. See, the Lion of the tribe of Judah, the Root of David, has conquered, so that he can open the scroll and its seven seals" (5:5). Here the language of conquest is appropriately connected with two images of power deriving from the Hebrew Scriptures: the lion of Judah and the root of David. The lion was widely used as a symbol of power in the ancient world (see Prov 30:30) and had become associated with the throne of David through Jacob's characterization of Judah (Gen 49:9). The root of David is first of all a metaphor for David's line (Isa 11:10), but it became a symbol for the restoration of the

Davidic monarchy (Jer 23:5). This is the language of tradition that sees the establishment of God's kingdom as an act of power—both the Jewish tradition and the Christian tradition use such language. Both have frequently imagined that only righteous violence can establish justice on earth. But this is not John's way.

John completely inverts this image. Rather than the lion who tears his prey (Ps 17:12), Jesus is the torn lamb. There is violence, to be sure, but it is endured not inflicted. Yet this lamb has conquered, has seven horns. This is a radical inversion of value and should guide us as we witness the action of subsequent scenes; we should not too quickly assume that the violence and conquest of this story are to be understood as the work of a lion. For this lion is a lamb-slain-standing-victorious.

THE FOLLOWERS OF THE LAMB

While the characterization of Jesus as the lamb is consistent throughout this section, the characterization of the followers varies from subunit to subunit. We will discuss the sequence of actions below (pp. 75–76); here we just note that there are four kinds of action portrayed: scenes in the throne room, scenes embedded in the opening of the seals and the blowing of the trumpets, scenes concerning the sealing of the elect, and scenes concerning the temple and the great city with its two witnesses. Each of these has a distinctive way of characterizing the followers of the lamb.

Those around the Throne

Apocalyptic writings describe throne scenes in varying levels of detail; some elaborate a host of beings in varying ranks, while others are more simple. John's description is one of the least elaborate. Two of the three categories of beings mentioned are standard features of most scenes: the angels and the four living creatures. The third order of participants is unique to John's vision: the elders.[15] The angels need little comment; they are the heavenly servants, the messengers of God. John does little more than note their presence: "Then I looked, and I heard the voice of many angels surrounding the throne and the living creatures and the elders; they numbered myriads of myriads and thousands of thousands" (5:11). The only noteworthy points are that, unlike in many apocalypses, they are not described in detail nor ordered in ranks and, second, that we have already seen in the first vision report that they function both as intermediaries between God and humans (e.g., 1:1) and as the heavenly counterparts of the churches themselves (e.g., 1:20).

The second group, the living creatures, are described more extensively. Again, such beings occur in many apocalyptic visions, deriving from the visions in Ezekiel 1 and Isaiah 6. Unlike in Ezekiel, where each creature exhibits four aspects, here each creature is identified with one trait: human, eagle, lion, and ox. These seem to represent something like four orders of creation: the domestic, the wild, the airborne, and the rational—with each of these representing the foremost of the species. A later Jewish writing comments: "[The Human] is exalted among creatures, the eagle among birds, the ox among domestic animals, the lion among the beasts; all of them have received dominion. . . . Yet they are stationed below the chariot of the Holy One."[16] So these four creatures set the scene in its broadest context, portraying all of sentient creation gathered around the throne of God.

The Twenty-four Elders

One accustomed to reading apocalypses would experience some surprise on finding these elders around the throne. The first surprise is simply their appearance—for elders do not appear in other throne scenes. But equally surprising is that there are twenty-four of them; one expects twelve, the number of God's people (see the section on John's symbolic use of numbers, pp. 6–10). Perhaps the reader is to think of the twenty-four heavenly beings associated with the zodiac; or perhaps the elders symbolize the twenty-four orders of priests who served the Jerusalem temple (1 Chr 24:4–6); perhaps they represent the addition of the twelve apostles to the twelve patriarchs of Israel (cf. Rev 21:14), or perhaps, they represent a combination of the numbers for earth (four) and for humanity (six, thus: 4 x 6 = 24). We should probably resist the urge to choose only one meaning, for it is a trait of our author to use multidimensional symbols. What should be noted is that in any case they are the heavenly counterparts to the earthly community. They continue to characterize that community as a community of priests (dressed in white, serving the deity) and of kings (thrones, crowns) as we have already seen (Rev 1:6; and see 5:10). This two-fold characterization corresponds to the two-fold significance of the scene (discussed on pp. 62–64).

Thus the inhabitants of the heavenly throne room all represent aspects of the earthly community, whether as general figures for the churches (angels), or as figures of the created orders (living creatures), or as specific figures for the new community in Jesus (elders as priests and kings). Because this is the ultimate (heavenly) identity of these believers it will shape their identity in the other scenes. We have a similar, but not the same, two-fold characterization of the faithful community in the story of the two witnesses (11:1–13).

The Two Witnesses

The author characterizes these witnesses by associating them with a number of important symbols, including two olive trees, two lampstands, fire coming out of their mouths, authority to shut up the sky so that it does not rain, the power to turn water into blood, and the power to strike the earth with any plague anytime they wish. They are specifically said to be witnesses who will prophesy for a limited span of 1,260 days (11:3–6), which is a standard symbol for the period of three and a half years of tribulation. We have already encountered the lampstands as symbols for the churches (1:20); their number has been shifted to two here because the emphasis now is not on their perfection but on their function as witness (for the legal requirement of two witnesses see Deut 19:15) and also to match the symbolism of the two olive trees, which John derived from another vision, one found in the Hebrew Scriptures:

> The angel who talked with me came again, and wakened me, as one is wakened from sleep. He said to me, "What do you see?" And I said, "I see a lampstand all of gold, with a bowl on the top of it; there are seven lamps on it, with seven lips on each of the lamps that are on the top of it. And by it there are two olive trees, one on the right of the bowl and the other on its left." I said to the angel who talked with me, "What are these, my lord?" Then the angel who talked with me answered me, "Do you not know what these are?" I said, "No, my lord." . . . "These seven are the eyes of the LORD, which range through the whole earth." Then I said to him, "What are these two olive trees on the right and the left of the lampstand?" . . . Then he said, "These are the two anointed ones who stand by the Lord of the whole earth."
>
> ZECHARIAH 4

Now the two anointed offices in Israel were the king and the high priest. We have already seen John characterize the community as a community of kings and priests (1:6 and 5:10), so the connection of these witnesses with the community seems clear.

John then uses three images associated with figures from Israel's past to characterize these witnesses: like Jeremiah they consume their foes by the fire that pours from "their mouth" (a curious plural pronoun with a singular noun); like Elijah they have the power to shut the heavens; like Moses they smite with plagues and turn water into blood.

> Therefore thus says the LORD, the God of hosts: Because they have spoken this word, I am now making my words in your mouth a fire, and this people wood, and the fire shall devour them.   JER 5:14

> Now Elijah the Tishbite, of Tishbe in Gilead, said to Ahab, "As the LORD the God of Israel lives, before whom I stand, there shall be neither dew nor rain these years, except by my word."   1 KGS 17:1

> The LORD said to Moses, "Say to Aaron, 'Take your staff and stretch out your hand over the waters of Egypt—over its rivers, its canals, and its ponds, and all

its pools of water—so that they may become blood; and there shall be blood throughout the whole land of Egypt, even in vessels of wood and in vessels of stone.'" EXOD 7:19

Now these three figures share two important traits in Jewish tradition. First, they are prophets, each called by God to announce salvation and judgment at crucial points in Israel's history: at the exodus (Moses), at the time when kings led Israel to worship foreign Gods (Elijah; Jezebel was queen, see 2:20), and at the time of the exile when Israel almost ceased to exist as a nation (Jeremiah). The beginning, middle, and end. Second, each was expected to return at the end times to proclaim the final restoration.[17] Ancient Jewish tradition was rich in the variety of expectations it held about how the end would come and how God's reign of justice and peace would be inaugurated. Various scenarios ranging from the conversion to the extermination of the wicked, from holy war to persuasive preaching, from a Davidic king, to a heavenly deliverer, to a suffering servant were imagined by different groups, and often by the same group.[18] One such expectation was that a final prophet—most often Moses and/or Elijah—would return and restore Israel to the true worship of God, thus inaugurating God's reign on earth. Evil would be removed; justice would prevail. This is another way John characterizes the community of those who follow Jesus.

That John should so combine images of prophet, priest, and king should not surprise us. That such images taken literally might mutually contradict each other should cause no concern. This is symbolic and evocative language and is not meant to be taken literally. John shares in the rich traditions of his people.

The Souls under the Altar

Like Jesus the lion/lamb-slain, the witnesses are people of unimaginable power who are also people defeated, killed, abandoned (11:7–8). And so John has another characterization of the community. In the midst of the destruction of the earth we catch a glimpse of the base of the altar of sacrifice in the heavenly temple:

> I saw under the altar the souls of those who had been slaughtered for the word of God and for the testimony they had given; they cried out with a loud voice, "Sovereign Lord, holy and true, how long will it be before you judge and avenge our blood on the inhabitants of the earth?" They were each given a white robe and told to rest a little longer, until the number would be complete both of their fellow servants and of their brothers and sisters, who were soon to be killed as they themselves had been killed. REV 6:9–11

This is a pathetic image of the community that we are too prone to forget. They are the slaughtered and the being-slaughtered; their number continues to grow. But even here John breathes new hope into the characterization: they are given *white* robes of those who conquer; they are told it is for only "a little longer"; and, most of all, their lives are poured out on the altar of the heavenly temple. They have become a sacrifice, whose death brings life. In this too, they imitate their Savior.

The Multitude—Numbered and Innumerable

When it comes time to seal the servants of God so that none of the troubles of the tribulation period may harm them they are characterized numerically: "And I heard the number of those who were sealed, one hundred forty-four thousand, sealed out of every tribe of the people of Israel" (7:4). The symbolic significance of this number (12 and 10 = all God's servants) has been mentioned already (see pp. 6–10). This group might seem to be contrasted with another group that John next mentions: "After this I looked, and there was a great multitude that no one could count, from every nation, from all tribes and peoples and languages, standing before the throne and before the Lamb, robed in white, with palm branches in their hands" (7:9). But we should not take these designations literally. One clue, of course, is the little wink that there are more people here than one could count—as if we might run out of numbers before we run out of true worshipers. But also, to understand these as a second group fails to do justice to the imagery of the first group, for they are all God's people.

Symbolically then, the worshiping community is at the same time "gathered from every nation" and "God's true Israel," just as they are at the same time innumerable and 144,000. This understanding of the community (including its gentile members) as Israel will shape the way John tells this story. For example, many readers notice that the images of palm branches, white clothing, and proclamation of salvation (7:9–10) are associated with the Feast of Tabernacles, the great Jewish pilgrim festival that celebrated Israel's safe passage through the wilderness and entrance into the promised land. It is just such a sure march to the new Jerusalem that identifies John's community.[19]

The further characterization of these people as dressed in white and carrying palm branches indicates that they are conquerors, victorious over the powers of evil. This is the other side of the image of the souls under the altar: the conquered and the conquerors.

Unlike the characterization of the churches in the first unit, the characterization of these followers contains not even a hint of criticism or judgment. All the negative characterization of the followers occurs in the messages to the seven churches. From the end of the letter scroll to the end of the work, an idealized picture emerges.[20] This is part of the author's larger strategy of resolving good and evil into ever clearer categories, so that by the time one finishes the story there can be no question of what is good and what is evil.

THE OPPONENTS

The final characters we meet in this section are those who oppose God, and thus make themselves enemies of the lamb and the lamb's followers. They remain vaguely characterized: implied in the slaughtered lamb and the souls (lives) under the altar (6:9), invoked by the four riders (6:1–8), imperiled by the various plagues and judgments, but only explicitly revealed at two points in the story. Our first glimpse of evil appears in the shapes that ascend from the bottomless pit, a blend of locust and scorpion, but built like horses with human faces, they torture without killing. They are ruled by one whose name "in Hebrew is Abaddon, and in Greek he is called Apollyon" (9:11). While the meaning of these details remains obscure, the clear image of a ruler of diabolical forces of evil that invade this world represents a dramatic shift in the telling of the story, where up till now evil has been largely seen in human terms.*

The shift is developed further in the second such reference where, upon the completion of their witness, the two witnesses are besieged and conquered by the "beast that ascends from the pit" (11:7). Whereas the locust army of Apollyon had attacked only those without the seal of God, the beast attacks and kills the witnesses of God. This is shocking, for we have been told that those who follow God will be protected. We will consider its meaning below when we explore the sequence of the action. Here we ask only what does it mean for our understanding of the nature of the opponents? And at minimum it must mean that the opponents' power must not be underestimated. Further, it suggests that John's characterization of evil has some complexity to it. We misread this story if we see only that aspect of evil that is easily defeated, is indeed already destroyed. For evil is at the same time alive and powerful.

Finally, we should note the audience's potential surprise by this sudden appearance of the beast, without explanation or elaboration—both of which must wait till the next phase of John's story when this character will be properly introduced (see chapter 13). It is only after we have heard the third of John's stories that we can understand this beast. This is further evidence that these stories must be heard together.

The Sequence of the Action

We turn now to a discussion of the significance of the order of the events told and of the way they are told, beginning with a notion of the plot of this

---

*We are accustomed to "flashbacks" in stories, when we realize a scene we are seeing really belongs to an earlier stage of the story. This is often done in dreams or memory-sequences in modern stories. What we have in this scene with the beast and the witnesses is a "flashforward" presenting a glimpse of John's third narrative movement.

section (4:1–11:18). For a general summary see p. 61. At the heart of the notion of plot is the idea of a causal connection between events in a sequence. (See pp. 10–16 of the Prologue for an overview of plot.) A reader tries to formulate the events of a story into a logical sequence and to follow the development of the action to some sort of conclusion.

My own reading of the dominant line of action in this section sees the central action as beginning, interruption, and then completion of a divine liturgy—a service of worship. John spends some time orienting us to the liturgy, with an elaborate description of the throne (4:1–8a) followed by a brief description of the worship events (4:8b–11). Then a problem arises: There is a sealed scroll and no one worthy to open it (5:1–4). This problem is solved by the appearance of the lion/lamb, whose presence is celebrated by continued worship (5:5–14). As this lamb opens the seals of the scroll, we get a story within a story. This embedded story has its own plot of suffering, judgment, and salvation carefully sequenced by a numbered series of seven (6:1–8:1). It is immediately followed by another embedded story also told as a numbered series of seven, now seven trumpets (8:2–11:18), but itself containing other stories, including an overlapping series of three woes (see 8:13) and an unnarrated series of seven thunders (see 10:3b–4). As the last trumpet sounds, a voice proclaims the reality of God's reign and the worship events resume (11:15–18).

The sequence of kernels[21]—the key story events that are connected by some narrative logic—then is: the divine liturgy; the dilemma of the sealed scroll; the revelation of the lion/lamb worthy to open the scroll; the unsealing of the scroll; the trumpets' signal; the proclamation of God's reign; the resumption of the divine liturgy. This is a plot of order, disruption, reestablishing of order—probably the most common plot in literature.[22] It is also the plot of the basic Christian story: God created the world good; humans forsook this goodness and turned away from the divine plan; God redeems the world through Jesus. In fact, if we probe the basic metaphor of a "service of worship" we will find the underlying connection between the ancient ideas of kingship and liturgy. In this "service" one becomes obedient to God the ruler when one worships God, thus bringing the reign of God into existence within the worship setting. This metaphoric interchange between worship and reign will appear many times in the Apocalypse, including the two references to the community as both priests (worship) and as kingdom (reign; 1:6; 5:10; see also 20:6).

If we take this sequence to be the basic plot-line of this section, then the other actions should be seen as auxiliary units (satellites) rather than as contributing to the forward movement of the plot. Their contributions are of different sorts: to explain, to elaborate, to redirect, to review. We must remember that everything we are seeing takes place within the divine liturgy and thus serves to interpret that liturgy. Now let us look more closely at these events.

Commentary on the Action

Having considered the significance of the setting of this action in the heav
enly throne room and discussed the primary characters and their traits and
the plot sequence, we now turn our attention to the individual scenes.

THE DIVINE LITURGY, 4:1–11

John carefully positions the action of this next section by repetition of the
words "after this." In Greek all of verse one is a single sentence, so the sentence opens and closes with identical words: *meta tauta*, after this. Thus the
scene in heaven occurs "after this" (John's vision of the Heavenly figure)
and John sees what will take place "after this" (a more vague reference).
Most take it as referring to the future, but this is doubtful, for what John
sees is the worship before God's throne in heaven. Surely John understood
that heavenly worship as a present event. Rather, *after this* should be understood to mean "as a consequence of this."[23] Both John's vision of heaven
and the true worship of God are a consequence of Jesus' witness, in John's
scheme of things.

The action of this scene opens slowly as the author retards the pace of the
telling by giving an elaborate description of the setting (4:1–8a). If we
imagine this as a film, we would see that nothing happens as the camera
pans the room, showing us item after item. Genette calls this a narrative
pause,[24] time is passing but nothing is happening. (We will discuss the temporal aspect of this section more fully on pp. 97–99.) Or more precisely,
what is happening is that the audience is being made aware of elements
of the story world that are necessary to interpret the action about to ensue.
By contrast, when characters and events are introduced they are told in
summary fashion, greatly accelerating the pace of the narrative (4:8b–11).

The action is itself very simple: the two major characters each praise God
in song and action. This strategy of summarizing the action and then presenting the words as if they were spoken emphasizes the content of their
songs, which focus on the being and the worthiness of God. The technique
of choral speaking is reminiscent of Greek drama, where a chorus summarizes and comments on the meaning of the action. In both these ways, then,
the audience is directed to pay attention to the words of the songs.[25]

REV 4:1–11 *Readers' Notes on the Divine Liturgy*

Rev 4:1–3

OPEN DOOR Enoch is shown ascending into heaven where he enters a great house
through an open door (*1 Enoch* 14:8–15), but a closer parallel is found in
Testament of Levi 5:1: "At this moment the angel opened for me the gates of
heaven and I saw the Holy Most High sitting on the throne."[26] John may also be

playing with motifs from the first section, where both a closed door (3:20) and an open door (3:8) figure in the action.

COME UP HERE John expresses his experience in terms of the "three-story" universe of his day. See pp. 64–65.

AFTER THIS Greek: *Meta tauta* (after these things), the same phrase used to open and close this first verse (4:1). Although it is common for modern interpreters to take this in a temporal sense, we should recognize that this scene is set in heaven, where temporal succession might not correlate with regular time. The real paradigm is not temporal but spatial: what is seen in heaven corresponds with what happens on earth. Seeing what takes place in heaven reveals what *must* take place on earth as a consequence. In fact, it is what John sees in heaven (the worship of God) that constitutes "what must take place after this." This scene of worship is the sum and symbol of all that is portrayed in this story.

POSSESSED BY THE SPIRIT See the Readers' Note on 1:10, p. 38. John ascends by going inward.

THRONE A frequent and central symbol in this story, signaling the political significance of these actions. See the reference to Satan's throne in 2:13. John's description is similar to that in the vision in Ezekiel 1.

STONE OF JASPER While we can no longer be certain just what gems John was referring to, we can still be startled that he chooses mineral metaphors for God.

RAINBOW Since ancient times a promise of divine protection; see Gen 9:12–13 and Ezek 1:28. See also at Rev 10:1.

Rev 4:4–7

TWENTY-FOUR ELDERS See the discussion on p. 71.

WHITE CLOTHING On the significance of white to denote victory see pp. 6–10 and 70–74.

CROWNS OF GOLD Greek: *stephanos*, crown or wreath. The kind of crown given to victors in the athletic contests (1 Cor 9:25), though this one is made of gold. Such crowns were worn by the high priest (Josephus, *Antiquities* 3.172), by companions of Gods in Greco-Roman festivals, and even by the king. It is a sign of status and honor rather than of power. Jesus wears both this type (14:14) and the kingly crown (19:12).

LIGHTNING . . . VOICES . . . THUNDERS The usual elements marking a manifestation of the divine presence (for which the technical word is theophany; see Exod 20:18).

SEVEN LAMPS . . . SPIRITS Lamps is literally "torches of fire" and here represent the Holy Spirit (see the Readers' Notes on 1:9–20, pp. 38–41). John seems to echo the images of Zech 4:2,10, where the notion is God's knowledge of the world.

Rev 4:8–11

FOUR ANIMALS Four because they represent the earth. On the identity of these see pp. 70–71.

HOLY, HOLY, HOLY This acclamation was built on Isa 6:3, and had become a traditional part of worship in Jewish and Christian contexts. See 1 Clement 34 where the writer uses the heavenly acclamation as a basis for community practice.

WHO WAS AND IS AND IS TO COME John's unique characterization of God; see pp. 30–34.

TO RECEIVE . . . POWER That God might receive glory and honor from humans is easier to grasp than how God might receive power, but the latter is worth reflecting on. For similar language see the prayer of David as given in 1 Chr 29:10–13.

CREATED This notion of God as creator underlies not only the whole of this scene, but also its prototypes in the prayer of David (1 Chr 29:10) and the vision of Isaiah (6:1).

THE PROBLEM OF THE SEALED SCROLL, 5:1–14

The action of this scene develops quickly, with little attention given to description beyond what is needed to establish the characters (on the characters see pp. 68–75). John now notices that the one on the throne holds a sealed scroll, and when the challenge goes out for one worthy to open the scroll no one is found. John weeps, but is comforted by one of the elders who announces that the lion of Judah has prevailed to open the scroll. What John sees, however, is the slain-standing lamb, who now takes the scroll from the one on the throne, causing the four animals, the elders, the angels, indeed all creation to join the heavenly worship.

I will note in passing the temporal distortion involved, for the resumption of worship narrated here is a proleptic glimpse (a kind of foreshadowing) of the final redemption which will be told in due course when all the actions implied in the taking of the scroll have been worked out. A more systematic discussion of temporal distortions will be found on pp. 97–99. It is as if all subsequent actions regarding the scroll were embedded in this initial taking (much as the author of Hebrews imagines that all subsequent descendants of Abraham were embedded in him and thus could be said to do whatever he had done—Heb 7:9–10). This understanding of action will produce a strong repetitive quality to this narrative, and makes it very difficult to deal with the concept of narrative closure, for the story "seems over" repeatedly before it finally is finished.

For in one sense this is all there is to the story of Revelation: the act of the lamb reestablishes the service of God. This redemption will be symbolized in many ways, from the revelations and comings of the letters to the earthquakes, wars, and devastation of the final scenes. But all these symbols point to the same reality: the reestablishment of God's reign. This is perhaps what Augustine meant when he said that John "repeats the same things in many ways, so that he appears to be speaking of different matters, though in fact he is found on examination to be treating the same subjects in different terms" (*City of God* 20). One who reads this scene with understanding understands the basic theme of the work, for it is the revelation of Jesus Christ (see pp. 2–3).

REV 5:1–14 *Readers' Notes on the Sealed Scroll*

Rev 5:1–3

RIGHT HAND A cultural code for power and favor. It is always the hand of God's deliverance and blessing (e.g., Ps 20:6; 44:3; 98:1); the Bible never mentions God's left hand. In ancient cultures the left hand was always inferior, often shameful (e.g., Eccl 10:2; Matthew 25; *Community Rule [1QS] VII*).

BOOK-ROLL How impressed the ancients were with the power of writing will often be reflected in the Apocalypse (3:5; 13:8; 17:8; 20:12, 15; 21:27), a power reflected in the writing of *this* book (22:9). The notion that God has recorded all history and that we only read as it unfolds is reflected already in the psalmist who wrote: "In your book were written all the days that were formed for me, when none of them as yet existed" (139:16). The fact that the scroll is written "on the inside and on the back" can be understood in two ways: that the writing is so extensive that the author had to use both sides of the sheet, so to speak (scribes seldom did this, for the fibers on the back of a papyrus sheet ran vertically, making it difficult to write on); that there is a short synopsis written on the outside, while the inside is protected by seals so it cannot be changed. This was the practice for wills and certain legal contracts. Such a document would only be opened when there was a conflict or some need to put the contract into effect (as in the death of the will maker). The imagery derives from Ezek 2:10, to which John will return in chapter 10.

SEVEN SEALS The primary meaning of seven symbolizes the completeness or perfection of the scroll and its contents. It is of some interest that Roman wills apparently were typically sealed with seven seals of witnesses; and there may be some irony in this writing revealing the will of God.

WORTHY Here meaning having the requisite power or accomplishment, as its parallelism with "able to open" makes clear. It is analogous to the Arthur legend wherein only the worthy one can extract the sword from the stone. The precise nature of the action that makes one worthy will be surprising (see Rev 5:9).

Rev 5:4–7

I WEPT A remarkable introjection of the prophet's own feelings into the scene.

LION . . . LAMB See pp. 69–70.

SEVEN HORNS, EYES, SPIRITS Power, knowledge and the spirit. See pp. 69–70.

FOUR ANIMALS Four is the number of the earth; see pp. 70–71.

TWENTY FOUR ELDERS See p. 71.

INCENSE Specifically defined here as meaning the prayers of the saints (5:8). This image will be worked into the story again at 8:2; see pp. 88–89.

Rev 5:8–14

NEW SONG Not just newly composed, but belonging to the new age; see Psalm 98.

SLAUGHTERED . . . RANSOMED . . . BLOOD This is the language of the sacrificial cult and of the slave market. One might profitably compare Lucius' understanding of himself as rescued from the slavery of passions by the Goddess Isis, who is worthy to do so because of her grand deeds.27 Only the grand deed here in view is the death of the hero.

KINGDOM . . . PRIESTS See the Readers' Note on 1.9 (p. 38) and the discussion of the elders in pp. 70–74.

WILL REIGN Many manuscripts have the present tense rather than the future. The present tense is probably the original, since it is more typical of the Apocalypse and it is easy to imagine why a scribe might intentionally change it to a future (by adding one letter) but not so easy to see why a scribe might change it to a present.

EVERY CREATURE Or "all creation," "everything created." However ruthless the rest of the story may appear to be in regard to the creation, this scene should color our understanding of the intention, which is redemption not destruction.

THE UNSEALING AND THE SEALING, 6:1–8:1

This lengthy section is bound together by the device of the breaking of the seals on the scroll; the first is broken in 6:1; the last in 8:1. Thus the main line of action is that which results directly from the breaking of the seals. But there also occurs a variety of other actions. Some refer to this additional material as interludes, interpolations, or as digressions, but we will persist in the categories of kernel and satellite.28 Kernel incidents directly follow from the opening of seals while satellite incidents revolve around these.

We should remind ourselves of how deeply into the narrative we are at this juncture. We have left the first level narrative (John addressing the reader), gone through the second level (John on Patmos), the third level (John's vision of heaven), the fourth level (what John sees in heaven), to the fifth level (things seen by characters in the scene John sees in heaven). All the actions stemming from the scroll occur at this narrative level.

The vision centers on a sealed scroll, which we should imagine as a lengthy sheet of papyrus (a kind of stiff paper) rolled into a tube and then bound with seven ribbons, each tied and then sealed with a wax impression. See pp. 79–81 for discussion of the scroll and the significance of seven seals. Some have questioned the logic whereby a part of the scroll seems to be revealed as each seal is opened, since any one intact seal would prevent opening the scroll to read it. But this is to fall prey to literal thinking. While it may be literally impossible to open the scroll one seal at a time, it makes perfectly satisfactory symbolic sense in a world where one action is seen as embedding all subsequent actions that spring from it.

I would segment the text into four interrelated sets of action: the four horses with riders, the two seals of judgment, the sealing for protection, and the seventh seal.

The Four Horses of Conquest, 6:1–8

One of the most influential symbols of Revelation, these four riders have often been celebrated in literature and art, including the magnificent woodcut by Albrecht Dürer. They form a logical and consistent series that has often been acted out in history: first a conqueror appears, followed by war, famine, and death. (Although some readers identify the rider on the white horse with Jesus, on the basis of the scene in 19:11–16, this makes no sense from a narrative perspective. Even if one spiritualized the war, famine and death would not follow in logical course. Nor does the rider possess the distinctive icon of Jesus: the two-edged sword.)

The first rider echoes traits of a Roman general (who would enter Rome on a white horse after a successful campaign); a Parthian king (whose riders were fierce bowmen); and the mystery God Mithras (whose mythology connected him with the sun and its struggle with darkness, and whose conquest over the lengthening night was celebrated at the winter solstice). All three may be appropriate, since Mithras was the prime God of the Roman army and was also worshiped in Parthia. Some images show him wearing a radiant crown, representative of the sun. The unconquerable sun became the military symbol for conquest, but John delegitimizes it by showing the disasters that follow: war, famine, and death. This is a logical sequence, often repeated in history even up to our own time. We would do well to reflect on this sequence, for however well-meaning the conqueror might be, the use of force breeds disaster. Even in the modern world we have recently seen the disasters of Africa and Eastern Europe—not to mention those of Hitler or Napoleon in earlier days. In the ancient world the cause-effect logic of the sequence was even more clear. Wars not only caused immediate death and destruction, they interrupted the agricultural cycle, and the ensuing social chaos often led to disease and death.

One might wonder how such an obvious sequence (conqueror-war-famine-death) could constitute a revelation, and the answer is important for understanding an apocalypse. An apocalypse does not so much give new information as it does interpret the information available. The root meaning of *apocalypsis* is to remove the veil; to allow one to see what is hidden, thus to reveal (see pp. 3–5 and 26–29). What John offers us here is not merely a picture of history, but an insight into what is going on behind history. This story tells us not so much how things happen as they do, but why.

Having shown us the forces behind history, John now turns to the consequences: suffering and judgment.

The Seals of Justice and Judgment, 6:9–17

Passing to the fifth seal we enter a vastly different narrative world: horses, riders, wars and their aftermath are all gone, not even alluded to. Clearly seals one through four are a self-contained unit. Nevertheless, the reader is prodded to make a connection with the previous scene not only because the two are put side by side but because they are numbered as part of the same series. We are left to imagine just how the "souls under the altar" are a consequence of the series of conquest-war-famine-death.

To imagine the relationship we must be clear of what happens in this vignette: we see under the altar the souls/lives of martyrs who cry out for justice by asking "how long?" They are given white robes, told to rest a little longer, "until the number would be complete" of those who would be killed. Both their question and the answer to it involve calculations of time: when will this madness end? And this would seem to be as appropriate a response to the first four seals as anything. The answer is baffling, requiring a deeper insight than the reader is prepared for. Does justice really await some numerical total? The logic of this response will only become clear as the story draws to its end (especially the scene of the grand prostitute in chapter 17). What is clear is that nothing is to be done (rest) but victory is assured (white robes).

The sixth seal now shows what the judgment will look like when it comes. All the elements shown here are typical of various visions of the final judgment: earthquake, darkening of the sun and moon, falling stars. The cosmic foundations of creation are coming undone.29

This is a dreadful scene and taken at face value raises questions about the ethics of this writing. Especially troublesome are the universal nature of the judgment, the destruction of creation, and the notion of "the wrath of the Lamb." Yet this last phrase also alerts us to the irony of the scene, for lambs are stereotypically gentle. Which side of this oxymoron do we trust: does the lamb redefine the wrath or does the wrath redefine the lamb? A further irony may be drawn from the earlier scene in which all creation was seen worshiping at God's throne (5:13). Here the creation is asked to hide those in rebellion against God.

The effort to hide itself may be understood ironically. Whereas the characters intend it to be an effort to avoid God's judgment, it echoes that earliest human action in the story of Eden, when Adam and Eve attempt to hide from God because they know their sin (Gen 3:8). This is only one of many echoes in this story to the stories of creation.

Those facing this dissolution of creation are terrified and cry out: who is able to stand before it? The following incident answers this question before proceeding with the final climactic seventh seal.

The Sealing of the Servants of God, 7:1–17

Some have called this an interlude, but its narrative function is more immediate, for it directly answers the question raised by the previous scene (who can stand?) and it prepares the audience for the third narrative segment in which there will be a cosmic war involving precisely these characters (see 14:1). It also plays verbally off the action of this sequence: as the scroll comes unsealed the elect are sealed. Fortunately the pun works in English as well as in Greek.

The action unfolds in three segments. Four angels with power to harm the earth appear and are told by another angel to wait until the servants of God are sealed on their foreheads. Those to be sealed are designated as 144,000 from Israel and an innumerable multitude from every nation. (On the characters involved, see the appropriate discussion on pp. 70–74.) As these worship God, one of the elders before God's throne asks John who these folk are. John cleverly replies that the elder knows, causing him to explain that "These are they who have come out of the great ordeal; they have washed their robes and made them white in the blood of the Lamb" (7:14). They will henceforth be cared for by the lamb who will be their shepherd (compare Psalm 23). John seems fond of such oxymorons.

This action of protecting the servants is a good example of temporal distortion in the telling of the story, for coming where it does it is out of place. We have already seen the earth harmed in the sixth seal, so this delay (7:3) must have occurred earlier. Also once done, one expects to see devastation, but the seventh seal is no such thing. Chronologically this action must come between seals five and six but John tells it between six and seven. Two things are gained by this narrative strategy. First, John enhances the cause-effect relationship between the action of seal five (prayers for justice) and that of seal six (divine judgment). Second, John enhances the readers' sense that the story is far more complex and drawn out than the simple series of seven seals is able to show. There is more to the story. And the seventh seal is truly surprising, perhaps one of the greatest anticlimaxes in all literature.

The Seventh Seal of Silence, 8:1

"When the Lamb opened the seventh seal, there was silence in heaven for about half an hour" (8:1). The logic of the series and the symbolic significance of seven lead the audience to expect a vision of God's kingdom, but instead: silence. John does not suggest any explanation for the silence, and readers attempting to imagine it have made two suggestions. First, silence may itself be an image of the new order. Another writer in this same time period, who shares many images with John, portrayed the coming new age thus:

> For behold, the time will come, when the signs which I have foretold to you will come to pass, that the city which now is not seen shall appear, and the land which now is hidden shall be disclosed. And every one who has been delivered from the evils that I have foretold shall see my wonders. For my son the Messiah shall be revealed with those who are with him, and those who remain shall rejoice four hundred years. And after these years my son the

Messiah shall die, and all who draw human breath. And the world shall be turned back to primeval silence for seven days, as it was at the first beginnings; so that no one shall be left. And after seven days the world, which is not yet awake, shall be roused, and that which is corruptible shall perish. And the earth shall give up those who are asleep in it, and the dust those who dwell silently in it; and the chambers shall give up the souls which have been committed to them. And the Most High shall be revealed upon the seat of judgment, and compassion shall pass away, and patience shall be withdrawn; but only judgment shall remain, truth shall stand, and faithfulness shall grow strong.   2 ESD 7:26–34

So the notion of a primeval silence before the new creation was known, though John's silence is considerably shorter. Viewed this way the silence fulfills our expectation that somehow the seventh member symbolizes the new order.

A second possible understanding of the silence views it as the silence between the opening of the scroll (now freed of the last of its seals) and the beginning of the reading of the scroll. This approach sees the intervening seven trumpets as anticipatory flourishes to prepare for the reading, which takes place at 11:15. The sequence of action then is: heavenly worship, worship interrupted by the sealed scroll, the worthy lamb opens the scroll, there is silence, trumpets, and then the reading of the scroll, followed by the resumption of worship. This suggestion has the advantage of tying the seals and trumpets series closely together. Of course our writer is a master of ambiguity and both understandings may be intended.

REV 6:1–8:1 *Readers' Notes on the Seven Seals*

Rev 6:1–8

HORSE The animal, but also used as a collective noun for the cavalry.

WHITE The color of conquest not purity. It is used nineteen times in Revelation, usually of clothing (3:4, 5, 18; 4:4; 6:11; 7:9, 13, 14) but also of hair (1:14), a stone (2:17), a throne (20:11), a cloud (14:14), and other horses (19:11, 14). In all the other instances the conquest is the positive conquest of good over evil, but the conquest symbolized by this horse leads to war, famine, and death.

BOW This is the only such weapon in the Apocalypse and is never an icon of Jesus. It seems a more general image for the military, but Parthian warriors were famous for their bows.

CROWN The sort of victory crown given in athletic contests (*stephanos*); as a symbol of victory it is appropriate to the conqueror.

RED The color of the blood shed in war.

BLACK The color of dead vegetation.

BALANCE The merchant's scale.

DENARIUS The equivalent of a day's wages for a working person.

WHEAT . . . BARLEY The yearly crops most at risk in war. An individual might survive on the bread made from the wheat but a family would need the larger quantity of the inferior grain. The famine is such that a working person would need most of the day's earnings for the day's food.

OIL . . . WINE Long term crops not needing yearly planting and thus not affected by this human-caused famine.

PALE The yellow-grey of rotting flesh.

HADES The place of the dead and thus by extension another name for death. In Greek writings it is used as a name for the brother of Zeus who rules the underworld.

ONE-FOURTH Part of the escalating idiom of John's visions of destruction; the next series (trumpets) will destroy one-third (8:7–12); the last (bowls) will destroy all (16:1–12).

WILD BEASTS The animals of prey that would haunt the battlefields along with disease and pestilence, but also—along with sword, famine, and pestilence—a sign of God's judgment (Ezek 14:21).

Rev 6:9–11

ALTAR Altars were of two types: one for sacrificing animals, whose blood would be poured at the base; one for burning incense. This is the heavenly counterpart of the sacrificial altar, with the lives of the martyred replacing the blood of animals. On the connection between blood and life-force, see Lev 17:11, 14. The symbolism here encourages the hearer to consider that what may appear to be a hapless death at the hands of the powers of this world is in reality a sacrifice on the high altar of that other world.

SOULS Hardly a picture of heaven, but rather of an intermediate state of waiting. The word could also be translated *lives* and is probably best understood as a picture of their battered lives giving testimony to the evils of their oppressors.

SLAUGHTERED Thus their lives have imitated Jesus (5:6). The word is especially appropriate for the killing of the animal of sacrifice.

TESTIMONY Another way they identify with Jesus (see 1:2). Being a witness (*martys*) who bears testimony (*martyria*) is central to the worldview of the Apocalypse.

HOW LONG? A crucial question for John's whole story. The same question followed Zechariah's vision of the four horses on which John has built (Zech 1:12).

AVENGE Retribution is a very important theme in the Apocalypse and it sometimes sounds vengeful. As here where the martyred ask for recompense on their oppressors, perhaps not a noble sentiment but one understandable by anyone who has witnessed any great evil. For a strikingly similar scene, see 2 Esd 4:35–37. Later in the story the justice of God's recompense will be declared in a fashion that casts new light on the action here:

> And I heard the angel of the waters say, "You are just, O Holy One, who are and were, for you have judged these things; because they shed the blood of saints and prophets, you have given them blood to drink. It is

what they deserve!" And I heard the altar respond, "Yes, O Lord God, the Almighty. . . . " REV 16:5–7

This suggests that retribution is more like Karma (inevitable consequence) than like revenge.

REST Their work is now done; they should await God's work. See their return at 20:4.

COMPLETE NUMBER Perhaps best understood in light of the meaning of avenge above: the more witnesses the system kills the more it hastens its own downfall.

Rev 6:12–17

AS A FIG TREE . . . LIKE A SCROLL Two wonderful similes that show John's power with images. If John's inspiration was Isa 34:4, he has considerably enhanced the feeling. Anyone who has worked with rolled paper can imagine the surprise of someone whose scroll suddenly snaps shut. Obviously one cannot take these images (including the sun turning black) literally for the consequence would be the end of all biological life on earth.

WRATH OF THE LAMB This oxymoron defines the basic moral issue of the Apocalypse. Does the wrath redefine the meaning of the lamb or does the lamb redefine the meaning of wrath?

Rev 7:1–8

FOUR The number of the earth, as this little scene makes clear. The word four is echoed in the one hundred and forty *four* thousand. Such happy coincidences seemed to the ancients to justify their belief in the mystical significance of numbers. On the four winds connected with four horses, see Zech 6:5–8.

SEAL The notion of sealing was a widely used metaphor in early Christianity, most often connected with baptism (see 1 Cor 1:13–15; Hermas, *Sim* 9.16), as a replacement for circumcision (Rom 4:11). It was also used of the Eucharist (John 6:27) and of having the spirit (2 Cor 1:21–22; Eph 1:13). The source of John's action may be Ezekiel's charge: "Go through the city, through Jerusalem, and put a mark on the foreheads of those who sigh and groan over all the abominations that are committed in it" (9:4).

FOREHEAD More than just a convenient writing space, the head is symbolic of the submission of the spirit (see the Readers' Note on the mark of the beast, 13:16, p. 130).

144,000 The number is based on 12 and 10, the first squared, the second cubed. The meanings of the root numbers have to do with being God's people and with totality; the effect of squaring and cubing is only to enhance the root meaning.

TWELVE TRIBES The sign of a regathered Israel had been taken over from expectations about the return from Exile and was widely expected in the last days (see Isaiah 43). This, however, is an odd listing of the tribes. Traditionally they included Dan and Ephraim (missing here) and did not number Levi or Joseph. No one has yet suggested a convincing reason for this anomaly.

Rev 7:9–8:1

GREAT MULTITUDE Since the 144,000 symbolize the whole people of God (see 14:1), I would see these as the same group, now construed under a new metaphor: an innumerable crowd. Lest one be tempted to take 144,000 quantitatively rather than qualitatively, we are told the quantity is beyond counting. Others see this as a second group of Gentiles, imagining John's community to be a divided community of Jews and Gentiles.

WORSHIPED GOD This is the same scene portrayed in chapters 4 and 5, here enhanced with images from the Feast of Tabernacles (Sukkot): white robes, palm branches, water and shelter (the word translated shelter also means tabernacle, 7:15). We will be repeatedly reminded that the demand to worship (only) God is at the heart of this vision story.

GREAT ORDEAL The time of troubles immediately preceding the coming end of the age. Note that it is underway in John's vision of things (and literally: the ones coming out . . . a present tense).

WASHED Perhaps a reference to martyrdom, but more likely to baptism, for in baptism Christians believed they identified with the death of Jesus (see Rom 6:1–4).

HUNGER . . . THIRST First an image drawn from expectations of a return from Exile (Isa 49:10), but then an image connected with the Eucharist.

HALF HOUR Hour most commonly means the twelfth-part of a day, but may be used for any time segment: part of the year, part of the month, season. This is a half segment.

THE WORK OF THE ANGELS, 8:2–11:18

In the silence that ensues, John witnesses preparations for a new series of visions: seven angels are given seven trumpets. But before that series unfolds, another angel appears and performs actions symbolic of believers at prayer. Perhaps another reason for the silence is to allow the prayers to be heard.

The Angel at the Altar, 8:3–5

We have already seen that one of the functions of angels in this story is to represent the heavenly counterpart to the faithful earthly community. (See the Readers' Notes on the Seven Letters, pp. 54–60.) In this short scene inserted into the opening of a new seven-series, John recapitulates the action of seals five and six (the martyrs' plea for justice and the divine judgment of earth). It is a wonderful miniature of some of the central themes of the book. Read it out loud.

It is striking that God does nothing in this scene, yet judgment is carried out. The prayers themselves, as they ascend before God, gain power and rebound to earth, shaking the very foundations of creation. Eugene Boring points out how rare is the reference to prayer in the Apocalypse (only mentioned in 5:8 and here), yet how powerful. He relates it to the ancient Jewish prayer called the Kaddish, which is a call for the sanctification of God's name, especially in the face of death: "Magnified and sanctified be his great name in the world that he has created according to his will. May he establish his kingdom in your lifetime and in your days and in the lifetime of all the house of Israel, even speedily and at a near time."30 This intrinsic connection between prayer and God's reign stands at the center of John's story. We should recall this scene whenever we are tempted to wonder why John repeatedly admonishes the hearers to "worship God."

The Angels with the Trumpets, 8:2, 6–11:18

Unlike the previous series, all of the trumpets are signals of doom and destruction. Like the previous series, they are divided into two subsets of four and three, the last three being characterized as three woes (8:13; 9:12; 11:14). In one sense, these trumpets are simply an amplification of the sixth seal: revelations of divine judgment on the earth. Though now the destruction has increased from one-fourth to one-third, indicating some forward movement of the action.

It is less important to grasp all the particulars of the plagues than it is to feel their power and horror. Perhaps the feeling here is best compared to watching a horror movie, as each disaster leads on to another more repulsive. The first four trumpets attack all creation: earth and vegetation; the sea and marine life; fresh water and humans; and the sun, moon, and stars. In each case they are assaulted and one-third is devastated. These disasters are not realistic, of course. One could not turn a third of the sea to blood without destroying all marine life (8:8–9) or dim the sun by a third without destroying all biological life on earth (8:12). These are images of disaster, repeated in differing spheres for their cumulative effect. And that cumulative effect is great.

Just when it seems that the devastation has spread everywhere, an eagle in flight announces three woes (in Greek: *ouai, ouai, ouai*) connected with the three final trumpets. And a new story element emerges, the demonic is unleashed. First from the pit (the abyss) deadly demonic locusts emerge, with power to torment but not kill humanity. These locusts are shaped like horses, with gold crowns, human faces, and hair like women have. With lions' teeth and scorpions' tails they wreak havoc for five months. They do not harm plants (the locusts' natural prey) but only such humans as are not marked with God's seal on their forehead (see p. 84).

The sixth trumpet takes us back to the altar of incense from where this whole series was launched (8:3). A voice from the altar itself instructs the angel to release the four primordial angels of destruction. Their mission is to kill a third of the human race. Now the story takes a very strange turn, raising important questions. For we are told:

The rest of humankind, who were not killed by these plagues, did not repent of the works of their hands or give up worshiping demons and idols of gold

and silver and bronze and stone and wood, which cannot see or hear or walk.
And they did not repent of their murders or their sorceries or their fornication
or their thefts.   REV 9:20–21

This is the first we have heard of a possible divine motive for these disasters;
till now the reader has assumed that they are merely for justice, God's
response to the cry of the oppressed. Now we wonder, is God tormenting
people to make them repent? Taken at face value, this is morality on a plane
with the Spanish Inquisition: torture the body to save the soul. Romans
would later torment Christians until they "repented" of their folly (see
Pliny's letter on pp. 166–67).

Another possible interpretation arises from the allusion to these torments
as plagues: the Exodus stories about the unrepentant Pharaoh (Exod 8:32
but also 10:20). In those stories also a series of plagues is visited on the
land, but the king hardens his heart and refuses to release the slaves. But
here too, on the literal level at least, we are not far from divine intimidation.
This is a strand of thought we must stay alert to as we read this story.

Just as the sixth seal was extended by the sealing of the faithful, so the
sixth trumpet is extended by symbolic acts of protection. Yet another angel
appears.

The Angel with the Rainbow and Open Scroll, 10:1–11:13

This section contains two complex and difficult scenes with little obvious
relationship to the immediate context. But John has created the need for
seeing them in this setting by embedding them within the sixth trumpet
(which logically does not end until the announcement of the completion of
the second woe in 11:14). Embedded narratives have a distinctive quality,
operating in another time and space than the primary narrative. They function as commentary on the primary narrative.

In fact, there seems to be a double embedding here. For in the primary
narrative John is in heaven, seeing a vision. In that vision he sees the
destruction of the earth and then an angel descends to the earth. Clearly the
point of view here is from the earth ("coming down from heaven") and the
John who sees it is on earth—where in fact John sees himself. Such spatial
disruption (John in heaven seeing himself on earth) can be confusing.

This descending angel first instructs John to eat a small open scroll that
the angel brings in its hand. Then John is instructed to measure God's temple, with an accompanying story of the fate of two witnesses. Sprinkled
throughout are moments of humor, irony, and mystery. Let us consider this
action more closely.

The angel has traits that echo those of the majestic human in John's
opening vision, without quite matching. They are alike, perhaps, but not
the same. This enormous figure places one foot on the sea and one on the
land and presents John with a small scroll, specifically said to be open (the

audience is perhaps thankful that we don't need to unseal it!). However, in response to the roar of the angel, seven thunders sound. Instead of revealing what they said, John is to seal it up. This has several effects. It adds to the mystery (something remains hidden); it adds to John's authority (he knows something we do not); it adds to the audience's expectation (there will be no more delay). The seventh trumpet will be the end. John is perhaps having a little fun with us, for in fact we are nowhere near the end of the story.

Now John is instructed to eat the scroll; and when he does it is sweet, but gives him indigestion. Immediately the interpretation is given: John must prophesy again. (See a similar scene in Ezek 3:1–3.) This is symbolic, I think, of the fact that a third scroll delineating the cosmic war is yet to be given. This third scroll is the story of the cosmic war in chapters 12–22. The first scroll entailed the seven messages (1:11); the second came in the heavenly worship (5:1).

After the scroll John is given a measuring rod and told to measure the temple, its altar, and its worshipers—but not the courtyard, for that has been given over to the nations who will trample the holy city for forty-two months. This short scene is probably built on the very lengthy vision that ends the book of Ezekiel (40–48), and will be recast at the end of the Apocalypse (21:15–27). In both cases the measuring carries a sense of restoration, and Ezekiel, especially, is very concerned about the purity of the temple and the exclusion of outsiders (44:6–8).

While ambiguous, the imagery of measuring the temple and altar yet leaving the courtyard unmeasured (and thus unrestored) clearly envisions a contrast between the inner and the outer reality, between true worship and mere place, between inward security and outward vulnerability, between the people of God and the nations. We might remember the conflict with those who would compromise with Gentile ways, so roundly condemned in the seven letters (see pp. 46–51).

John elaborates this inward/outward dynamic with a marvelous short story of two witnesses who appear in the city. Like the story of the angel at the altar of incense that was interjected into the beginning of the trumpet series, this story symbolizes the underlying themes of the Apocalypse. John leaves no doubt about the import and meaning of these witnesses, piling symbol on symbol: witnesses, olive trees, lampstands, with special abilities to speak fire, shut the sky, and cause plagues. These images are easy to trace. The olive trees and lampstands are drawn from Zech 4:3, 14, where they symbolize the priest and the king (see Rev 1:6; 5:10; 20:6). The lampstand has already been said to represent the church (1:20). They are now said to be two (rather than seven) because John is interested in their function as witness, and two witnesses are required under the Law (Deut 19:15). Their special abilities represent those of Elijah (shutting the sky; 2 Kings 17) and Moses (bringing the plagues; Exodus 7–12). Elijah and Moses were widely expected to return in the last days as the final prophets of God's call for repentance. The fire from their mouth is the word of their testimony and is, like Jesus' sword, ironic (for a description of the prophetic word as fire, see Sir 48:1; Jer 5:14).

In short, John tells the story of the church at work in the world; they are the final prophets long expected. Their witness and power seem unbeatable, but then they are devastated:

> When they have finished their testimony, the beast that comes up from the bottomless pit will make war on them and conquer them and kill them, and their dead bodies will lie in the street of the great city that is prophetically called Sodom and Egypt, where also their Lord was crucified.   REV 11:7–8

And so John combines two antithetical images: their unstoppable testimony and their annihilation. This contradiction will now be mediated by a third action: after lying dead in the street for three and a half days, they are called up to heaven, accompanied by a great earthquake that destroys a tenth of the city. Seven thousand (7 and 10) are killed and fear causes "the rest" to give glory to God.

This is a well-crafted little story that will repay several readings.

A bodiless voice announces that the second woe has ended but that the third comes quickly (11:14). But no further disasters occur in this series. With the sounding of the seventh trumpet, great voices in heaven announce: "The kingdom of the world has become the kingdom of our Lord and of his Messiah, and he will reign forever and ever." This is the announcement we have awaited since we first saw the sealed scroll. Now heavenly worship resumes. The great thanksgiving (Greek: *eucharisteo*, the origin of the word Eucharist) is given:

> We give you thanks, Lord God Almighty, who are and who were, for you have taken your great power and begun to reign. The nations raged, but your wrath has come, and the time for judging the dead, for rewarding your servants, the prophets and saints and all who fear your name, both small and great, and for destroying those who destroy the earth.   REV 11:17–18

Notice how complete the victory is; even God is described without a future (contrast 1:8). For a discussion of the possible relation of this story with the symbolic action of the Eucharist see the Epilogue, pp. 171–75.

REV 8:2–11:18 *Readers' Notes on the Work of the Angels*

Rev 8:2–13

TRUMPETS What we would call a bugle today.

CENSER Either a cup-shaped device on a long handle or a pot set on a tripod. Spices were burned on smoldering coals to produce a pleasant smell.

ONE-THIRD An increase from the one-fourth of the first series (6:8), but still only a partial destruction.

WORMWOOD Bitterness or bitter herb; the English name derives from its use in folk-medicine to kill intestinal worms, which of course has nothing to do with John's use. Closer to John's meaning is Amos 5:6–7, where justice is made bitter by corrupt governors.

EAGLE Such as that used on the Roman standards to symbolize Rome. See also 12:14.

Rev 9:1–12

STAR . . . FALLEN Apparently a reference to the myth of Lucifer, the fallen angel/star. For other references to the myth see Isaiah 14 and Luke 10:18. (For other star imagery in Revelation see 2:5 and contrast 22:16.)

LOCUSTS One of the plagues on Egypt (Exod 10:12–20) and modeled on Joel 2.

TWO HUNDRED MILLION Literally, two myriads of myriads. An impossibly large number. Rome's standing army in John's time numbered about 150,000 troops plus perhaps that many auxiliaries.

FIVE MONTHS Oddly more than a third of the year, this is the only use of five in the whole story (except the five fallen kings of 17:10). It is apparently the normal lifespan of locusts.

ABADDON/APOLLYON The former is a Hebrew term for the grave or the pit; the latter seems to be a modification of its usual Greek translation (*apoleia*, destruction), changing it to reflect the proper name Apollo, the sun God favored by the emperors. See pp. 64–65.

Rev 9:13–21

POWER IN MOUTH . . . TAIL Some suggest that the image derives from the Parthian cavalry technique of charging at the enemy on horseback, shooting one arrow, then retreating and shooting the second arrow.[31]

WORKS OF THEIR HANDS The specific works they refuse to repent of make a curious list: idolatry, murder, sorcery, fornication, theft.

WORSHIP DEMONS AND IDOLS Our writer here covers two opposite views of Greco-Roman religion held by various Jews: either they really worshiped demons or they worshiped inanimate objects.

Rev 10:1–11

NO DELAY An admission that we were right to expect the end at the completion of the first series of seven and a promise that the next seven will really do so. But of course even that is not the end of the story.

FORTY-TWO MONTHS Same as three and a half years or 1,260 days. All three are symbols for the period of evil, a period represented by the broken seven for evil can never be full. The writer seems to choose the expression that gives the best rhetorical effect in the context.

Rev 11:1–18

OLIVE TREES . . . LAMPS They have a perpetual supply of oil (see Zech 4:12).

PROPHECY Not predicting the future but announcing the judgment and justice of God.

THE BEAST THAT COMES UP FROM THE BOTTOMLESS PIT The first reference to this character who will dominate the next story. Notice the present tense verb.

MAKE WAR This is the action of the third section (chapters 12–22), here reduced to one sentence.

THE GREAT CITY A multifaceted symbol in the Apocalypse. Here it stands for Jerusalem ("where the Lord was crucified"); later it symbolizes Rome (17:18). Or perhaps it is more accurate to say it symbolizes both in both places, for the great city is the city in opposition to God and the antithesis of the truly great city that will appear at the end of the story (chapter 21).

PROPHETICALLY CALLED SODOM Literally: "spiritually" but probably best taken as "symbolically." All John's geography is spiritual not physical. See pp. 64–65.

THREE AND A HALF DAYS Yet another figure for the period of struggle against evil. The same as three and a half years, forty-two months, or 1,260 days. John's time too is spiritual.

DESTROYING THOSE WHO DESTROY . . . Divine justice.

The Drama of the Scroll

It is too easy to get bogged down in all the details of John's visions and miss the grand drama of the story. The best antidote for this is to read the story out loud and to invest it with as much drama of voice and action as you can. You will feel the difference in the story.

Three additional factors work against our experiencing the drama of this section. First a good deal of effort is spent on characterization rather than action. Nearly all of chapters 4 and 5 are concerned with characterizing God and Jesus, with a good deal of descriptive material. Second, while there is conflict, there is no struggle: the outcome is never in doubt. We meet God seated on the throne and John never allows us to entertain the possibility that God's rule will not finally prevail. Third, the material is highly repetitive, or if not exactly repetitive, repetitious. Different scenes make the same point over and over again. It is not that the plot does not move forward, but it also circles back, rather more a spiral than a linear development.[32]

This iterative quality of the narrative can give one a sense of wandering, but this is far from the truth. Nor would I agree with those who speak of interludes to the story, for those elements that are not directly connected to the forward movement of the action serve definite narrative strategies of the author. These satellite incidents provide exposition, development, and commentary on the kernel incidents and characters. (For a discussion of the difference between satellite and kernel incidents, see pp. 10–16.) But, of course, it is not absolutely clear which incidents should be taken as central and which as supportive.

John is a generous author and allows the reader great freedom in construing the relationship between the incidents. Thus various readers may construe the sequences differently. One way to focus the issue is to ask what is the central conflict of the section.

The clear protagonist is God and God's agents; the clear antagonist is humanity; the struggle is for God to overcome human intransigence and evil: wars and their aftermath (6:1–8); idolatry and social disruption (9:20–21); destroying the earth (11:18). Thus John addresses the oldest and most profound of human questions: Why is the human species worse than all others? Can anything be done about our injustice, oppression, and destruction? Why has God not done something? Can God do anything short of forcing us into obedience, thereby depriving us of our basic humanity (freedom)?

John's telling begins by imagining the ideal: all creation gathered around the throne of God, a harmonious and balanced universe. But this harmonious order is threatened when no one is capable of opening a sealed scroll. The seals that bind the scroll include: conquest, war, famine, and pestilence; the call for vengeance and judgment. Who can remove such seals? Just here we meet the central claim of the work. For the hero is introduced as the lion of the tribe of Judah, but shown to be a lamb—slaughtered and standing. And this one does remove the seals, but the end does not come. Terrible scenes of divine power ensue in the seven trumpets and three woes, but still there is no change in humanity (9:20). Then the two witnesses reenact the experience of the lamb: they are slaughtered but stand (11:11). And this testimony causes some to give glory to God. God's reign and judgment are then announced. And the heavenly liturgy resumes.

I would set this forth visually in Table 9 (over), using indentations to represent subordinate actions. The actions in the left-most column are the kernel incidents that drive the story.

One caution I would suggest is not to be overly attracted to the patterns of seven. While these series are clearly convenient for ordering the material and while they would facilitate the listening in an originally oral situation, they do not control the action. In terms of action, they are repetitive rather than sequential. Their primary action is dramatizing human failings and divine judgment.

What Could Possibly Come after This? A Completed Action

On the one hand the final scene of this section sounds like the end: God's kingdom and judgment have come. On the other hand, there is much more to the story. It is worth asking how much closure this section achieves.

Closure is the sense that a story is over, what Aristotle called a fitting place to stop, an action that does not require further actions to satisfy us.

TABLE 9 *The Action of the Second Scroll*

The vision of universal harmony: worship in heaven
The dilemma of the sealed scroll: disruption
The revelation of the Lion/Lamb worthy to open the scroll
   The unsealing of the scroll
     1 White horse
     2 Red horse
     3 Black horse
     4 Pale horse

     5 Altar
     6 Earthquake/day of wrath
       Israel sealed
       Multitudes before the throne
     7 Silence
The trumpets signal
(Angel at the incense altar)
   Seven trumpets
     1 Hail, fire, blood
     2 Sea turned to blood
     3 Star turns rivers bitter
     4 Sun, moon, stars darkened by one-third
   Eagle announces three woes
     5 Locust swarm—end of first woe
     6 Four angels and armies kill one-third
       Angel announces no more delay
       John eats small scroll
       John measures the temple
       Two witnesses—end of second woe
     7 Voice announces kingdom
The proclamation of God's reign
The resumption of the divine liturgy

This last scene meets all these criteria. It could well have been the end of some previous edition of this work, for it fulfills all the expectations the earlier story has raised.

The only loose end, perhaps, is the promised third woe (11:14). This last scene hardly seems aptly characterized as a woe, nor are we told that the third woe has come, as we were told in the case of the first two (9:12 and 11:14). But this is a loose end that will never be wrapped up; we are never told that the third woe has come (although 12:12 might imply that the whole final scene should be understood as the third woe).

This sense of closure, or near closure, raises the question about the relationship between these three basic actions of the Apocalypse. For, in fact, the same sort of near closure existed at the end of the seven messages: nothing more was required to complete the story. Nor was John's transition especially helpful ("after this" 4:1). There is little to connect this second action to the first, except for John and an occasional repetition of descriptions or ideas (conquest, for example).

The reason for this lack of obvious connection with what comes before and what comes after is that logically nothing can come before or after this action. It begins in the primal time when all is harmony and ends in the final time when all is restored. All other actions must be contained within this action. Thus the seven messages reveal an intermediate time when the "two witnesses" bear their testimony in the face of opposition; and the third scene (cosmic war) focuses anew on the opposition to the witnesses. It is not that the final closure of the whole work will be more complete than this near closure, but that the final closure is already contained in the near.

Such a suggestion raises acutely the question of time in the Apocalypse.

Story Time and Discourse Time: Temporal Distortions

Stories always distort time; if nothing else they radically shorten the events told, compressing days and even years into a sentence or two. But they often also rearrange the events, so that they are told out of their natural order; and they distort in other ways also. One way to analyze temporal distortions is to consider the difference between story time (the time-frame of the story) and discourse time (the time-frame of the telling). The story time of Alexander Solzhenitsyn's novel *One Day in the Life of Ivan Denisovich* is radically compressed as we follow one of the residents of Stalin's concentration camps through one day's labor. But the discourse time is compressed even further, for one can read it in about two hours. Some things are told in great detail; others are passed over in summary.

Critics often speak of three aspects of temporal distortion: order, duration, and frequency.[33] Any story can be told in its natural *order:* beginning at the beginning and proceeding to the end. But a story may also contain various kinds of anachronisms, such as flashbacks, when the audience learns of events that happened earlier. Some stories have what we might call flashforwards, when we learn of things before they happen (perhaps by a dream or intuition). Stories are also told with repetitions, gaps, and indeterminate events.

In regard to *duration,* we can distinguish between the scene (when the time of the telling seems realistic, normal), the summary (when the reading time is shorter than story time), and the stretch (reading time is longer than story time). The last has an effect similar to slow motion in film and is achieved by description or the narration of other non-linear material (such as what the character is thinking). We can think of the relationship between the duration of the story time and the duration of the narrative time as the pacing of the narrative, from the accelerated pace of the summary to the suspended pace of the stretch.

In regard to *frequency,* we can speak of the singular (in which one event is narrated only once), the repetitive (when one event has multiple narrations), and the repetitious (when there are multiple narrations of events so similar that they are identified in the audience's mind), and the iterative (when many events are captured in one telling: every evening George spent an hour watching the night sky).

Now let us consider how we experience temporal distortion in the story of heavenly worship.

THE ORDER OF EVENTS

Certain events are clearly told by flashback. We are told that the lamb has won the power to open the scroll, because he was killed (5:5, 9). The first four seals seem to be in order, but in seal five we are told of those "who had been slaughtered" (6:9). Even the great climactic ending to the story seems to be told in a combination of flashback and flashforward: "The kingdom of the world *has become* the kingdom of our Lord and of his Messiah, and he *will reign* forever and ever" (11:15). One might observe that at this climax of the story there is no present.

Other flashforwards are also evident, perhaps including the whole story (4:1—"what must take place after this"). The temporal location of the story of the two witnesses in chapter 11 is somewhat ambiguous, but two elements seem future: they "will" be given authority to prophesy (11:3) and the beast "will make war" on them (11:7). In fact, we will soon see that this is the action of the third story soon to be narrated, but here anticipated in this flashforward.

While other temporal relationships are sometimes ambiguous, the rest of the events narrated here seem to be in a natural order, at least there are no temporal indicators indicating otherwise.

THE DURATION OF THE TELLING

Notice how slowly the action begins; nearly the whole of chapter 4 involves description, so that when characters speak it has the effect of jarring us out of slow motion into normal time. With the introduction of the scroll (5:1) we shift from stretch to scenic time, but still with retarding descriptions. Only with the unsealing of the scroll (6:1) does the pace accelerate. The sealing of the faithful (7:1–8) again slows the action, coming to a virtual stand-still in the naming of the tribes.

The first four trumpets tend toward the summary, greatly reducing the time it takes to tell of such catastrophic events. Interrupted by the scene of the eagle pronouncing woe (8:13), the pace slows again as action is interspersed with description. This retarding pace does little to convince us that "there will be no more delay" (10:7). It reinforces John's effort to defer the final closure. The section ends with a real-time scene in which we hear the actual words of the heavenly liturgists, so that story time and narrative time are identical.

The pacing of the story focuses our attention on the heavenly worship; other events speed by. This can be experienced in miniature in the short scene of the angel before the altar of incense (8:3–5). The pace focuses our attention on the actions of the angel in the heavenly sanctuary (the apocalyptic counterpart to the praying of the community) and then rushes the consequences of this action past us in kaleidoscopic summary: "there were peals of thunder, rumblings, flashes of lightning, and an earthquake." John is more intent in focusing the audience's attention on what they are doing than on what God will do as a result.

THE FREQUENCY OF THE TELLING

It is useful to distinguish between the repeated and the repetitious: very little in this section is repeated; quite a bit is echoed in other incidents. The scene of the twenty-four elders worshiping before the heavenly throne is repeated (4:10–11 and 11:16–18), though with different words. The earthquake is repeated (6:12; 8:5; 11:13, 19). The incense bowls full of the prayers of the faithful is repeated (5:8–9 and 8:3–4).

The repetitious, however, is everywhere. On one level, there is a repetitiveness to the first four seals, as each proceeds in verbal synchrony with the previous. This is the repetitiveness of the drum, hammering home the message. Much the same can be said of the first four trumpets. But there is a deeper level of the repetitious.

Seal six, for example, symbolizes the final judgment, as does the angelic hurling of the censer to earth (8:5), as does each of the first six trumpets, as does the earthquake following the ascent of the two witnesses (11:13). This is not drumming, but more like the musical variations on a theme in a symphony. Each repetition states, refines, and enhances the theme so that we understand it in new ways. Understanding the action of the Apocalypse in this way leads to a radically different understanding of its purpose than trying to construct a linear sequence in which each later development must symbolize something new.

Conclusion

John has told us a symbolic and truly apocalyptic story, a prophetic story in the rightful sense of that word. Everything in this story is symbolic, often with symbol piled on symbol. John ascends to heaven and witnesses a heavenly worship scene. Such heavenly worship symbolizes the actual worship of

God in the assemblies of Asia Minor. But that worship itself is symbolic of bringing life under the control of God. Such "service of God" symbolizes the true reign of God, including the conquest of evil. But conquering evil is itself a symbol of life lived "for the word of God and the testimony of Jesus." These two acts are now symbols for the witness against evil marked by both word and action, a life of "patient endurance" or "consistent resistance" to those powers of injustice in the world.

So we see an angel throw a golden censer against the earth, causing thunder, lightning, and an earthquake. And the symbolic echoes ripple out: the prayers of the faithful bring judgment to the earth; the saints' prayers stem from their own suffering; such suffering stems from their consistent resistance to injustice; such resistance to evil leads not only to their suffering but to the overthrow of evil.

John's symbolic story is apocalyptic in the root sense: it takes away the veil and lets us see behind history to the inner dynamic. It is also apocalyptic in the obvious ways: it features a trip to heaven, visions of the throne of God, arcane symbols that need to be interpreted by characters in the drama. But an apocalypse is a revelation.

The four horses and their riders are a revelation, not because we do not know the foibles of human conquest, war, famine, and death. We read of such folly in our daily newspapers. The revelation is that such persistent idiocy is not the last word; it is only the fourth of seven words. John draws aside the veil that hides such conviction and allows us to see God at work.

This is prophetic in the rightful sense: a proclamation of a useful future based on the conviction of what God has done in the past and is doing in the present. It is not a fortune teller's trick of trying to tell you what will happen tomorrow or the day after. Prophecy is not really about predicting the future. Prophecy is articulating a vision of life and announcing what faith in God means in the present circumstances. If the prophet knows what is going to happen, it is because the prophet understands something about the nature of God and can thus foresee what that predicts about how the present must unfold.

John's prophecy is one of justice and judgment.[34] When John sees the lives of the faithful that have been forfeit on the altar of sacrifice, he predicts that God will avenge them. But God does not act immediately. They must wait till the injustice is complete. John knows that a system that kills its best kills itself.

John prepared for this story by first telling one about the divine messages for those who would be faithful (chapters 1–3). That story sets the audience up to read this story by enabling them to see themselves in the role of the faithful witness. Now John turns to another story that helps the audience grasp more clearly what it means to be faithful. This third story is a story of war, conquest, and renewal. It too is symbolic, apocalyptic, and prophetic.

The War Scroll

> For the common soldier, at least, war has the feel—the
> spiritual texture—of a great ghostly fog, thick and perma-
> nent. There is no clarity. Everything swirls. The old rules
> are no longer binding, the old truths no longer true. Right
> spills over into wrong. Order blends into chaos, love into
> hate, ugliness into beauty, law into anarchy, civility into
> savagery. The vapors suck you in. You can't tell where you
> are, or why you're there, and the only certainty is over-
> whelming ambiguity. In war you lose your sense of the def-
> inite, hence your sense of truth itself, and therefore it's safe
> to say that in a true war story nothing is ever absolutely
> true.[1]
>
> TIM O'BRIEN, *The Things They Carried*

A New Story

At the climax of the scene of heavenly worship, as the voice announces that
God's reign has come and everything would seem to be over, John moves
deeper into the heavenly mystery, shifting our focus into the innermost
sanctuary of the temple. In John's time many people imagined that the
heavenly reality corresponded to the earthly (though they would have said
it the other way around). Thus the temple in heaven was like the Temple in
Jerusalem, constructed in three parts: an outer courtyard open to all, an
inner sanctuary accessible only to the priests, and an innermost room, the
Holy of Holies, accessible only to the high priest. A near contemporary of
John described this shrine briefly:

> Behind the second curtain was a tent called the Holy of Holies. In it stood the
> golden altar of incense and the ark of the covenant overlaid on all sides with
> gold, in which there were a golden urn holding the manna, and Aaron's rod

101

> that budded, and the tablets of the covenant; above it were the cherubim of
> glory overshadowing the mercy seat. Of these things we cannot speak now in
> detail.   HEB 9:3–5

It is apparently the action of section two in which the lamb removes the
seals and enables the worship of God that allows John to see into this most
holy place.2 What he sees there seems familiar at first, then we recognize
that something completely new has begun:

> Then God's temple in heaven was opened, and the ark of his covenant was
> seen within his temple; and there were flashes of lightning, rumblings, peals of
> thunder, an earthquake, and heavy hail. A great portent appeared in heaven: a
> woman clothed with the sun, with the moon under her feet, and on her head
> a crown of twelve stars. She was pregnant and was crying out in birth pangs,
> in the agony of giving birth. Then another portent appeared in heaven: a great
> red dragon, with seven heads and ten horns, and seven diadems on his heads.
> His tail swept down a third of the stars of heaven and threw them to the earth.
> Then the dragon stood before the woman who was about to bear a child, so
> that he might devour her child as soon as it was born.   REV 11:19–12:3

Lightning, thunder, and earthquake we have seen before, but never have we
seen such a wonderful woman, nor such a monstrous dragon. We have
entered a new story, returning to the theme of conflict and victory that so
permeated the scroll of the letters.

One of the most shocking things about this third story is that God is no
longer the main actor. The dragon acts and God reacts. This can be seen
already in the short sketch above; the only active verbs are those connected
with the dragon. This is the dragon's story.3

It is as if John, having sketched the need for struggle in the scroll of the
letters and having shown the mode of God's victory in the scroll of worship,
turns now to look more deeply into the conflict. It is as if the storyteller
having finished the tale of God's coming rule should turn to the audience
and say: "and do you wonder how this came about? Well, let me tell you
another story." Let us now examine that story more closely, first sketching
an overview of the action, then investigating the story elements of genre,
character, setting and plot, before turning to a commentary on the action.
We will also raise some questions about the morality of the story told and
the extent to which this end is final.

Overview of the Unit: The War Scroll

When the dragon fails to destroy either the newborn child or the mother, it
turns to "make war on the rest of her children, those who keep the commandments of God and hold the testimony of Jesus" (12:17). The two
primeval beasts, one from the sea and one from the land, are summoned to
the aid of the dragon. They have enormous powers and cause all the earth

to worship the dragon. Then the lamb gathers its army, the 144,000 who bear God's name. After three angelic announcements made in mid-air, the majestic human figure from the first section appears, only now he is seated on the clouds and directing the harvest of the earth. First the grain (bread) and then the grape (wine).

Then John sees a third sign (the first was the woman; the second was the dragon): seven angels with seven bowls containing the final plagues file out of the heavenly temple. The pouring of these bowls wreaks complete havoc on the earth: all is destroyed.

Then one of the angels comes to John and offers to show him the judgment of the great harlot, whose destruction is shown in brutal detail. Some lament her passing; others rejoice. Now a rider on a white horse appears out of heaven. The kings of earth gather their armies to do battle, but the beast is captured and cast alive into the lake of fire. The rest are killed. The dragon is seized by an angel, chained, and cast into the bottomless pit, where he remains a thousand years. There follow a thousand years of peace.

At the end of the thousand years, Satan is released and again gathers an army for battle. They encircle the camp of the saints and the holy city, but fire comes down from heaven and consumes them, with the Devil now also being cast into the lake of fire. Humanity is judged and all whose names are not found written in the lamb's book of life are cast into the lake of fire. A new heaven and a new earth appear.

Then another of the angels comes to John and offers to show him the bride, the wife of the lamb. What John sees is a vision of the holy city, a new Jerusalem descending out of heaven. After a lengthy description of the city, John returns to his own voice and brings the whole book to a rapid end.

Story Elements

This section is without doubt the strongest section of John's writing. Nearly all the aspects of Revelation that have entered the popular imagination come from this section: the seven-headed beast, 666, the debauched woman, final judgment, streets of gold, the lake of fire—to name just a few. There are several reasons for this, which we will explore more fully in the Epilogue (pp. 152–54), but one reason is the techniques, devices, and strategies with which the story is put together. Thus before looking at *what* John has written, we want to explore *how* he has written it. Let's begin with the broadest level of *how* with the question of the genre of this segment.

WAR STORIES, COSMIC AND MUNDANE

The genre of war stories is as ancient as the *Iliad* of Homer at the beginning of the western literary tradition and as new as the latest film about

Vietnam. Conflict is the basic ingredient of stories, and war lends itself to this narrative mode. But there are many different kinds of war stories, and two characteristics of the kind of war story we find in Revelation are important for understanding what is happening. First, in this kind of war story the actions of spiritual forces are as important as the actions of humans; and second, this is a cosmic battle determining the whole future of world.

Every group, I suppose, believes its God fights on its side in war, but in the ancient world where each group had its own God this belief had special force. Thus we read in the *Iliad* that the battle between the men on the field is only the mirror image of the battle between the Gods; first one side prevails and then the other as first the Gods who favor the Achaians prevail and then those who favor the Trojans.[4] In Israel this was transformed somewhat, with the fighting being done by God's angels rather than by God (see Dan 10:7–21, where Daniel learns how Michael, Israel's prince, fights against the prince of Persia). Or listen to the reported words of the King of Assyria when he besieged Jerusalem:

> Has any of the gods of the nations ever delivered its land out of the hand of the king of Assyria? Where are the gods of Hamath and Arpad? Where are the gods of Sepharvaim, Hena, and Ivvah? Have they delivered Samaria out of my hand? Who among all the gods of the countries have delivered their countries out of my hand, that the LORD should deliver Jerusalem out of my hand?
>
> 2 KGS 18:33–35

Battles below are reflections of battles above.[5]

And this basic image of the world as consisting of an *above* and a *below* permeates the thinking of the Apocalypse. (See the discussion of worldview on pp. 3–5 and the discussion of space on pp. 65–67.) We have already observed this sense of correspondence in scenes like the angel at the altar of incense (8:3–5). So in this section John is using a well-known idea of a heavenly war that corresponds to earthly struggle, only John writes an apocalypse that will reveal what is really going on at the spiritual level.

The second aspect of this war story that would be familiar to ancient audiences is related to this: this is a cosmic war. This is not a war that corresponds to some conflict between nations, as in the illustrations from the *Iliad* and from Kings above. This is a war of cosmic proportions; it founds the world, overcomes evil, abolishes chaos, establishes order and justice.

The oldest instance of this type of war comes from ancient Babylon, from a story more than a millennium old by John's day. In the Babylonian creation myth *Enuma Elish* we learn that the world came into being through a primordial war. It seems that Tiamat (Chaos), mother of the Gods, has decided that her children have grown too raucous and noisy so she makes plans to destroy them all. She creates monsters to fight on her side: serpents, dragons, the sphinx, and others. She works other magic. Learning of this the Gods cower in fright, then band together to try to do something about it. They decide that they will choose a champion, invest him with each of their special powers, and he will challenge chaos. They choose the young Marduk, son of the sun, God of the storm and the four winds, wisest of the Gods.

Marduk meets Tiamat in combat and, after lengthy battle, kills her, driving a storm wind into her mouth and puncturing her inflated torso with his arrow. From her split carcass he creates the heavens and earth. He fixes all of the Gods in their own spheres, orders the heavens, and then, from the blood of Tiamat's consort, he creates humans to be the servants of the Gods. He makes order out of chaos. There follows the enthronement of Marduk as king of the Gods, the establishing of a new temple, his marriage banquet, and signs of his universal rule.6

We will see in the course of our comments on the action (pp. 122–45) that John reflects many of these motifs and sequences (and rejects others), but it is even more important to observe that John's story functions in an analogous way: it is the story of the creation of "a new heaven and a new earth" (21:1). We must always keep in mind that this whole story is an extension of the situation at the end of the second narrative section, where the voice announces that God's reign has begun. This story is designed to show us how that came to pass.

The form in which the story is cast is that of a war story. But it is a particular type of war story, one in which the fighting is shown to occur on two levels, above and below. As humans engage the forces of evil, spiritual powers grapple for control of the cosmos. And it is a particular sub-type of this genre; rather than imagining a spiritual counterpart to some human war, this story works the other way. It imagines the human counterpart to the cosmic struggle between good and evil. In technical terms, this is a cosmogony, a story of the founding of the universe. Obviously, such a story requires a far different cast of characters than the two earlier stories John has told.

CHARACTERS OLD AND NEW

The defining characteristic of the major characters in this third segment is their fantastic nature. They are quite literally characters of fantasy—visionary, dreamlike, imaginative: a woman clothed with the sun (12:1); a great red dragon (12:3); two evil beasts (13:1, 11); a heavenly rider on a white horse (19:11); a debauched woman (17:1); and a heavenly bride (21:9). Just a listing of these characters alerts us to the fact that we are reading a story that is neither historical nor realistic. I think we can take it as a given that any story in which one of the (major) characters is a dragon will be received by the audience with a knowing nod.

I do not mean that such a story is less serious or less true than other kinds of stories, only that it speaks to a deeper part of the psyche than the rational mind. It is mysterious, fantastic, horrible, terrifying. It is different in quality from the story of John on Patmos (realistic) and even from the story of John in heaven (strange, mysterious). Angels, animals, and elders are mysterious, but they are qualitatively different from dragons and seven-headed beasts. Let us look at these new characters more closely.

Characters of Destruction

It is common in literature like this to characterize the participants as good and evil or as the children of light and the children of darkness; these are not inappropriate for the present story, but they do not seem primary. Rather, the dualism here seems to be between characters who are agents of destruction and characters who are agents of preservation. At the head of the agents of destruction stands the *dragon,* who first appears as a beast of prey, ready to eat the woman's newborn child; failing that, it pursues the woman herself into the wilderness and attempts to destroy her. Stymied again, it turns its anger on her other children, making war on them. The dragon's one goal seems to be to destroy. This characterization is reinforced by other things we learn about the dragon. It is red, the color of war (see pp. 6–10 and 82). Its seven heads and ten horns represent the extent of its claim to authority and power. Its tail has already obliterated a third of the stars of heaven. In fact, we learn by flashback (see pp. 117–21) that it has already been in a war in heaven and been defeated, cast down to the earth. Here we learn the dragon's motivation: "woe to the earth and the sea, for the devil has come down to you with great wrath, because he knows that his time is short!" (12:12) Ironically, this characterization of the dragon means that the wrath of the dragon is itself a sign of its impending doom.

We also learn here the other aliases of the dragon: the great dragon . . . that ancient serpent, who is called the Devil and Satan, the deceiver of the whole world (12:9). We see here the ancient pedigree of this character. In the first instance the character of the dragon reaches all the way back to the Babylonian creation story, for Tiamat is portrayed as a dragon. And in other cultures too, the chaos monster is portrayed as a dragon. But John makes an even more subtle connection when he identifies the dragon with "that ancient serpent." Israel's creation story has no primeval battle with chaos.[7] But John insinuates that the serpent of the Eden story is really the dragon (and it seems to have been envisioned with legs; see the curse of Gen 3:14). Additionally, by alluding to Satan as the accuser, John incorporates later developments by which the figure of Satan became a figure of evil. At one stage, Satan was merely one of God's agents whose job it was to bring charges against any who fell short (a sort of prosecuting attorney such as we see in Job 1). But the figure evolved from accuser to deceiver to one who would willfully lead astray.[8] By John's time the evolution was complete.

It is marvelous how John picks up such ancient motifs and incorporates them into his new story, creating a new character as old as memory. This is a character of deception and disguise. In fact most of the rest of the acts of destruction will be carried out by others acting as agents of the dragon. The two most prominent agents are characterized as beasts.

The two *beasts* are a study in contrasts, one from the sea and one from the earth. The first beast looks very like the dragon itself (compare 13:1 with 12:3), while the second beast looks like the dragon's enemy, the lamb (13:11), but it is clearly a superficial resemblance. The first beast is further described as a composite animal, with leopard, bear, and lion parts (13:2). These images are drawn from Daniel's visions (see Dan 7:1–7), where the image of the beastly (nations) is meant to contrast with the human-like (Israel; see 7:13). For anyone familiar with Daniel these images characterize this beast in the worst possible way, as Israel's enemy and the opponent of God.

This seven-headed beast presents us with a marvelous aspect. Like the slain lamb it seems to live beyond death: "One of its heads seemed to have received a death-blow, but its mortal wound had been healed. In amazement the whole earth followed the beast" (13:3). What is not quite clear in English is that it is the beast and not its head that is healed (in Greek, the pronoun translated "its" agrees grammatically with "dragon" but not with "head"). The meaning here becomes transparent when we recall that the first "head" of the Roman Empire (Julius Caesar) was struck down by senators who thought Rome should be a republic and not an empire, but the empire lived on. Julius Caesar may be mortal but Caesar is not: the king is dead; long live the king.[9]

In fact, Julius was declared to be divine and every Caesar thereafter was "son of the divine Julius." Hence the names of blasphemy on each head (13:1, 5). John's story veers toward allegory, without ever becoming that unidimensional. Thus John complicates the story by introducing a second beast, one from land.

This second beast is characterized as a land-beast, which, while looking like a lamb, speaks like a dragon. It possesses all the authority of the first beast and works miraculous signs so that people worship the first beast. In addition, it has a special sign of its own, a number: 666. Here we come to one of the most enigmatic and provocative symbols of the Apocalypse, one that has captured the imagination of interpreters in every generation. I will discuss the action involved here in the commentary below (pp. 122–45); here we concern ourselves only with the way this number characterizes the beast.

There are two major alternatives, depending on how we understand the Greek phrase: *arithmos anthropou estin* (literally: number of human it is). The question is whether *human* here should be understood as referring to an individual or to the collective; in the first case we might translate: it is the number of a human; in the second case it could be read: it is a human number.

Most readers have taken it as referring to some one person. A number could refer to a person because each Greek letter also had a numerical value—the Romans being the first to invent a separate system for writing numbers (Roman numerals). Both the Greeks and the Hebrews used the letters of their alphabets to represent numbers. Thus any name could also be said to be a number (one simply added the letters together to get a total). Under this scenario one would look for a person whose letters added up to 666.

The most likely candidate is Nero, but with some manipulation one can get the name of most of the emperors to add up to 666! The manipulation in Nero's case involves writing his name in Hebrew letters (but then John said it called for wisdom and calculation). None of the potential candidates adds up to 666 without some manipulation, so if John intended to refer to an individual we must assume that the identification was already known to the audience. But there is another possibility.

The number six is commonly used to refer to humanity, created on the sixth day of creation according to Genesis (1:27–31). Read this way, the number represents the humanity of the beast whose claim is divinity. The very name of the beast is evident testimony to the falsity of its claim. Pretending to be 7 it remains ever 6—even if intensified to 666. While John does not mention it, people able to compute such numbers would surely know that the name Jesus adds us to 888.[10] The eighth day, of course, is the beginning of the new week, and by symbolic extension, the new creation. Read in this light we would understand that Jesus is what the emperor claims to be. The implicit comparison is carried further in the contrasted "marking" of the followers of the beast and the "sealing" of the followers of the lamb.

Like the dragon, these beasts derive from ancient stories. Not only does the chaos figure in ancient myths regularly call on monstrous allies, but these two specific beasts play a role. Known in the Hebrew tradition as Leviathan and Behemoth,[11] they represent archaic forces of chaos that God keeps in check.[12] As in John's story Leviathan the sea monster looks like a dragon and has seven heads (see Ps 74:13–14). Although Leviathan was defeated at creation, final defeat awaits the coming day of God's judgment: "On that day the LORD with his cruel and great and strong sword will punish Leviathan the fleeing serpent, Leviathan the twisting serpent, and he will kill the dragon that is in the sea" (Isa 27:1).

In short these three are well-known characters deriving from very ancient Canaanite and Babylonian stories of creation and conflict. They were used by earlier biblical writers to express God's victory over chaos—both at the beginning and in Israel's historical struggles, as well as at the end. John echoes all three contexts (creation, history, new creation), only the historical struggle now is with the Roman empire and its religious claims.

The fourth major agent of destruction is a more complex figure whose ancestry is not so easy to trace. She is introduced with the ironic expression: the great prostitute. She is said to sit on many waters, reminding us of Tiamat/Leviathan, but her chaos is described as sexual. The kings of the earth have lain with her and the inhabitants of the earth have had to drink "the wine of her fornication" (17:2), so that all are drunk. She is described in detail, showing both the most elaborate and refined dress and the most repulsive behaviors. She is a figure divided, both attracting John and repelling him, a figure of desire and death: a great prostitute.[13]

She rides the beast with seven heads, whose initial support turns violent and abusive: "they and the beast will hate the whore; they will make her desolate and naked; they will devour her flesh and burn her up with fire" (17:16). This is an ugly scene; we will consider its implicit misogyny when we look at the action below. It adds a radical new element to the characterization of the agents of destruction: that of the pathetic victim.

John clarifies and refines this characterization by adding one final element to the description: "The woman you saw is the great city that rules over the kings of the earth" (17:18). This element of the great city occurs four times in the story, first appearing as a description for Jerusalem (11:8); then there is an oblique reference to the great city being split into three parts in the final battle (16:9); the third is the present reference; the final reference is in the lengthy description of the destruction of Babylon (18:10–24). In this final reference certainly, but also in the present reference, the most likely city signified by this image is Rome ("the great city that rules over the kings of the earth" 17:18). But we should not get trapped in the false question of whether the great city is Rome or Jerusalem; in fact it is crucial to John's purpose that the image elide from one to the other. It was, after all, Jerusalem that shed the blood of Jesus, just as it was Jerusalem that was devoured and burned by the kings—but this was just an historical instance of this cosmic event. Rome too will be devoured. The despised whore is also a victim.

These agents of destruction, then, are both cosmic and historical. The struggle with Rome is also the struggle with the ancient monster of chaos.

Characters of Rescue

Given the characterizations of the antagonists discussed above, especially the dragon, one expects the protagonist to appear as a young warrior from heaven. Such a figure will appear, but we will have to be patient, for our hero will be characterized in four other figures before we meet the heavenly warrior at 19:11.

The dominant characterization of the dragon's foe is the lamb, who is referred to nineteen times in this segment (and only eleven times in the previous segment where it rightfully belongs). Our first view of the lamb shows it standing on Mount Zion with the 144,000 sealed witnesses (14:1–5). Our familiarity with the idea should not dull us to the preposterousness of the situation, the audacity of casting a lamb in the role of defender of the faithful against the attack of a dragon. Nor is it comforting that this scene of gathering is followed by a voice from heaven announcing: "'Write this: Blessed are the dead who from now on die in the Lord.' 'Yes,' says the Spirit, 'they will rest from their labors, for their deeds follow them'" (14:13). Yet the lamb will conquer (17:14) and even marry the woman at the end of the story (19:7). This characterization is carried over from the story in segment two, the worship scroll, where we saw John subverting and reversing the usual images of conquest (see the discussion at pp. 69–70). It functions in a similar manner here.

The dragon's foe is also characterized as the woman's child that the dragon wishes to devour (12:4–5). We are told three things about this child: it is a son, a male (and the text is redundant here); it will shepherd the nations with an iron rod; and it is rescued from the dragon by being taken up to heaven—seemingly following birth—where it shares God's throne. Of course it was the lamb who was called shepherd and who shared God's throne in the worship scroll (7:17). Consequently, one begins to understand that this "rescue" is of a rather odd sort, for the lamb arrived in heaven slain. Again John subverts his own images. The iron rod connects this figure both with the Jesus of the letters and the heavenly warrior (see 2:27–28 and 19:15).

The next characterization of the dragon's foe does not, at first glance seem to be Jesus. In fact it is said to be Michael, who engages in a heavenly war with the dragon that resulted in his expulsion from heaven (12:7–9). Now Michael is a common figure in stories like this, usually representing the heavenly prince who defends the interests of Israel in the spiritual struggle (see Dan 10:13, 21; 12:1; *Ascension of Isaiah* 3:16; *Testament of Dan* 6:2).[14] On the face of it we have a traditional image of divine conquest of evil by superior power, but again John subverts the image. Listen to the voice that announces the victory:

> Now have come the salvation and the power and the kingdom of our God and the authority of his Messiah, for the accuser of our comrades has been thrown down, who accuses them day and night before our God. But they have conquered him by the blood of the Lamb and by the word of their testimony, for they did not cling to life even in the face of death.   REV 12:10–11

Thus the apparent victory by superior power in war is said to be a victory "by the blood of the Lamb." The action attributed to Michael is now attributed to Jesus, meaning that it is probably best to understand Michael here as another image for Jesus; at least the work of Michael and the work of the lamb are identical. (This victory will also be connected with the image of the heavenly warrior below; see also pp. 137–38.)

The next characterization of the hero reaches back to the opening vision, for John sees one like the majestic human being, but with new characterizing traits. He is seated on a cloud, wears a crown, and holds a sharp sickle in his hand (14:14). These are all images of messianic deliverance. This is a very gory scene, as both the (ordinary) harvest of wheat and the (extraordinary) harvest of grapes (one doesn't harvest grapes with a sickle!). We will deal with the action below, only noting here that this seems to be an image of power, the grim reaper at work. It leads naturally to the next characterization, the one we have been anticipating.

The heavenly warrior descends out of heaven on a white horse to do battle with the beasts (19:11). This is a stock figure, as we will see when we discuss the action below (pp. 128–30 and 137–38). Let's limit our present concern to how John has characterized the figure, for he has invested him with traits from the earlier figures. Like the majestic human figure of 1:13–16, he is in human form, has eyes like flames, and projects a sword from his mouth.15 Like the male child and lamb he will shepherd the nations with an iron staff.16 Like the lamb he is king of kings (17:14; 19:16). The bloodied robe has no exact parallel, but reminds us of the slain lamb (see 7:14; 19:13). Perhaps because this figure is central to the story, John insures that we see in him all the other characterizations of the rescuer. Ultimately all these figures are one, representing different ways this one character impinges on the story John tells.

One additional characterization must be mentioned, that of the enthroned judge (20:11). After the battle is done, one on a great white throne judges all the dead according to what is written in the heavenly books. While popular interpretation has seen this as another image of Jesus, there is no trait or icon internal to the story to support this identification. The comparison with the scene of the sixth seal (6:16) suggests that the figure here is God (see also 21:5, where the one seated on the throne seems to mean God).

The characterization of the rescuer throughout this section is deeply ambiguous. On the one hand we find a conqueror, a warrior, a ruler. On the other hand we find a lamb, a baby, one like a human being. It is John's art to make the reader feel that these are one and the same.

Characters Rescued

Perhaps the most surprising—indeed shocking—aspect of the characterization of those rescued is that they are characterized as female. No feminine imagery was used of the churches (in the letter scroll) or of the followers of the lamb (in the worship scroll). Yet in this war scroll there are two powerful feminine images: the woman clothed with the sun and the bride, the wife of the lamb. (There is also the strong negative image of the woman as the great prostitute discussed on pp. 106–9).

One could argue, of course, that given the story we are being told these are not surprising characters at all, for they portray the stereotypical feminine states: being rescued and being married. This is true, but it does not account for the way they frame and dominate the section. These are powerful feminine images of mother and wife. Let us consider them more carefully.

The first is described as "a woman clothed with the sun, with the moon under her feet, and on her head a crown of twelve stars. She was pregnant" (12:1–2). This is an awesome woman. She is further characterized as bearing a son, fleeing into the desert, pursued by the dragon, receiving two eagle's wings, and having other children. Who is the woman?

Perhaps the closest analogy in John's world would be either Isis or Roma, both known as queen of heaven. We will see below when we look at the action that she also shares much with Leto, the mother of Apollo. These three Goddesses were well known in John's time and our woman here would surely remind the audience of them. At the least we might think of her as John's version of the queen of heaven.

Other traits remind us of Israel: the twelve stars, the birth of the son/messiah, the preservation in the desert, even the two eagle's wings (Exod 19:4). The ancient prophets regularly personified Israel as a woman, even as the wife of God. Interestingly, the two images are as wife and as faithless wife (e.g., Isa 54:5; Jer 3:20), which are also the two images that will appear in this story (17:1; 21:9). It is of course quite appropriate to think of Israel as the mother of the messiah.

But there is even a more archaic possibility, for *the* mother of the messiah is Eve. In the story of Adam and Eve in the garden, there is a devious snake who leads them into disobedience to God. When God returns to the garden and sorts things out, both the snake and the woman receive special notice. To the snake God declares:

> Because you have done this, cursed are you among all animals and among all wild creatures; upon your belly you shall go, and dust you shall eat all the days of your life. I will put enmity between you and the woman, and between your offspring and hers; he will strike your head, and you will strike his heel.
>
> GEN 3:14–15

Notice that all the elements of our story are encapsulated here: the dragon/serpent, the woman, the dangerous son. Now we understand why the dragon cannot afford to let this child be born.

These three images—Eve, Israel, queen of heaven—are not mutually exclusive. John seems to have combined elements from each in creating this magnificent character of woman as ancestor of the community.

The other major characterization of the community as woman looks to the future, the bride. This characterization does not bear too close an examination, for we have a woman, described as a city, marrying a lamb. Clearly the various strands of John's symbolism do not weave together very well here. But such mythic war stories end with weddings, and John follows the pattern.17

She is called Jerusalem, the holy city, and descends from the sky—the true heavenly counterpart to the earthly city. She wears the glory of God and like God is described in terms of minerals and gems (cf. 21:11, 18–21 and 4:3). She encompasses both ancient Israel (twelve tribes) and the new people of God in Jesus (twelve apostles). All her dimensions are multiples of four, the number of the earth, and twelve, the number of God's people. The city is described in the most extravagant manner imaginable—in fact beyond the imaginable (from what oysters would one get pearls large enough to stand as a city's gate!). Perhaps we can just say that this city is as much beyond ordinary cities as a bride is beyond ordinary women.

She is the clear antithesis of the great whore, who as we saw above could symbolize Jerusalem as well as Rome (p. 109). Both are introduced in the same stylized manner (21:9 and 17:1).

These two overarching images of woman bracket this whole action, symbolizing the community's past and future. All the images in between are male; each occurs in only one scene, some with mere passing reference.

Satan, for example, is described as "the accuser of our brothers" (12:10, literal trans.). And when the dragon fails to destroy the woman in the wilderness, it sets off to make war on "the rest of her seed" (12:17, literal trans.). This is quite unusual, for women were not thought to possess seed (Greek: *sperma*) in the ancient understanding of childbirth. The agricultural metaphor persisted, with the man planting seed in the fertile soil of the woman. It is probably an allusion to the Eden story, where the seed of Eve would destroy the serpent (Gen 3:15). Though "brothers" is grammatically masculine and "seed" is neuter, neither is intentionally male. Such is not the case with the third minor characterization.

We again encounter the 144,000 sealed followers of the lamb, whom we first met in relation to the sixth seal in the worship scroll (7:1; 14:1). But now they are further characterized, and in a rather troubling fashion, as those who "have not defiled themselves with women, for they are virgins; these follow the Lamb wherever he goes. They have been redeemed from humankind as first fruits for God and the Lamb, and in their mouth no lie was found; they are blameless" (14:4–5). So the elect turn out to be an all-male band, and in fact the characterization of women here (those who defile) raises the question of just how women are regarded in this story world.

To some degree our story reflects the rather widespread misogyny of the Greco-Roman world. Women were often regarded as corrupt and corrupting and their general social oppression was pervasive.18 We find a similar view among the Essenes, whose vision of the new Jerusalem was pervaded by the Temple, from which women were excluded.[19] But there's more to the story. For this band is pictured as gathered for battle against the beasts, and the ancients believed that holy war required special precautions. In brief, it was believed that the divine was involved in such battles and that the divine could not come in contact with impurity. Thus any soldier in a ritually impure state must be excluded from battle. Any sexual activity, even within marriage, even a nocturnal emission, made one impure and thus excluded from holy war.[20] The elect are characterized as warriors in a ritually pure state.

Further, they are said to be "blameless" or literally "without blemish." This is sacrificial language, for the lamb of sacrifice must be such an unblemished creature (see Lev 1:10 and 1 Pet 1:19). In this way both their purity and their status as warriors begins to take on new meaning, for like the lamb these warriors seem to conquer by their own death (see 12:11).

The only other characterizations of the rescued in this section are as "God's people" who are to come out of fallen Babylon (18:4) and those who sit on thrones and reign with Christ (20:4). These are the martyred and remind us of the martyrs we met in the fifth seal of the second scroll (6:9–11).

There are then a range of characterizations for those rescued. Vibrant female images bracket the characterization of the group as a celibate male army, an army marked by the requirements of holy war and of sacrifice. This is in some way a vague temporal sequence, for the woman in the wilderness looks back to the history of the people of God while the woman on the mountain (the bride) looks forward to the consummation of history. The warriors picture the present struggle with the forces of evil.

Characters on the Sidelines

In addition to heavenly beings, usually described simply as "another angel" (14:6, 8, 17; 18:1) or a strong angel (18:21) or some such general reference (15:1; 19:17), and the great host in heaven (19:1), there are several minor characters who do not fit easily into the categories above. For instance, there are the "small and great, rich and poor, free and slave" who are marked by the beast (13:16). There are also the "merchants of the earth" and the "shipmasters and sailors" who join in the lament for the fallen woman Babylon (18:11, 17). And there are "the rest of the dead" (20:5), all those not martyred by the beast. These are bit players on a large stage, each making a contribution but none is very important.

Finally, we should notice that John himself turns up as a character in his own drama. Twice an angel comes to him and invites him to move to a new site from which he might see new things (17:1; 21:9). And then in response to an angel's instruction to write, he tries to worship the angel only to be rebuked (19:9, see also 22:8). At one point God seems to directly address him (21:6). We must remember that this John in the story operates on different temporal and narrative levels than the John who is addressing us as author. Let us look more closely at the settings of these stories.

We have discussed the settings of these stories briefly (pp. 19–21) and then in more detail when we considered the worship scroll (pp. 61–68). We have noted that setting is not just backdrop for a story but is an essential element of the action, shaping our sense of the meaning of the story. We have further noted the complexity of John's settings and their ever increasing strangeness. Finally, we have been careful not to confuse settings in stories with settings in the real world, even when they share the same name. Stories are fictions and the places and times they contain are also fictions. This is abundantly clear in this third narrative segment.

The Places

Both the two earlier story segments were easier to place than is this one. The letter scroll is set on Patmos (1:9). The worship scroll is set in heaven in God's throne room (4:1–2). But it is not possible to say exactly where the war scroll is set. It opens with three references to "in heaven:" the temple of God in heaven is seen to open; a portent is seen in heaven; a second portent is seen in heaven (11:19–12:3). But even this is ambiguous, for the Greek expression *en to ourano* can equally well mean in heaven or in the sky. And these last two references to portents are particularly suited to the sky, for they could describe astrological phenomena. John may well see in Scorpio's pursuit of Virgo through the sky a sign of the dragon's pursuit of the woman.[21] I think it likely that he did, but whether he did or not, my point here is that the setting is ambiguous.

Having given birth (where?), the woman flees into the wilderness (12:5), so here surely the action is on earth (also, her child is taken up to God and to the throne). But immediately our attention is focused back on heaven, where war has broken out (12:7). As a result of that war the dragon is expelled from heaven to earth—to earth's great woe. Now the dragon pursues the woman into the wilderness and then goes off to make war on the "rest of her children" (12:17). Now clearly from the point of view of this story, these children live in Asia Minor; they are surely the very people John is writing to. While there will be numerous and rapid shifts to heaven, Palestine, and other locations, most of the action of this story should be understood as occurring in the life-space of the audience: Roman Asia Minor.

The audience is meant to feel that it is their place where the beasts emerge, their place where the elect are gathered, their place where the final battle is fought, their place to which the new Jerusalem descends. But of course all these things occur in places of their own. We need to understand that any connection between these story places and actual places is figurative, symbolic, metaphorical.

Thus the 144,000 are gathered on Mount Zion (14:1), which should place them in Palestine, but they also sing "before the throne" (14:3), which should place them in heaven. Both heaven and Mount Zion exist in Asia Minor, symbolically. (See the similar ambiguity of the "great city" which is simultaneously Jerusalem, Sodom, Egypt, and Rome [11:8; and the discussion above on pp. 64–67]). Mount Zion is also in Asia Minor, spiritually as John would say.

In a similar way, the final battle is said to be fought at a place called in Hebrew *Harmagedon*. In spite of much scholarly ingenuity, Harmagedon has never appeared on any map of the known world; it is a fictional place. Scholars have offered two solutions to this problem, neither of them convincing. One view is that John meant Har Mo'ed (often written in Greek as Har Moged), meaning "Mount of Assembly"—a fitting place to gather for the final battle to be sure. But John didn't write Moged; he wrote Magedon. A second solution notes that the Greek translations of the Hebrew Bible spelled Megiddo as Mageddon. We only need to imagine that John misspelled it, using one d where he needed two. (And John made more serious mistakes in his writing of Greek.) Further, Megiddo provides a nice allusion, for the plain of Megiddo was the scene of many battles including Deborah's victory over Sissera (Judges 5) and Josiah's loss to Egypt (2 Kings 23). Zechariah even alludes to it in a description of the final turmoil on the day of the Lord (12:10). But the problem is obvious: Megiddo is located on a plain not a mountain. There is not a single reference to any Mount Megiddo extant. The closest mountain is Mount Carmel (itself an auspicious enough place, see 1 Kgs 18:19–40). But no one ever referred to it as Har Megiddo, let alone as Harmagedon. Neither of these solutions seems likely.

And even if they were possible, how likely is it that anyone at Ephesus could have figured them out? The Greek inhabitants of Asia Minor could have made little of the mysterious name, except to somehow connect it with the river Euphrates (16:12), a place they *could* locate on a map. Now the Euphrates marked the eastern frontier of the Roman empire. Beyond it lay Parthia, Rome's enemy. But perhaps Rome's enemy is God's friend. At least such feelings are more crucial to folks living in and about Ephesus than any supposed setting in Palestine. The war is fought in Asia Minor.

And the war originates in heaven, more specifically in the temple. The story begins with a vision of God's temple in heaven (11:19) and ends with a vision of a new heaven, a new earth, and a new Jerusalem without a temple (21:22). And it is from the temple that judgment is meted out, both with the dual harvests (14:15–20) and with the seven final plagues (15:5), resulting in the pronouncement from the temple: it is done (16:17). While this spacial setting serves to advance the plot of the story, it is both ambiguous and indeterminate. God's temple is nowhere and everywhere. It is wherever people gather to worship. And in the final vision one can no longer even speak of a temple, for God is present in the city. Let us take a closer look at that city.

We have already discussed the city under the category of characters, for one of the characters is a place. The bride is the new Jerusalem (see pp. 111–14). We discussed her characterization above; now let us consider her as place. Three things about the city seem important as setting. First, John reports, "I saw no temple in the city, for its temple is the Lord God the Almighty and the Lamb. And the city has no need of sun or moon to shine on it, for the glory of God is its light, and its lamp is the Lamb" (21:22–23). Now this is surprising, for in the Greco-Roman world every city had a temple, many temples. A city's status was partially measured by the number and quality of its temples. They were often magnificent structures, centrally located. But the prime function of a temple is to represent the divine and since God fully inhabits this city there is no need for temples (nor for sun or moon, since God is light). Second, the city is a garden, containing the river of life and the tree of life (22:1–2). We return to the origins of humanity, to the garden of Eden, but now transformed into a city, the paramount achievement of human civilization. This final destination of the human race is no mere return to a pastoral ideal. Third, this is a permeable city: the gates are never shut (21:25). This is surprising, for John has been very keen on establishing boundaries for this community, drawing clear lines of who is in and who is outside. One might suspect that this means there is no longer an outside, but this is not true: "Outside are the dogs and sorcerers and fornicators and murderers and idolaters, and everyone who loves and practices falsehood" (22:15). Now this is truly shocking. Here, at the very end of the story, after the battle, after the judgment, after the destruction of evil, there is still an outside. This image of a completely sacred space with doors open to the outside, where evil lurks, is important for understanding John's Revelation.

The action of this story segment takes place in an ambiguous space, suspended as it were between heaven and earth, participating in both at once.

The Times

Part of the reason for the spacial ambiguity of this section is the temporal distortion that marks the story. In order to sort out the temporal setting, let us first consider the temporal point of view from which the story is told, then look at frequency, order, and duration. (These terms are defined and discussed on pp. 97–99. Temporal point of view was discussed on pp. 30–34.)

As a spacial point of view indicates *where* the narrator stands to observe the action, the temporal point of view indicates *when* the narrator observes it: what parts of the story are in the past for the narrator, what parts are in the present, and what is yet to come. We see this clearly in the opening action of the dragon and the woman when we are told: "the woman fled into the wilderness, where she has a place prepared by God, so that there she can be nourished for one thousand two hundred sixty days" (12:6; see also verse 14). Notice she *fled* (in the past), *has* a place (present), and *can be nourished* (present stretching into the future).

The same scheme can be seen in the little biography of the dragon. It *has come down* but it *knows* that its time is short (12:12). And it *went* off *to make war* on the woman's children (12:17). Some things are past; some are present. In the same way, the verbs associated with the first beast are in the past tense (13:1–7) while those associated with the second beast are largely in the present (13:12–16).

Surprisingly little is future from the point of view of the narrator; such future actions include: universal worship of the beast (13:8, 12); judgment on those who worship the beast (14:10); rest for the martyrs (14:13); universal worship of God (15:4); war and the lamb's conquest (17:14); the destruction of the whore (17:16–17; 18:8–9, 21); the rule of the lamb (19:15); the rule of the martyrs (20:7); Satan's release and deception of the nations (28:8–9); the destruction of Satan (20:10); God's full dwelling with humanity (21:3–7; 22:3–5); and a curse on anyone changing this writing (22:18–19).

We may conclude then that this story stands in the time of struggle, after the beast is established, while the beast is leading many astray, and before the beast has either apparent success (universal worship) or real defeat.

But of course temporal relations are not quite this clear in the actual telling of the story, for the story is not told simply or in order. Probably the most baffling aspect of this story is its use of repetitions. It is often difficult to say whether John is being repetitive (narrating the same event over again) or merely repetitious (narrating events so similar the audience identifies them), but there can be no doubt that the narrative gives the impression of redundancy. The most significant redundancy touches the major theme of this narrative section: the war. John narrates the "final battle" at least three times—maybe more. Consider the listing of John's uses of the battle motif in Table 10.

Three times the same pattern holds: the forces of evil gather for battle against God's forces and are utterly defeated and destroyed (16:14; 19:19; 20:8). They seem more like three ways of telling the story rather than three stages of the same war. In addition to these three, we are told predictively that the ten kings will make war on the lamb and the lamb will conquer them (17:14). Plus there is the predictive statement by the writer of the letters (2:16). Finally, there is the report of the war in heaven (12:7–9),

which on the face of it involves other combatants but which on closer examination reflects this same war (12:11). Thus there are as many as six repetitions of the war incident, each told as if it were the whole war.

In addition, there are three other incidents that show the beasts/dragon
launching war on the saints, two with adverse outcomes. At the end of the
narrative segment on heavenly worship we had a scene of two witnesses and
in the course of that scene we were told that the beast from the pit will war
with the witnesses *and conquer them* (11:7). At the end of the dragon
episode we see it setting off to make war on the rest of the woman's children (12:17), with no outcome indicated. But the sea beast is said to be
allowed to make war on the saints and to *conquer them* (13:4, 7).

Perhaps we could simplify and say there are two phases to this war. The
dragon and its allies war with and conquer the saints; the lamb and its allies
war with and conquer the dragon. But of course the point is John does not
simplify. The narrative effect of this repetition is to make the war appear
complex, even while still emphasizing the final outcome as the conquest of
evil. The deeper complexity rests in the conviction that these two seemingly
opposite outcomes are the same, for it is precisely the dragon's apparent victory in the death of Jesus and his followers that is the dragon's ultimate
defeat.

In a similar way, the fall of Babylon is given six times. First it is
announced that it is fallen and will burn forever (14:8–11); second, it is
shown to be destroyed by an earthquake (16:18–21); then we are shown

TABLE 10 *The Wars of the Apocalypse*

Ref.	Description	Outcome
2:16	Christ will come and war against Nicolaitans	Christ's victory assumed
9:7–9	Locusts of fifth seal sound like horses rushing into battle	None given
11:7	Beast from pit will war with witnesses	It will conquer them
12:7	War in heaven: Michael and dragon	Dragon beaten and expelled
12:17	Dragon goes to make war on woman and her children	Not said
13:4, 7	Sea beast allowed to make war on saints	It conquers them
16:14	Demonic spirits of sixth bowl gather kings for war	"It is done"
17:14	Ten kings will make war on Lamb	Lamb will conquer them
19:11	Heavenly warrior makes war	Not said
19:19	Beast and kings gather to make war against rider	Beast captured and destroyed
20:8	Released Satan gathers nations for battle against saints in beloved city	Fire from heaven destroys them; Satan destroyed

the kings stripping and devouring her (17:16–18); then we are shown the city abandoned, with a call to leave it (18:2–4); fifth, we are told the city will be burned and mourned by the merchants and sailors (18:8–20); and finally Babylon's destruction is symbolically enacted by the angel who throws a large millstone into the sea (18:21–24). As is immediately evident, these six scenes are incongruous in terms of image, action, and time. Clearly the temporal sequence is not linear: proclaimed to have fallen in the first incident, there is still the call to abandon the city in the third. Again, it seems best to understand these incidents as repetitions of the same event narrated in a variety of ways.

There are several doublets that could be understood either as repetitions or as narrations of similar incidents. There are two conjurings of beasts (13:1, 11). There are two harvests of the earth (14:14–16, 17–20). There are two openings of the heavenly temple (11:19; 15:5). There are two descents of the heavenly Jerusalem (21:1; 21:10). There are two incidents in which John attempts to worship the heavenly messenger (19:10; 22:8). The introductions of the two visions of the symbolic women are strikingly similar (17:1; 21:9). And the vision of the second woman is a vision of the new Jerusalem, which had already been narrated (21:1–4).

Finally, there are strong parallels between the whole sequence of the seven bowls and the earlier sequence of the seven trumpets. With both the trumpets and bowls, the stages are: earth, sea, rivers, sun, abyss/throne of the beast, Euphrates River. But whereas in the earlier sequence the author is careful to spell out that only a third is destroyed, here destruction seems to be complete. (Compare 8:7–11:15 and 16:2–17.)

We have, then, a highly repetitive narrative, with incidents narrated multiple times and with incidents imitated by other similar events. Still there is the sense of forward movement, even of closure. While such redundancy risks boring or confusing the audience, it also has the effect of enhancing the certainty that these events are real.

A corollary effect of this repetition is that the order of the telling of this story is not straightforward. The war in heaven that results in the dragon being expelled to the earth is certainly prior to the dragon's pursuit of the woman on earth, although it is narrated afterwards as a flashback (12:1–13) and includes a flashforward to the time when God's kingdom has come (12:10). The pronouncement of the angel that Babylon has fallen (14:8) is likewise a flashforward, for the fall of Babylon will be narrated later in the story (perhaps at 18:2, making 17:16 another flashforward).

John's story seems organized more to emphasize character than action. It opens by introducing two prime characters and closes with another (12:1–3; 21:9–14). At each stage of the action we are first carefully introduced to the characters (13:1, 11; 14:1, 14; etc.). Thus different characters, or—in the case of the characterizations of Jesus—different versions of the same character, will precipitate the telling of the appropriate story segment, even if that is out of order or redundant.

This also means that there will be great fluctuations in the duration of the scenes, ranging from summary to frequent narrative pauses. In fact, these two extremes dominate the action; there are few scenes in what we might think of as normal narrative time. (For a discussion of the concept of duration see pp. 97–99.) We often move directly from an elaborately descriptive scene to a summary scene, nearly skipping a narration of the action (e.g., 19:11–20). This only increases the audience's sense of temporal disorientation.

We have then a highly repetitious narrative, with both flashbacks and flashforwards, told in a style that alternates between lengthy descriptions that retard the narrative and dramatic summaries that rush it forward. The reader of such a narrative will not likely be able to maintain a clear sense of time—and it is even less likely that the original oral audience could do so. We will return to the significance of this observation when we discuss the sense of an ending (pp. 147–48).

In summary, both the places and the times of this story segment remain obscure, reflecting the experience of the audience as they are forced to enter another dimension. We have been successively removed from normal time and space (the first narrative segment on Patmos), through extra-normal time and space (the second narrative segment in heaven), into this meta-time and meta-space of cosmic war, disaster, and renewal. These events are not in some linear future, connected to normal time in a historical fashion. These events occur above and within the events of time. This story is not some prediction of a logical future but rather a revelation of the true significance of the present. We will return to this theme below. Now let us look more closely at the plot of the action.

THE PLOT

With all the doublets, repetitions, flashbacks and flashforwards, still the sequence of significant incidents (kernels) is reasonably clear. After a war in heaven, a dragon is cast down to earth where it first attempts to kill an infant, then pursues the mother, and finally turns to make war on her other children. First it creates allies, two beasts from sea and land, who act in the dragon's stead making war on these other children. An opposing army gathers on Mount Zion, the lamb and 144,000 male virgin warriors. From the heavenly temple come seven angels who attack the earth, sea, rivers, sun, the beast's throne, and the Euphrates River. A heavenly warrior appears on a white horse and the beasts and kings gather for war. The beasts are destroyed and all their followers are killed by the sword coming from the mouth of the heavenly warrior. Satan (the dragon) is bound and imprisoned, producing a thousand years of peace. However, Satan is released and gathers the nations for battle. But fire from heaven consumes them and Satan is destroyed. All are judged from the heavenly books. A new creation appears and a new Jerusalem comes down out of heaven. John sees the lamb's bride and describes her in great detail, culminating in the declaration:

> [The Lamb's] servants will worship him; they will see his face, and his name will be on their foreheads. And there will be no more night; they need no light of lamp or sun, for the Lord God will be their light, and they will reign forever and ever. And he said to me, "These words are trustworthy and true, for the Lord, the God of the spirits of the prophets, has sent his angel to show his servants what must soon take place." "See, I am coming soon! Blessed is the one who keeps the words of the prophecy of this book."   REV 22:3–7

There follows the closing scene that parallels the opening in which John directly addresses the readers and calls them to imitate this action by their worship (22:8–9).

The basic plot is ancient and common to stories of cosmic warfare (see pp. 103–5). While versions of the story differed significantly, the overall pattern has been reconstructed thus:[22]

Appearance of dragon or pair of dragons
Chaos and disorder
The attack
Appearance of the champion
The champion vanquished
The dragon's reign
The recovery of the champion
Renewed battle and victory of the champion
Fertility of the restored order
Procession and victory shout
Temple built for the warrior God
Banquet (wedding)
Manifestation of the champion's universal reign

The story of the Apocalypse is different, but enough like this general pattern to be considered a version of it. For discussion of points of comparison and contrast see the discussion in the next section.

Commentary on the Action

We are now ready to examine the incidents of this story in detail. Earlier in this chapter, we saw that such stories of cosmic warfare are a common story type, and that the plot of this story fits that type. We have carefully surveyed the characters and the settings, both spacial and temporal so that we have a context for this more detailed discussion. The following divisions are somewhat arbitrary, as all story divisions are, but they are a convenient way to analyze the action.

THE DRAGON'S WAR, 11:19–12:17

This narrative segment sets the stage for all that follows, explaining how this horrendous war came about. There are three phases of hostility leading up to the present war. First, we meet two characters: a woman about to deliver her child and a dragon who is trying to destroy her child. Then we witness a war in heaven where the dragon is defeated and cast to earth. Finally the dragon attempts to destroy the woman. When this proves impossible, the dragon sets off on a new war on her other children. The rest of the story provides the details of this new war.

The Two Signs in the Sky: Woman and Dragon, 12:1–6

While it is never possible to speak of an author's sources with any confidence, it is possible to explore the resonances a given scenario would elicit in certain readers. The resonances of this scene are rich and complex. In addition to the explicit traditions of cosmic warfare and creation stemming from Babylonian and Canaanite mythology outlined in pp. 103–5, there are several other possibilities. There is first the resonance with astrology. In the zodiac, in which there are twelve stars or constellations, Scorpio follows Virgo through the sky. Zodiacal imagery was well-known, even being used as the subject matter for floor mosaics in synagogues. Perhaps looking up at this night sky John has seen a deeper significance, a significance borne out by other stories as well.[23]

There is, additionally, the echo with the Egyptian tale of the daily cycle in which the sky Goddess Hathor (or Isis) gives birth to the sun (Horus) but is pursued by the red dragon Typhon (or Seth) who swallows the sun each night. There is the similar story connected with the birth of Apollo, also a sun God, in Greek tradition. His mother Leto was pursued by the dragon Python. Leto is provided refuge on the island of Delos; Apollo is born and eventually slays the dragon. In both these cases the focus is on the birth of the sun, which Roman readers would likely connect with the Caesar who was portrayed on coins as a sun God. The irony of John's story is clear, for in his version the emperor is clearly an ally of the dragon not his opponent.[24]

But perhaps the thing the reader might notice most is that the woman not the newborn is the focus of this story. This aspect of the story finds its closest parallel in Jewish tales. Since this is clearly the story of the birth of the messiah, readers might well think of Mary. Whether there were such stories of Mary this early we do not know; this would be the first evidence for them if it referred to her. But certainly we can see here the ground for later stories that exalt Mary as queen of heaven and adapt Isis imagery to her.25

Another Jewish parallel would see the woman as Israel and the twelve stars as the tribes. The prophets commonly portrayed Israel's enemies under the figure of the dragon, and Israel's pursuit into the desert where she is kept safe by God is an essential element of the Exodus story (e.g., Ezek 29:3, Deut 1:30–31).

A final Jewish tale with a direct conflict between a woman and a serpent goes back to the primeval story of creation when Eve is pursued in the garden of Eden. This conflict was said to produce a lasting enmity between the woman's seed and the serpent, resulting eventually in the crushing of the serpent's head (see Gen 3:15; and compare 3:16 with Rev 12:2).

None of these contexts is essential for understanding John's story but each of them adds potential meanings and nuances.26 Readers familiar with these other stories would have seen that John's story points to an enduring truth concerning the war of darkness with light, of oppression with liberty, of false loyalty with true worship. (For discussion of ways these allusions might influence character, see the discussion on pp. 111–14.)

The action of this section remains a little obscure. The dragon seeks to eat the child but the child is snatched away, apparently rescued. But the child goes to God while the woman flees into the wilderness where she has a place prepared for her for the set time of the period of evil. This action is then interrupted by a flashback.

The War in Heaven, 12:7–12

This is an interesting incident that follows John's penchant for inserting a short scene that summarizes the action of major sections of the book. Just as the action of the worship scroll could be summarized by the angel at the altar (8:3–5), so the action of the war scroll is summarized here. Although the action is attributed to Michael (12:7), it is clear that the victory was won by the lamb/Jesus (12:11). Although it reports the war as that primeval battle of the distant past in which one of God's heavenly courtiers rebelled, the victory is clearly the future victory of the messiah (12:10).

There were numerous stories about Satan's expulsion from heaven, most apparently built on the mythological elements in an ancient dirge for a fallen tyrant (Isa 14:12–21). For a version of the story told from Satan's point of view see *The Life of Adam and Eve* 12–16.27 Most involve simple expulsions, but Luke reports Jesus saying he saw Satan fall from heaven like lightning (10:18). John of course casts it as a war, for that is the motif of this story. But it is not simply a war that happened in some mythic past; it happened in the death of Jesus and happens in the deaths of those who witness to Jesus. Above and below, before and after, all correspond in John's world-view (see pp. 3–5 and 64–65).

The Pursuit of the Woman, 12:13–16

Two actions are narrated: the dragon pursues the woman (but she is saved by being given two wings that allow her to escape into the wilderness); the dragon tries to destroy the woman with a flood of water from his mouth (but the earth opens her mouth, swallows the flood, and helps the woman). While the former rescue has echoes of the Exodus (see Exod 19:4), the latter is unparalleled. All other biblical references to the earth opening her mouth have to do with destruction not rescue. Also unparalleled is the notion of one woman rescuing another (earth being in Greek a feminine noun with a feminine pronoun).

That the woman flees "into the wilderness" (12:14) even though she has already been said to have fled there (12:6) indicates two things. First, it shows that the war in heaven incident is really a flashback that interrupts the conflict between the woman and the dragon. (See the discussion of time on pp. 117–22.) Second, it illustrates the symbolic importance of this place. Not only is the wilderness the place of escape in the Exodus tradition, it is the place where salvation begins anew in the prophetic tradition (see Isa 40:3 and Mark 1:1–15).

The New War, 12:17

Having failed to destroy either the infant or the woman, the dragon sets out on a broader war on the rest of her children. The story is careful to designate who these children are: "those who keep the commandments of God and hold the testimony of Jesus" (12:17). Such a description, clearly meant to characterize the implied audience, points to a dual heritage, resting both on their identification with Jesus and on their allegiance to Jewish Law—thus on the border between Christians and Jews. We will discuss the implied audience more fully on pp. 159–60, just noting here that a community that imagines itself in such a position on the boundary between communities may well find validity in metaphors of war and fighting for space.

In summary, this segment portrays four stages to the dragon's war, but they are not told in order. The first stage is the war in heaven which results in the dragon being expelled to earth. The second stage is the attempt to destroy the messiah-child, who is instead snatched up to heaven. The third stage is the attempt to destroy the woman, who is protected in the wilderness. The fourth stage is the attack on her remaining children—clearly marked as the intended audience of this writing. Thus this story functions as a charter story for the community explaining how they have come to be in the situation they occupy. They are a community under attack, or so our story would have them believe.

REV 12:1–17 *Readers' Notes on the Dragon & Woman*

PORTENT A sign, mark, or token. The word was used especially of an omen from the divine, including the constellations of the zodiac.

HEAVEN The Greek word can refer either to the sky or to heaven as the abode of God.

BIRTH PANGS At once an allusion to the Eve story (Gen 3:16) and to the travail that would accompany the birth of the new age (Matt 24:8).

RULE THE NATIONS A messianic allusion, see Psalm 2. Literally the phrase here is *shepherd* the nations.

WILDERNESS Both the place of safety after the Exodus and the place of the beginning of salvation. See Isa 40:3 and Mark 1.

1,260 DAYS The period of evil understood as an incomplete time: half of seven years. This period will be variously cast as three and a half years, forty-two months, or 1,260 days. The different designations seem to be used for variety rather than with any different meaning. It was standard to think of a period of immense evil just before the final end. Often this period was called the "birth pangs of the messianic age."

TESTIMONY Witness, in Greek *martys*, is well on its way to getting its technical meaning of martyr. Jesus is the *martys* par excellence but his followers add their own testimony to his.

TIME, TIMES Another designation of the three and one-half year period of evil.

FLOOD Perhaps a metaphor for the flood of imperial propaganda designed to support the emperor's position and power. If so the earth's ability to absorb it could point to the inability of the political system to live up to its promises.

THE DRAGON'S ALLIES, 12:18–13:18

The action here continues the dragon's withdrawal from the attack on the woman in order to make war on her other children. The first act of that war is the gathering of allies (or creating of agents). Two beasts rise up in response to the dragon's presence, one from the sea and one from the land. These are the primal agents of chaos who appear in many ancient stories, known sometimes as Leviathan and Behemoth (for a discussion of the identity and descriptions of the beasts, see the explanation of characters on pp. 109–11).

These two agents act in distinctive, but complementary, ways in the dragon's war against the woman's children. Both receive the dragon's power and authority, but the first acts by force, the second by deception, seduction, and coercion. The first beast survives death, utters blasphemies against God's name and dwelling, makes war on the saints *and conquers them* (13:7). It enjoys universal dominion and all will worship it. This development elicits a narrative aside, reminding us of the rhetoric of the letter scroll: anyone who has an ear should listen (13:9). There follow two maxims, on the futility of escape and of armed resistance. Endurance is called for.

The second beast works by miracles and deception to gain worship of the first beast. Those who refuse are killed (13:15). Those who acquiesce are marked, on their foreheads and hands, with the mark/name of the beast: 666. Whether we understand this as an individual or corporate reference (discussed in the section on characterization, pp. 107–8), the meaning is to be found in the ancient metaphorical use of the body's parts. The head was the seat of authority and volition and thus the center of the spirit. The mark on the head signifies spiritual devotion to the beast. The hand represents action, production, and commerce. The mark on the hand signifies economic support for the beast.[28]

To understand how everyone is tainted by these marks one needs to understand how life was lived in first-century Roman Asia Minor. Literally every activity would involve one in some token recognition of the emperor (and his divinity) and of the Gods. Education began with reading Homer's ancient tales of Gods and heroes. Medicine was practiced in the name of Asclepius, God of healing. Entertainment consisted of sporting events (both the bloody arena and the Olympic Games) dedicated to the Gods and of the theater dedicated to Dionysus. Each performance began with a sacrifice to Dionysus whose altar stood at the front of every theater. To ply a trade meant to belong to a guild, but trade guilds were devoted to a patron deity regarded as the founder and protector of the craft. Mutual assistance societies (the ancient form of insurance) would gather in the name of some God or Goddess. The very coins by which one bought and sold, and paid one's taxes, testified to these Gods and Goddesses. And these coins most often bore some image of the emperor and an inscription claiming him to be "son of the divine Julius." Even if one avoided the direct worship of these "beasts" one's hand might still be marked in the daily round of commerce.

In this scene of the two beasts John paints an almost wholly pessimistic picture: who can fight against the beast (13:4). Those who have followed the story this far might suspect they know the answer, and that suspicion is confirmed in the next scene.

REV 12:18–13:18 *Readers' Notes on the Beasts*

BEAST . . . SEA Probably a symbol of the Roman empire. See pp. 106–9 for details.

ONE OF ITS HEADS Clearly an individual ruler who is killed. Some relate this to a legend of Nero's return, but this seems unlikely. The Nero legend does not seem to envision a return from death but rather a return from exile (see *Sibylline Oracles* 5.90–235). More importantly, what is said to be healed here is not the head but the beast (clear in Greek if not in English translations). The point is that cutting off the head does not kill the beast; even as killing the emperor does not destroy the empire. Probably the assassination of Julius Caesar is a better parallel than the death of Nero.

ENDURANCE Consistent resistance to the powers of evil. See Readers' Note on 1:9, p. 38.

BEAST . . . EARTH This beast functions as minister to the first, and later seems to be called the false prophet (see 16:13 and especially 19:20). Perhaps we can think of it as the system of institutions, individuals, and ethos that supports the domination system of Rome.

MAKES . . . WORSHIP There is little evidence of enforced imperial worship in this period and we must be careful of reading later periods of persecution back into this story. Surely some died for refusing to recognize imperial claims (13:15), but this would have been rare. The coercion of the beast is more subtle.[29]

HEAD A symbol of the will and the center of the spirit.

HAND A symbol of one's work, activity, duty, purpose.

666 The triple six is an intensification of the significance of six as incomplete and imperfect. It also echoes the sixth day of creation, when humans were created. Here it can be understood in either an individual or a corporate sense, referring to the emperorship or to some individual emperor. See pp. 106–9 for details.

THE APPEARANCE OF THE CHAMPION, 14:1–20

We begin a sequence of actions here that runs on through the final battle and the ultimate defeat of evil (20:15), but I have for convenience divided them up into smaller logical units, beginning with the introduction of the one who will ultimately defeat the dragon. It is crucial to understand the various images used to characterize this agent throughout this section, beginning with the image of the lamb (14:1), followed by the son of humanity figure coming on the clouds (14:14), and reaching a climax with the divine warrior from heaven (19:11) before returning to the figure of the lamb (21:22; 22:1; etc.). This story frames images of destruction and holy war with images of sacrifice and martyrdom. (See the discussion on pp. 109–11 and 69–70.)

The action of this segment continues the introduction of the combatants. Just as the dragon has manifested its allies, so now we see the lamb with its allies: the 144,000 sealed from the tribes of Israel (first encountered at 7:1). On the highly problematic characterization of these as male celibates, see the discussion on pp. 111–14. (See also pp. 70–74.)

The lengthy introduction of these characters causes a narrative pause in which nothing happens, but also contains a flashback by reintroducing the worship scene from the second major narrative segment that I call the worship scroll (compare 14:3 with 4:4–8). This reminds us that these two scenes are interrelated and simultaneous (see the discussion of time at pp. 117–21).

Time is further distorted by the appearance of three angels, acting in their primary function as heavenly messengers. Each makes a proclamation. The first makes a demand; the second announces something that has happened; the third makes a prediction: seemingly present, past, and future events. The first makes a present demand, cast as an "eternal gospel." It declares, "Fear God and give him glory, for the hour of his judgment has come; and worship him who made heaven and earth, the sea and the springs of water" (14:7) This is surely the heart of the conflict portrayed in this story, a conflict of who and how one ought to worship.30 This present demand is reinforced with two other messages.

A second angel announces that Babylon has fallen. The tense of the verb in Greek has no exact counterpart in English; it is called an aorist and indicates an action that occurred at some definite point in the past. Here is an instance where the story world and the real world are radically disjunctive, for the worldly city that corresponds to Babylon is Rome and Rome has surely not fallen. It is as if this character greets the audience from the future and assures them that things will change.

The third angel's time once more corresponds to that of the audience, announcing the future judgment of those who worship the beast and receive its mark. But then the pronouncement slips from future to present tense: it is as if they are already burning, already beyond rest (14:11).

Now the narrator explains the purpose of this interruption: it is a call for endurance (14:12). Then a voice from heaven makes the ominous announcement: Blessed are the dead who from now on die in the Lord. We are reminded of the battle in heaven (12:11) and of the sacrificial imagery used to describe the lamb's army. But just when we might think we have it figured out, the scene shifts dramatically.

Our attention shifts back to the sky, where there is a white cloud and seated on it is the majestic human being from the inaugural vision (14:14; 1:13). The figure wears a golden crown (of victory; see Readers' Notes on 4:1–11) and carries a sickle. An angel emerges from the temple and tells him to harvest the earth, which he does. Then there is a second harvest, but not of grain and not by the human figure. Another angel comes from the temple carrying another sickle and is told by yet another angel (from the altar, see the discussion of 8:3–5) to harvest the grapes. This is truly odd. Further when these grapes are harvested they are thrown into the "great wine press of the wrath of God" which is "trodden outside the city" with the wine/blood flooding out "as high as a horse's bridle" covering 1,600 stadia—a figure equivalent to about 200 miles. This is a truly horrible scene, a war scene that both repulses and compels. But why is it told thus? Why does the human figure not perform the grape harvest? Why are grapes harvested thus? Why is it outside the city? Why is there so much blood?

The answers to these questions can be found in the symbolism of the story. First the human figure surely stands for Jesus and the harvest of grain and grape evokes echoes of the bread and wine connected with Jesus—the Eucharist. We know that the expression "outside the city" was used by some Christians in this period to refer to the death of Jesus (Heb 13:11–16) and probably stems from a concept of impurity (Lev 14:40). Thus while on one level the blood here would seem to be that of the wicked of the earth, it is symbolically aligned with the blood Jesus shed to redeem the wicked. The blood that covers the whole earth (1,600 being rooted in four, the earth's number) is the blood of Jesus—everywhere available in the eucharistic wine.

The champion has appeared. Victory is assured. But everything is not as it at first appears.

REV 14:1–20 *Readers' Notes on the Champion*

LAMB See the discussion on pp. 69–70.

MOUNT ZION The place from which the deliverer was to come (Ps 14:7; Isa 59:20 and Rom 11:26) and also a symbol for the community of faith (Heb 12:22).

144,000 See the discussion on pp. 70–74 and the Readers' Notes on 6:1–8:1, pp. 85–88.

THRONE . . . CREATURES . . . ELDERS See the discussion in pp. 70–74.

DEFILE A purity not a moral concern, though the two are confused in English. As warriors in a holy war these men must not have contact with women, based on the ancient laws of purity.

FIRST FRUITS . . . BLAMELESS Both are images of sacrifice (Lev 2:14; 1:3; 3:1, etc.). The word translated blameless means literally "without blemish."

BABYLON The ancient destroyer of Israel now used metaphorically for the new destroyer of Israel, Rome.

MARK OF THE BEAST See the discussion on pp. 106–9 and 126–28.

WHITE CLOUD The heavenly figure coming on the clouds derives from Daniel (7:13) and was widely used in early Christian writings (Matt 24:30 and parallels). John adds the element of white, symbolizing victory.

SON OF MAN See the Readers' Notes on 1:9–20, pp. 38–41.

OUTSIDE THE CITY Indicates rejection, exclusion, impurity (1 Kgs 21:13; Heb 13:11–12; Lev 14:40).

TWO HUNDRED MILES Not a good translation since it misses the symbolic significance of the number, which in Greek is 1,600 stadia, a number built on the root of four, signifying the earth. This blood then covers the earth.

THE ATTACK ON THE EARTH: SEVEN FINAL PLAGUES, 15:1–16:21

This incident signals a resumption of the main action by announcing it as "another portent" seen in the sky (compare 12:1–3). As noted above, the first two sky portents probably had astrological significance (see pp. 115–17). This third sign may also rest on astrological phenomena. Once again the action is delayed by a lengthy description and preparatory events. And once again the scene harks back to the heavenly worship scene with its sea of glass (15:2; 4:6). Again the heavenly temple is opened (15:5; 11:19), and again angels come out of it (15:6; 14:15–18).

Some have objected that the angels are introduced as having the seven plagues (15:1), but they are then given the seven bowls of wrath (15:7). It seems best to regard their introduction as a summary of what is about to be shown in detail. The action itself is straightforward: a voice from the temple instructs the angels to pour their bowls on the earth and they each do so in turn.

The sequence echoes the seven trumpets (see the comparison in pp. 117–21), but the action is more climactic, more final (note the introductory statement at 15:1 that these are the last plagues, for with them God's wrath is ended). The seven stages show a successive bombardment of the earth, destroying every aspect of it until the dominion of evil is overthrown. Rather too much like the bombing of cities in our day, these scenes raise serious ethical concerns, which we will consider shortly (pp. 145–47). Each scene begins with one of the angels pouring out its bowl.

The first pours on the earth, causing painful sores on all who have the mark of the beast and worship its image. The second pours into the sea, which turns to blood killing all sea life. The third pours into the rivers and springs, which also turn to blood. This provokes a response that briefly interrupts the series. The "angel of the waters" (reminiscent of the Greek tradition of nymphs who represented the life force of rivers, trees, and mountains) comments on the justice of this destruction. We might expect this guardian spirit of water to object, but instead the angel defends the devastation. The logic of the comment is crucial for understanding what is happening: "because they shed the blood of saints and prophets, you have given them blood to drink. It is what they deserve!" (16:6). However outrageous the story becomes, this principle guides it. We get what we deserve. It is as if there were a law to history: those who live by the sword die by the sword (as 13:10); those who shed blood wind up bloody. (Compare the need for waiting until the full number of martyrs has been killed; 6:11, discussed on pp. 82–83.)

The series resumes its final four stages. The fourth pours on the sun, causing scorching heat and cursing of God, but no repentance. (We will discuss the morality of this implication that people are being tortured to bring repentance on pp. 145–47.) The fifth pours on the throne of the beast, plunging its kingdom into darkness; again they curse God but do not repent. The sixth pours on the river Euphrates, which dries up allowing invasion from the east. Demonic spirits from the mouths of the dragon, the beast, and the false prophet (seemingly another name for the second beast) gather the kings of the whole earth for battle. An unattributed voice declares, "I am coming like a thief." They assemble at Harmagedon. The seventh angels pours its bowl into the air, eliciting a loud voice from the temple declaring, "It is done."

But of course it is not done; much remains. We have seen that each series of seven seems to bring the end, but that somehow the end always remains just over the horizon. In this regard, it is important to note that the final battle is never fought. The narrative moves directly from the gathering of the armies to the victory pronouncement. Or perhaps it is more correct to say that for John the final battle has already been fought and the victory secured in the death of Jesus. Much of the symbolism of this work is designed to interpret the meaning of Jesus' death.

The victory pronouncement elicits scenes of extraordinary disasters: lightning, thunder and an earthquake more violent than any earlier quake. The great city splits into three parts; cities fall; islands and mountains disappear; hailstones weighing a hundred pounds fall on people, who respond by cursing God. It would seem that all is destroyed; and in fact the narrative now pauses to show us in greater detail the destruction of Babylon.

REV 15:1–16:21 *Readers' Notes on the Seven Bowls*

SONG OF MOSES . . . LAMB The same duality as reflected in the description of the saints as those who keep the commandments and the testimony of Jesus (12:17; 14:2, etc.). For the song of Moses see Exodus 15 and Deuteronomy 32, which is verbally echoed here along with two Psalms (111:2; 86:8–9) and Jeremiah (10:6–7; 16:19). The original setting of the song of Moses is one of extolling God's vengeance on the enemies in very harsh terms.

TEMPLE . . . TENT A conflating of the idea of the original tent (tabernacle) of Moses with the later stone temple.

SMOKE . . . GLORY The scene is reminiscent of that in Isaiah 6.

BOWLS Greeks drank their wine from bowls.

HARMAGEDON Consciously labeled a Hebrew name, it would translate Mount Magedon. But there is no such mountain. See the discussion on pp. 115–17.

THE GREAT CITY An ambiguous symbol standing primarily for Rome (17:18), but also including Jerusalem (11:8). See the discussion on pp. 64–65, 106–9, and 133–36.

A HUNDRED POUNDS Literally a talent weight, a measure of 125 Roman pounds (12 ounces each), thus roughly 90 pounds by our measure. But the expression is best understood to mean they were impossibly big. In our idiom, we might say they weighed a ton.

THE ENEMY DIVIDED: THE GREAT WHORE DESTROYED, 17:1–19:10

Just as the great city has been split into three parts (16:19), so now we watch the dragon's coalition fall apart. The story focuses this disintegration through the character of Babylon, viewed as a grand, richly attired prostitute. On the characterization as both vicious and victim, see pp. 106–9. Here we trace the action of the story.

The fall of Babylon was proclaimed by an angel when the 144,000 gathered on Mount Zion (14:8) and shown as destroyed in the great earthquake (16:19). Now it will be enacted four separate times in four different images: an abused woman, an abandoned city, a burning city, and a millstone thrown into the sea. Let's look at each in turn.

The Abused Woman

This is the longest incident and also the one with the most powerful imagery and most detailed interpretation. The scene is carefully linked to the series of seven bowls by having one of these angels address John and transport him into the wilderness where he sees the woman. (One wonders vaguely whether John intends the audience to think of that other woman we left in the wilderness at the beginning of this story; 12:14.)

We begin with a summary in which she is labeled "the great whore" (17:1). Next she is described in detail. She is seated on the sea beast, the one with seven heads. She is clothed in purple and scarlet and wears gold, jewels, and pearls and holds a gold cup. She is clearly an aristocrat, since only the richest and noblest citizens were allowed to wear these colors and such jewelry.[31] This is her fascinating, alluring side. But there is also the repulsive side. Her cup is full of impurities; she is marked on her forehead as a whore; and she is drunk—drunk with blood. John gives his response but it is hard to express it in English. The Greek is literally: I marveled seeing her a great marvel. It indicates astonishment and wonder moving towards awe. It is the same verb used at 13:3 to indicate the enchantment with which the whole earth followed the beast. The angel immediately moves to disillusion John (17:7), by a lengthy interpretation of the image.

There are three parts to this interpretation. First there is a detailed explanation of the beast, then a description of the coming war, and finally a prediction of the woman's fate. The angel gives an unparalleled double interpretation of the seven heads of the beast: they are seven hills as well as seven rulers. Of these seven, five have fallen, one is, and one is yet to come. Thus the present ruler is the sixth.[32] The beast itself is described in messianic terms (it is an eighth) and appears to have come back from the dead, echoing John's conviction that evil imitates good. (See similar ideas expressed in the introductions of the two beasts in chapter 13.) The ten horns stand for ten kings who ally themselves with the beast, yielding to him their powers (as in the story of Marduk, only reversed, for they are joining the monster; see pp. 103–5).

The angel adds that they will make war on the lamb and the lamb will conquer them (17:14). Again we lack any semblance of a war narrative, moving directly from the fact of the war to the fact of victory, justified only by the explanation that the lamb is Lord of lords (notice the tense).

Finally, we are told the fate of the woman, and a dark and horrible fate it is. For her allies turn on her: "they and the beast will hate the whore; they will make her desolate and naked; they will devour her flesh and burn her up with fire" (17:16). It is unfortunate that these acts are carried out on a human figure. For even though they are carried out by the monsters of the story, the audience understands that she got what she deserves—and later in the story there will be rejoicing over her demise (19:1–3). But there is no rejoicing here, and I think we are meant to feel the horror of this scene; it is the sort of thing that happens in war. John may feel the danger of experiencing these terrors on the literal level, for he adds a postscript to the story: The woman you saw is the great city that rules over the kings of the earth (17:18).

Thus on one level John is retelling history, for it is just this fate that befell Jerusalem: stripped, devoured, and burned. But the great city is also Rome and John is convinced the same fate awaits that city also. John will symbolize this destruction under three more literal images, and then portray two opposite responses, first a dirge, then a hallelujah.

The Abandoned City

What was earlier told in summary is here portrayed more fully, as an angel announces that Babylon has fallen (18:2; compare 14:8). Now the desolation of the city is elaborated, for it is inhabited only by wild animals and demons. Or would be if God's people obey, for they are called to leave the city (18:4) so as to avoid sharing in her sins and the plagues they bring. Once again the call for justice: render to her as she herself has rendered (18:6).

The Burning City

The judgment of the city comes swiftly and unexpectedly—in a single day. Pestilence, mourning, and famine . . . and fire (18:8). The eternal city becomes an eternal smoking ruin (19:3). To this spectacle there are three sets of witnesses, who see the smoke and mourn. The *kings* of the earth stand afar off, weep for her, and cry "alas" (18:9). The *merchants* too stand afar off and mourn for her. But their loss is more evident, for no one buys their cargo any more. The cargo is listed with grave irony:

> gold, silver, jewels and pearls, fine linen, purple, silk and scarlet, all kinds of scented wood, all articles of ivory, all articles of costly wood, bronze, iron, and marble, cinnamon, spice, incense, myrrh, frankincense, wine, olive oil, choice flour and wheat, cattle and sheep, horses and chariots, slaves—and human lives. REV 18:12–13

This is clearly the commerce of the upper class, people who would as soon trade in human lives as in spices. But the merchants also weep for the city, now described in the same terms as the great whore, "for in one hour all this wealth has been laid waste."

So too the *sailors* who deliver these goods stand afar off and mourn, crying out, "What city was like the great city?" (18:18). But in one hour all has been laid waste. Now just at this most dismal part of the narrative, when we are perhaps beginning to feel some of the loss, the audience is directly addressed: "Rejoice over her, O heaven, you saints and apostles and prophets! For God has given judgment for you against her" (18:20). We are called to remember that the fate of the city and the fate of the saints are antithetical. So John portrays once more the destruction of Babylon.

The Millstone

A mighty angel symbolically enacts Babylon's destruction by throwing a millstone into the sea as an image of the violence with which the city will be thrown down. Once more we are given a picture of the desolation of the city, a haunting, melodic ode to lost pleasures (18:22–23). The scene ends with a rationale for the destruction, for the city contains all the blood of prophets and saints who have been slaughtered on earth.

These scenes of mourning are followed by one of rejoicing, as the setting shifts from earth to heaven. Once again the climax of the action is a worship scene, as we are taken back to the throne room of heaven, with the same characters as in chapter 4. Only here the theme is rejoicing, with the repeated hallelujah. The rejoicing is over justice (God has avenged the blood of the faithful on the whore; 19:2), over God's universal reign (19:6), and the coming marriage of the lamb (19:7). This is the first mention of the marriage and is a bit surprising given the description of the warriors as celibate virgins (14:4). We get here our first glimpse of the bride, who will be described in great detail later (21:9–27). Her simple linen apparel contrasts starkly with the great whore's lavish purple and scarlet robes and jewels. In one of several instances of breaking his own symbolism, the writer tells us that this apparel "is the righteous deeds of the saints" (19:8; see Table 1 on

p. 7 for other interpreted symbols). Such an overt breaking of the symbolic frame reminds us that what is being discussed here is not brides and whores and battles, but the on-going life of the followers of Jesus whose actions can either clothe Rome in lavish ways or clothe their own community in faithful deeds.

The section ends with an important but almost humorous scene in which John tries to worship the messenger who has given him this vision, only to be rebuked sternly: "You must not do that! I am a fellow servant with you and your comrades who hold the testimony of Jesus. Worship God! For the testimony of Jesus is the spirit of prophecy" (19:10; see 22:9). Once more we hear the basic theme of the narrative stated boldly and simply: worship God.

REV 17:1–19:10 *Readers' Notes on the Fall of Babylon*

SEVEN BOWLS A reference back to the incidents narrated in chapters 15–16.

IN THE SPIRIT The third use of this phrase in the Apocalypse. See 1:10 and 4:2. It will be used again in the parallel vision of the bride at 20:10. The phrase seems to mean something like "in a trance" and is used when John wishes to emphasize the spiritual nature of what he is seeing.

WILDERNESS Ordinarily the place of salvation, but also the haunt of demons.

BEAST Introduced in chapter 13. See the discussion in pp. 106–9.

SEVEN KINGS Probably best understood symbolically rather than as referring to actual rulers we could count (and thus date the writing). There are to be seven emperors (a complete series) but the present is always the sixth, human. Also see endnote 32 on p. 193.

DRUNK WITH BLOOD See the third bowl, 16:6.

MYSTERY Hidden knowledge; secret meaning.

TESTIMONY OF JESUS Both the testimony by Jesus (his life and especially his death) and the testimony about Jesus which his followers carry on by their words and imitation of him.

SPIRIT OF PROPHECY The spirit that inspires prophecy. As a rebuke to John's attempt to worship the messenger this sentence reminds him that the source of the message is the testimony of Jesus.

THE NEW CHAMPION WINS THE VICTORY, 19:11–21:8

We come now to the final phase of the war, the central conflict. The warrior appears from heaven in all his military splendor and wins an easy victory over the beasts. A period of peace ensues, but it is not to last. The renewed evil leads to a final conflict in which the evil one is destroyed, ushering in the complete victory of God. Or so it seems. Let's examine each segment in detail.

The Word Destroys the Beasts, 19:11–21

The pattern for the figure of the heavenly warrior was well established in the ancient stories of John's time. In those stories a dragon attacks a woman; her son is removed (either killed, taken to heaven or the underworld); the son then returns and slays the dragon. The tale originated in the agricultural cycle where annually the vitality of spring is eventually destroyed by the dry season that saps life from all vegetation, only to be vanquished when the new rains bring new life. With variations it is the tale of Baal and Asherah, Isis and Osiris and Horus, Tammuz and Inanna. As myths will, it conflated with other myths like the creation story of the battle between Marduk and Tiamat (see the discussion in pp. 103–5) and the solar myth of the sun's daily victory over darkness (see pp. 123–24).

The heavenly warrior here fulfills all our expectations: appearing out of heaven on a white horse, with exalted names, an honorable reputation, in command of heavenly armies, bearing the accouterments of war. We have shown (pp. 109–11) how he manifests traits of all the other figures of rescue in this story. He is a culminating figure.

And his actions match his character. He judges and makes war, he will rule with a rod of iron; he treads (a present tense in Greek) the wine press of the fury of the wrath of God; he killed all the warriors of beast. All this is typical, expected; perhaps the only surprise is the ease with which it is done.

But closer examination reveals some anomalies. First, his robe is dipped in blood even before the battle begins. Second, his name is the Word of God. Third, once again no war is narrated; the story moves directly from the statement that they gathered to make war to the declaration that the beast was captured. Fourth, the means by which all the rest of the followers of the beast are killed is striking: "And the rest were killed by the sword of the rider on the horse, the sword that came from his mouth; and all the birds were gorged with their flesh" (19:21). We will return to the birds in a moment, but we must first consider the meaning of this mode of execution. The followers of the beast are killed by the Word of God that comes from the mouth (testimony) of Jesus. This has been a consistent theme of the story. Just when we think that good might prevail over evil by the use of force ("The Lion of the tribe of Judah") the story reverses its images and we see evil defeated by weakness ("The Lamb standing as though slain"). See the discussion in pp. 69–70. In this story the power of good over evil is the power of suffering (2:10; 6:9–11), the power of faithful testimony (12:11), the power of steadfast resistance (2:2; 13:10). It is the word of God that slays, not the coercive power of government (1:9; 12:17; 20:4). This story does not deny the power of good; it redefines it.[33]

This insight makes sense of the anomalies. Of course the warrior is named the Word of God, for it is that word that has power. Of course no war is narrated, for the battle is already won by the faithful testimony of

Jesus. Of course, the warrior wears a bloodied robe, for he has bled for this victory. John is not here predicting that some horse will someday drop out of the sky and set everything right. Such a literal reading of the imagery completely misunderstands the story. Rather John is showing how the death of Jesus has the power to destroy evil, using the graphic imagery of holy war.

So graphic is the imagery that it borders on the grotesque, as when the widely anticipated messianic banquet is caricatured as a feast by birds of prey on the battlefield. The notion of an ultimate feast celebrating a new creation was widespread with many variants. It was already a part of the holy war story in ancient Babylon (*Enumah Elish* 6.69–94). It developed in various ways in Jewish traditions. The *War Scroll* (1QM) from Qumran describes the attack of the Sons of Light against the "forces of the Sons of Darkness":

> On that day when the Kittim [Romans] fall there shall be a battle and horrible carnage before the God of Israel, for it is a day appointed by Him from ancient times as a battle of annihilation for the Sons of Darkness. On that day the congregation of the gods and the congregation of men shall engage one another, resulting in great carnage. The sons of Light and the forces of Darkness shall fight together to show the strength of God with the roar of a great multitude and the shout of gods and men: a day of disaster.[34]
>
> REV 1:9–11

While there is no parallel in the scrolls to this grotesque banquet, the sect clearly regarded their common meal as a prefiguration of the final messianic banquet.[35] For Christians, too, the eucharistic meal is a proleptic messianic banquet, a meal anticipating that final meal (see 22:17). That Christians spoke of eating the body and drinking the blood of Jesus at this meal perhaps sheds some light on what is parodied here. There were also versions of the messianic banquet that saw the destroyed sea beast Leviathan as the menu for the final banquet.[36] The reference to the birds feasting is probably drawn from Ezek 39:4, 17–20, though John saves the rest of Ezekiel's imagery for the next battle.

Both the battle and the feast ought to indicate we have come to the end of the story, but still it goes on.

A Time of Peace, 20:1–6

Instead of a final victory, this battle achieves only an interim period of peace. With the beast defeated, the dragon appears helpless. An angel descends with a chain and a key and the dragon, "that ancient serpent who is the Devil and Satan," is bound and locked into the abyss for a thousand years, when it will once again be freed. This thousand years is a marvelous and paradoxical symbol, for as a multiple of ten its suggests a complete and total victory. But as a period that comes to an end it symbolizes the temporariness of the victory over evil. No other New Testament writing refers to such an interim period and no other surviving work uses this paradox. 2 Esdras imagines an interim period of four hundred years, for example, a figure more closely connected to the earthly (7:28). But the thousand is clearly important, for it is mentioned six times in this brief scene.37 Such a paradoxical symbol points to the deep persistence of evil.

The story here represents another expulsion of Satan, who was earlier cast from heaven to earth by the angel Michael (12:7–12). Now Satan is thrown down into the abyss, which was earlier unlocked to release the locust plague (9:1–2) and from which the beast came (11:7).

The removal of Satan opens the way for a reversal of fates. Finally the souls/lives under the altar get their due, as they are raised to new life and "reign with Christ a thousand years" (20:4; 6:9–11). These are the faithful witnesses, those who refused the mark of the beast and so paid with their lives (13:15–18). Now they are beyond the reach of death (20:6) and they reign for a thousand years.

We now come to a remarkable twist in the story, one that well illustrates the movement of the plot. For on the one hand the plot cycles back on itself and we have one more portrayal of the final battle. On the other hand, there are new developments. And so the plot spirals forward.

Hostilities Resumed and Final Victory, 20:7–21:8

Why Satan *must* be released from prison (20:3) and why once released Satan again takes up this futile war and why nations still gather to his side are not taken up in this story. Part of the answer probably rests with the prototype of this story, found in Ezekiel 37–48, which begins with the resurrection of Israel, proceeds to the battle with Gog/Magog, and ends with a vision of the new temple. But of course John has substantially revised the story, even eliminating the temple, so there is no reason to think he would be bound by the source.

The reason for this renewal of evil probably lies deeper, in John's very notion of the battle in which final victory was won with the death of Jesus but which must be won anew whenever Jesus' followers are called on to add their testimony to his (see 12:11).

The sequence of action here is clear and logical. Satan is released, gathers an army, and after a swift march, lays siege to the camp of the saints. Then, as in the rescue of Elijah, fire falls from heaven and consumes them (2 Kgs 1:10–11), ironically one of the signs performed by the beast to induce worship (Rev 13:13). Again there is no battle in the final battle. Now the Devil is thrown into the lake of fire just as the beast had been earlier.

Two contrasting scenes follow. First all the dead are raised and judged; Death and Hades are thrown into the lake of fire, as are all those whose names are not found written in the book of life. Second, there appears a new heaven and a new earth—an earth without a sea (without chaos). And a new Jerusalem comes down from heaven, symbolizing that God now dwells among humans. There is an eloquent verse on the end of death, pain, and tears: the one seated on the throne is making all things new. Then this one on the throne speaks directly—for the first time in this story:

> Then he said to me, "It is done! I am the Alpha and the Omega, the beginning and the end. To the thirsty I will give water as a gift from the spring of the water of life. Those who conquer will inherit these things, and I will be their God and they will be my children."   REV 21:6–7

All this sounds like a fitting conclusion, but the speech goes on with shocking implications:

> But as for the cowardly, the faithless, the polluted, the murderers, the fornicators, the sorcerers, the idolaters, and all liars, their place will be in the lake that burns with fire and sulfur, which is the second death.   REV 21:8

It seems that the wicked are still with us.

REV 19:11–21:8 *Readers' Notes on the Victory*

HEAVEN OPENED Or the sky opened.

WHITE HORSE John had earlier seen a white horse, but with nearly the opposite significance. In the first seal vision (6:1–2) the white horse represented the conqueror, the one who started war, famine, and death (see the discussion on p. 82). Here the symbolic significance of white as victor remains, but the meaning is almost the opposite: the one who ends war.

FAITHFUL AND TRUE Terms connected with the death of Jesus, see Readers' Note on 3:14, p. 60.

EYES LIKE A FLAME See Readers' Notes on 1:14 (p. 40) and 2:18 (pp. 57–58).

A NAME NO ONE KNOWS Name here is the external symbol of the person; this person is beyond ordinary understanding. There was also the notion that to know someone's name was to have some power over that person, hence this person is uncontrolled.

DIADEMS These are the crowns of the ruler in contrast to the usual crown of the victor which is much more common in this story. The dragon also has diadems (12:3).

SHARP SWORD The iconographical mark of the human figure in the first vision (1:16; 2:12).

ROD OF IRON The iconographical trait of the woman's son (12:5).

WINE PRESS Earlier used as a reference to Jesus' death (14:20).

FALSE PROPHET This figure seems to have replaced the second beast, whose job entailed proclaiming the glories of the first beast (see 13:5–8 and 16:13).

LAKE OF FIRE A heightening of the vision of Daniel (7:11) by interpreting the fire that destroys the beast in conjunction with the Greek idea of hell as a place of fiery suffering.[38]

AN ANGEL That Satan is bound by an angel (rather than by Jesus) corresponds to the image of 12:7 where Michael is the protagonist. This use of angel imagery may be related to John's temptation to worship angels (19:10; 22:8).

ABYSS The lowest part of John's three-storied universe. See the discussion in pp. 64–65. The ascent of Satan from the abyss parallels that of the beast in 11:7.

FIRST RESURRECTION Jewish notions of the afterlife were in flux in this period as the older ideas of resurrection were combined with Greek ideas of immortality. Some believed that all would be resurrected; some believed that only the just would be resurrected; some believed that first the just and then the rest would be resurrected.[39]

SECOND DEATH An image deriving from the notion that all people would be raised in the endtime, some to new life but others to new death.

BOOK OF LIFE A remarkable metaphor (as if God could not remember who was who) showing the power of books in this culture making the transition from oral to written forms of authority.

THE BRIDE REVEALED: NEW CREATION, 21:9–22:7

This is an unusual scene in which all the action is limited to the scene setting; the rest is description, a lengthy narrative pause that enhances the audience's sense of an ending. All the action occurs at the beginning and ending and involves John. At the start he is addressed by one of the seven bowl-carrying angels (exactly parallel to the vision of the whore in 17:1), who offers to show him the bride, the wife of the lamb. But instead of a woman he sees a city. Or we might say that whereas in the whore scene John saw a city in the figure of a woman, here he sees a woman in the figure of a city. Instead of the wilderness, the scene is set on a great high mountain. John then provides an elaborate description of the holy city Jerusalem (see also 21:1).

In elaborate and fantastic detail John describes the symbols of the city. The Readers' Notes below will help interpret these symbols, but their general meaning is clear. Here is the earthly city of God (four-square), containing—or perhaps better, consisting of—the people of God (twelve by twelve, reminding us of the 144,000). In addition to the physical description, some important things are said about the city.

First we are told what it does not contain. It has no temple, no sun or moon, and no lamps; God's glory and the lamb provide all the light needed. While it has gates, they are never shut because there is no night (21:25). Nevertheless, "nothing unclean will enter it" (21:27). So even at this late stage of the story when we might have thought the world purged of all uncleanness, the unclean remains.

Then we are told some things it does contain. For within the city is the river of the water of life and the tree of life—images from the Eden story of creation (22:12; Gen 2:8–14). So at the end of the story we return to the beginning, only now the garden of God is incorporated into the city of humans.

The scene ends with a direct address to John. While the identity of the speaker remains ambiguous, the content of the speech can only come from Jesus:

> And he said to me, "These words are trustworthy and true, for the Lord, the God of the spirits of the prophets, has sent his angel to show his servants what must soon take place. See, I am coming soon! Blessed is the one who keeps the words of the prophecy of this book."   REV 22:6–7

The first sentence is a clear echo of the opening statement (1:1) while the second repeats the blessing on the reader with which we began (1:3). We have come full circle.

REV 21:9–22:7 *Readers' Notes on the Bride-City*

SEVEN BOWLS The reference ties this scene to the plague series of 16:1–21.

MOUNTAIN Mountains are places of revelation, going all the way back to the Sinai tradition of Moses receiving the Law (Exod 19:20–25). But the immediate inter-textual reference is to Ezekiel's vision of Jerusalem restored (40:2; 47:1–12).

GLORY OF GOD Technical expression for God's presence in the temple; see Ezek 10:18 and 43:4 for a vision of its departure and return.

JASPER As God was described at 4:3.

TWELVE GATES The means of entering the city are twelve because God's people enter here.

TWELVE ANGELS The heavenly counterparts to the earthly messengers.

TWELVE TRIBES Identified with the gates because those who enter are those "who keep the commandments of God" as well as the testimony of Jesus.

TWELVE FOUNDATIONS It is not entirely clear how to picture this except to say that the image is of the undergirding of the whole city.

TWELVE APOSTLES This group, now understood as a select institution and not just as twelve people, is seen as the foundation of God's new work.

MEASURING ROD The angelic surveyor provides the symbolic figures that help us understand the meaning of the city. The detail is drawn from Ezek 40:3.

1,500 MILES Literally 12,000 stadia. The English translation misses the point, for the number is clearly chosen for its symbolic significance not its realism. Every facet of this description is built on twelve, the number for God's people. Keep in mind that the whole of Palestine is only about 150 miles long and 50 miles wide, so this city is more than ten times that length. Also, Herodotus says that ancient Babylon was 120 stadia square (*Hist.* 1.128), so this city is over a hundred times that size.

144 CUBITS Here the translators have kept the symbolic number, showing that we are talking about God's people. The resulting picture is somewhat ridiculous if taken literally, for 144 cubits would be about 300 feet high for the wall. That would be a big wall around an ordinary city, but this city is 1,500 miles high! Of course, these images are not meant to be seen so much as to be understood. Any attempt to take John's numbers as computations is mistaken; they are qualities not quantities.

EVERY JEWEL The jewels named here correspond, in reverse order, to the jewels associated with the twelve signs of the zodiac.[40] That the zodiacal signs should somehow correspond to the people of God would fit John's view of the world. See also the list of the jewels in the breastplate of the high priest (Exod 28:17–21; 39:10–14).

GLORY AND HONOR OF THE NATIONS That there should be room in the new city for the works of the nations is in keeping with John's sense of renewal. See also 22:2–3.

I AM COMING SOON A sense of urgency has permeated this work from the opening phrases declaring that the time is near and that these things must happen soon (see also 2:5, 16, 3:11; 16:15). But at this point in the story it is no longer possible to understand it in the naive, literal sense. Rather the promise is that Jesus' presence will be known to those who live this story.

THE END, 22:8–21

John now returns to his own voice, echoing his direct address to the audience at 1:9. There are numerous other parallels to the opening as well (see the discussion and Table 3 in the Prologue, pp. 10–16). We have completed the fantastic journey through these three stories and John now assures us that this is all true. The book is to be left unsealed but not unprotected: a double curse is put on anyone who would change it.

The action packed into the brief closing is remarkable. John again attempts to worship the angel and is again rebuked with an explanation and the simple command that provides the theme for the whole work: worship God. John is told not to seal up the book for the time is near, the works of the evil and the righteous are then contrasted. Then a voice, eventually identified explicitly as "I Jesus" declares he is coming soon, with rewards to repay each worker. Those who wash their robes may enter the city; "outside are the dogs . . . " (22:14–15). Jesus identifies himself as the root of David and the bright morning star, followed by a short liturgy inviting the thirsty to come, drink of the water of life. Again the voice declares, "surely I am coming soon," to which is added the acclamation: "Amen, come, Lord Jesus." The work ends quickly with the sentence commonly used to conclude a letter: "The grace of the Lord Jesus be with all."*

And so we come full circle back to the outermost frame of the letter. But perhaps circle is not the right metaphor, for although we have returned to the opening frame, the story has changed. (For a discussion of the structure, see pp. 147–49.) Within the story world we have gone from a world controlled by evil to a world ruled by God, yet John's address to the audience within that story world remains just the same as it was at the beginning, with the same call to worship God, avoid evil, and do righteousness. We will consider this curious open-ended end more fully in pp. 147–48. But something has changed: Jesus is coming (note the present tense verb, 22:20).

If one takes this bold declaration together with the implied setting of Revelation in a service of worship and the repeated use of liturgical language throughout the work and the concentration of specific liturgical language in this closing (specifically the language associated with the Eucharist), one must entertain the notion that Revelation ends with a call to the eucharistic meal—the messianic banquet. Such an implied setting would make this story function as an explanation of what happens in the Eucharist: Jesus comes, evil is overthrown, the new Jerusalem descends out of heaven. We will examine this idea more fully in pp. 159–80.

The action of this section emphasizes the need to worship only God and shows the role of this book in achieving that worship. It is an unsealed word from Jesus, containing the very voice of Jesus, inviting all who are thirsty to come and drink of the water of life. For the new Jerusalem is now open.

REV 22:8–21 *Readers' Notes on the End*

WORSHIP THE ANGEL Angels are exalted figures in this story, representing the heavenly counterpart to the earthly community, but they are nonetheless servants. Angels sometimes perform messianic functions (12:7; 20:1). See the duplicate scene at 19:10.

SEALED BOOK A standard device in apocalyptic works, stemming in part from their claim to be written by some ancient prophet. The idea was that the book was written long ago (by Enoch, Abraham, Moses, Isaiah, Adam and Eve, Daniel) but was sealed and kept hidden until the time of the end (see Dan 12:4, 9; 8:26). Thus the very fact that one can now read such a work would mean that the end

---

*Various Greek manuscripts present seven different versions of the ending sentence (in spite of the curse!): on all, on all of you, on all of us, on the saints, on you saints, on all of the saints, on all of his saints. The shortest reading is probably to be preferred because the scribal tradition was far more likely to expand than to contract such formulas, especially in light of similar sentences at the ends of Paul's letters. The final amen in numerous manuscripts is probably not original, because it is omitted in many important manuscripts.

is near. John consciously avoids this device, probably because the author is actually known by the audience.

I AM COMING SOON Note the present tense verb in both instances of this phrase here (22:12, 20). The word translated *soon* can mean either after some relatively brief period of time (see e.g., Mark 9:39; Phil 2:19) or quickly, swiftly (see e.g., James 1:19). The present tense verb favors the latter meaning: I am coming swiftly. For a parallel ambiguity see John 11:29, "she quickly/soon got up and went to meet him."

WASH THEIR ROBES Having white robes is a complex symbol in the Apocalypse. They are given to those who conquer (3:5); but they are made white by being washed in the lamb's blood, with the implication of martyrdom (7:14).

TREE OF LIFE An image both from Eden (Genesis 3) and the new Jerusalem (22:2) and a symbol for the cross of Jesus (see 2:7).

I JESUS That both John and the reader of this story here speak directly in the voice of Jesus is important for understanding how this story makes Jesus present.

ROOT OF DAVID Both a messianic and eucharistic title. See Isaiah 11 and *Didache* 9:2.

MORNING STAR Also a messianic title. See Num 24:17.

SPIRIT AND BRIDE The invitation has both heavenly and earthly sources.

WATER OF LIFE An image both from Eden (Genesis 3) and the new Jerusalem (22:2) and a symbol for the cross of Jesus (see Readers' Notes on 2:7, pp. 54–56).

AMEN Literally an acclamation: "let it be so," but stylized in liturgical usage in connection with prayer and the Eucharist.

Is This a Moral Story?

Those who raise moral objections to the Apocalypse do so on the basis of this story segment. D. H. Lawrence called it "a rather repulsive work" not content till the whole world be destroyed, except that lake of fire in which those who fail to get in line might suffer eternally.[41] C. S. Peirce declared:

> But little by little the bitterness increases until in the last book of the New Testament, its poor distracted author represents that all the time Christ was talking about having come to save the world, the secret design was to catch the entire human race, with the exception of a paltry 144,000, and souse them all in brimstone lake, and as the smoke of their torment went up for ever and ever, to turn and remark, "There is no curse any more." Would it be an insensible smirk or a fiendish grin that should accompany such an utterance? I wish I could believe St. John did not write it . . . [42]

And more recently the feminist writer Tina Pippin has lamented:

> The irony of the grotesque burning of the whore is that the Christian utopia is itself an oppressive world (for women). . . . But in the Apocalypse narrative, gender oppression is left untouched by the sword of God.[43]

She goes so far as to call it a "misogynist fantasy" and to conclude: "The Apocalypse means death to women."[44]

What these and countless other readers share is their revulsion to the images of violence and coercion in this story. Whether it be the beast's vicious destruction of the whore (17:16) or God's ultimate consignment of humanity to the lake of fire (20:15) or the warrior's defeat of the armies of the nations with its gory feast for the birds (19:17), the ultimate value in this story seems to be power, power exercised ruthlessly. One even has the sense that God is willing to engage in torture in an effort to persuade humanity to repent (see 9:21; 16:9, 11). There can be no question that this is a war story and that John uses conventions of war, with all their repulsive details. This is disconcerting, but the moral problem goes deeper.

If God triumphs over evil only because God has more power than evil, then power—not love or goodness or truth—is the ultimate value of the universe. This is the moral dilemma never faced by the popular readings of Revelation. For in the popular readings it is really the lion of the tribe of Judah that appears. The heavenly warrior replaces the lamb; conquest is by power. Evil is crushed by superior force.

But in John's story just the reverse is true. It is the lamb who replaces the lion (5:5–6); visions of the lamb bracket that of the heavenly warrior (14:1; 19:11; 21:9, 22); and even the warrior conquers by what comes from his mouth not his arm (19:21). Surely this story is built on the mythology of holy war (and that itself may be ethically problematical), but just as surely John consistently demythologizes the war—or perhaps more accurately, remythologizes it. For the warrior now appears in the image of the suffering savior so that the death of the warrior and not some later battle is the crucial event of the war. At every juncture in this story where good triumphs over evil, a close examination will show that the victory is finally attributed to the death of Jesus (perhaps most obvious at 12:11).

The actions of the Apocalypse are never arbitrary, never do they rest on simple power. There is a logic of judgment finally articulated by the angel of the waters when the third bowl causes the water to turn to blood: "because they shed the blood of saints and prophets, you have given them blood to drink. It is what they deserve!" (16:6). If our waters are polluted it is not because God is exercising some tyrannical power over us; it is because we foul our own streams. This is the same logic of justice that undergirded Amos' visions of Israel's destruction. Amos first saw a vision of locusts, but when he prayed God stopped the locusts. Amos then saw a vision of fire, but when he prayed God stopped the fire. Amos then saw a vision of a crooked wall, and Amos could not pray for relief. For crooked walls fall as an evitable result of their crookedness (see Amos 7:1–9).

So in our story the martyrs have to wait till their "number would be complete" (6:11). There comes a time in every oppression when the amount of coercion needed to maintain a system will itself destroy the system, as we ourselves have seen in the Soviet Union and South Africa. So the great whore has become drunk with the blood of the saints (17.6), Rome's very act of killing becomes her own death. Such is John's vision.

Surely many of us, myself included, are not comfortable with John's violent images, with the easy equation of blood and wine, with the intolerable depiction of a lake of fire. But ancient sensibilities are not the same as modern; and war stories are not polite reading. This story is profoundly disturbing; nevertheless, when one reads through the symbols this story is not immoral.

Near Closure: Rethinking the End

This story trains the reader to be wary of endings, for the end seems to be repeatedly offered only to be withdrawn. The seven messages seemed like a complete story, but the story simply shifts to a new level. Already at the end of the first series of seven seals, the silence of the seventh event seems to offer resolution after the conflict (seals one through five) and judgment (seal six). But the story goes on. Then as we approach the end of the seven trumpets and John announces that he has heard seven thunders, but that he cannot write these down because there will be "no more delay" (10:6), the end seems close. When the heavenly voice then declares that God's kingdom has come (11:15), the end seems to have arrived. But still the story goes on, once more shifting to a new level. Several times in that long story we seem to have the destruction of evil and the victory in the final battle, but still the story continues (see the discussion on pp. 117–21). Even at the culmination of the story, when evil seems completely destroyed and there is a new creation, when God dwells among humans, we are told that "Outside are the dogs and sorcerers and fornicators and murderers and idolaters, and everyone who loves and practices falsehood" (22:15). That such miscreants can remain outside the walls of the new Jerusalem challenges the audience to rethink the story. As a modern literary critic has observed, when endings are not neat, when they entail the unexpected, they demand that the reader rethink the meaning of the story and "reinterpret the work so that the ending in fact serves as an appropriate conclusion."[45]

It is just such rethinking that is continually called for in this story. For this story is never about what it seems to be about. We read about whores and virgins and monsters and angels throwing objects on the earth, but these are means of revelation. We are also reading about Rome and Jerusalem and the followers of Jesus and prayer and justice. Revelation is a story that requires thinking and re-thinking.

No less does the ending require thought, for the ending is no less symbolic than the rest of the story. If one asks where it is that God dwells among the people, one can begin to grasp where it is that the new Jerusalem comes down out of heaven. If one asks where it is one finds the water of life and the tree of life, one begins to understand the new creation. If one asks when it is that Jesus comes to his followers, one understands when the end comes. For all these occur in the context of Christian worship. It is in worship that the churches hear the messages of the risen Christ (letter scroll). It is in worship that one contemplates the throne of God and the Lamb reveals the will of God (worship scroll). It is in worship that one fights the dragon and its minions and where the final victory is won: worship God. The worship of God is the primary theme of the Apocalypse, contrasted with the worship of the beast.[46]

The power of this idea of worship as a means to conquer Satan can be seen in an incident that occurred about fifteen years after the completion of the Apocalypse. A Christian leader from Antioch was being transported to Rome for trial. Pausing at Smyrna, he wrote letters to several of the same cities John had addressed in the Apocalypse. In one of these letters addressed to Ephesus he wrote:

> So be zealous to meet together more frequently and to give thanks [*eucharisto* in Greek] to God and to glorify him. For when you meet together frequently, Satan's powers are destroyed and his destructiveness comes to naught through the harmony of your faith. There is nothing better than peace, by which every war of beings in heaven or on earth is nullified.
>
> IGNATIUS, *To the Ephesians* 13:1–2[47]

Clearly the original audience of the Apocalypse would be familiar with the idea that meeting for worship and "giving thanks" (Eucharist) led to victory in the war with Satan.

The ending of the Apocalypse is not simply a vision of some far-off future; it is a symbolic portrayal of the victory of those who through persistent resistance to the powers of domination maintain their loyalty to God and God's justice.

Conclusion

John has taken us on a fantastic journey, the most fantastic phase of which has been this final narrative segment detailing the cosmic war between the dragon and the lamb. The action is in many ways surprising, both in the degree to which the dragon is the active agent of the war and in the many twists of the plot when victory seems certain and final only to be delayed. In other ways the action is perfectly expected as an appropriation of the story of the cosmic holy war.

John uses this war story genre to bring a sense of closure to the story of the coming of God's universal rule in the life and death of Jesus. This story

TABLE 11 *The Concentric Structure of the Apocalypse*

Letter frame
   Vision report frame
      Letter scroll: Vision of the majestic human on Patmos
         Worship scroll: Vision of the throne in heaven
      War scroll: Vision of the dragon's war and defeat
   Vision Report Frame
Letter frame

segment explains why it is that Jesus can instruct the churches (letter scroll) and enable the worship of God (worship scroll). It is because Jesus has done battle with evil and conquered.

We have seen that the action of the Apocalypse moves in several stages, through two frame devices (letter and vision report) and through three story segments: a letter scroll, a worship scroll, and a war scroll. Table 11 represents the structure of the Apocalypse graphically, thus highlighting the correlations between these sections. When we lay out the structure of the work in this concentric fashion, two implications appear. First, the worship scroll forms the heart and center of the work. It is here that God's will is most perfectly realized. It is here that the reader sees most directly the correspondence between the above and the below. This fits with the repeated theme of the whole work: worship God.

Second, we see there is an implied correlation between the letter and the war scrolls. The correspondence is not one of theme or character or action, but of response. For the stories in these scrolls call the audience to decision, to persistent resistance, to the fight for victory. The war scroll dramatizes in concrete and vivid imagery the struggles abstractly indicated in the letter scroll with its repeated promise "to the one who conquers. . . . "[48] In both these stories the audience is expected to conquer; in the worship scroll all conquest is attributed to the lamb.

Thus the war scroll provides a fitting climax to the broader story, functioning to dramatize victory, to reveal where final victory lies, to encourage those who bear the testimony of Jesus to persistent resistance, and to show how the true worship of God comes about.

Epilogue

THE APOCALYPSE AS STORY

The whole Scheme of this prophecy then is so far from
being an Encouragement for Enthusiasm that it is a wise
Preservative against it; for the general Doctrine of the
whole Book is this, that the Patience of the Saints is the
Way to Victory.[1]

MOSES LOWMAN, *Notes on Revelation,* 1745

Afterthoughts

Many have been the enthusiasts who claim some special insight, inspiration,
or key to unlocking the secrets of the Apocalypse. History is littered with
their failed timelines, fanciful charts of ages and dispensations, and futile
predictions of world-changing events. Would-be prophets have been offering so-called literal interpretations that see the events of the Apocalypse taking place in their own day since the early second century, and continue to
do so in the late twentieth century. In spite of the *universal* failure of their
predictions, people continue to be taken in by them.

The struggle between those who would view the Apocalypse as a work of
literature with symbolic significance and those who would take it literally is
very old. This is a strikingly inappropriate use of the word literal except in
its secondary sense of *prosaic,* non-poetic. What this designation of a literal
reading really means is an interpretation that assumes the events of this story
refer to actual events in the world, albeit in symbolic form. The term grows
out of the fundamentalist controversies of the early twentieth century
wherein belief in a "literal second coming of Christ" was made a touchstone
of faith. Of course all literalists allegorize the text by the process: this symbol means this event. Such literalists claim that 666, for example, means
Hitler or Saddam Hussein or some other historical villain. But of course this
is literally what the text does not say.

151

We can catch something of the animosity between the two camps in the remark by Eusebius, a fourth-century historian, writing about a second-century interpreter named Papias:

> He says that after the resurrection of the dead there will be a period of a thousand years, when Christ's kingdom will be set up on this earth in material form. I suppose he got these notions by misinterpreting the apostolic accounts and failing to grasp what they had said in mystic and symbolic language. For he seems to have been a man of very small intelligence, to judge from his books.   *Church History* 3.39.11–13

But the literal reading of the Apocalypse is not so much the result of limited intelligence as it is of hidden political agendas, thirst for power and gain, and faulty understandings of this genre. In this final chapter we will take a brief look at the use of apocalyptic literalism in America, examine the ancient genre more fully, and consider what can be said about the social and historical situation that provided the context for the earliest audience.

The Apocalypse in America: A History of Deception

A narrative analysis of the Apocalypse should make clear that anyone who claims to predict the future based on this book is at best deceived and at worst a deceiver. The rash of such books that appear around world crises do little more than make their authors a considerable sum of money. Writers like Hal Lindsey have become wealthy selling false scenarios to a public ready to believe that they have some secret knowledge drawn from the Apocalypse and other biblical writings. There is a certain hypocrisy in building elaborate mansions in southern California all the while predicting the imminent end of the world. Such deception has a long history in America, and will no doubt flourish as we approach the end of the millennium.

The most egregious example of failed apocalyptic literalism is the case of William Miller (1782–1849). Miller was a retired military officer and Baptist lay preacher who became fascinated by the Bible and the possibility of computing when Christ would return. Basing his calculations on a literal reading of Revelation and Daniel (especially Dan 8:14, interpreting the days as years), Miller predicted Christ's return to earth "about 1843." When nothing had happened by March of 1844, he at first admitted he was wrong, but then he recalculated and predicted the exact date: October 22, 1844. Perhaps half a million Americans awaited the fateful day with strong expectations, and as many as fifty thousand sold or gave away their earthly possessions, quit their jobs, and went to the countryside to await their transport to heaven.

The date is known as "the great disappointment" and Miller died discredited a few years later. But Miller was only the most successful example of a phenomenon repeated every few years. When one takes these stories as predictions of actual events there is a strong temptation to specify them and relate them to events in one's own time. While this temptation proves too strong for a few, many more maintain a literal interpretation without predicting exact dates. In *The Late Great Planet Earth*, Hal Lindsey originally predicted the date as 1988, forty years after the founding of the state of Israel in 1948. But as 1988 drew closer he equivocated and then stopped talking about a date. Such interpreters are content to predict that the end of the world is near at hand, that it could happen at any time, and that surely it will happen in their lifetime.

Aside from the fame and money to be made by claiming to have secret, divine information about the future, such would-be prophets have another agenda, for such proclamation serves the ends of social and political stasis. Miller lived in a time of great social crisis; the Civil War was approaching and no doubt the great financial panic of 1837 helped provide a ready audience for his book, first published in 1838.[2] Great movements of social reform—abolition, temperance, labor—were sweeping the country; many were using the Bible to advocate change. But apocalyptic expectations of the sort Miller advocated work against change.

The Apocalypse presents an image of the world as a very evil place, so bad that only a new creation can possibly remedy the wrong. Instead of improvement, one can look only for a decline in morals. But this is not a cause for concern, for God will soon intervene and change everything. Instead of working to improve the world, Miller taught that it would soon end. "Obviously, such expectations did not lead to long-range programs of social reform."[3] Much the same attitude was articulated by James Watt, Secretary of the Interior under Ronald Reagan, when he said there was really no need for a long-range plan to preserve the national forests for our grandchildren since Jesus would return and change the world before then.[4] A literal reading of Revelation is not necessarily a harmless reading.

The remarkable persistence of the literal reading, in spite of the repeated failures of the predictions of the espousers of this view, is a wonder. Generations of Americans have been told that they live in the last days, that the events pictured in the Apocalypse will happen in their lifetime. As we approach the second millennium of the Christian era we will no doubt see a renewal of such enthusiasm. The end of the first millennium was also intensely apocalyptic. Literalists will no doubt delight in adding the four millennia that can be calculated from the time of Jesus back to the creation by using the biblical numbers and thus point expectantly to the beginning of the seventh and final millennium! And so we find ourselves in a new cycle of deception.

Rather than submitting to such claims, we must become familiar with the nature of apocalyptic and learn to read the Apocalypse for the exciting story it tells. The following details are provided for those readers who have read through the above commentary and the Apocalypse itself and want to go further.

The Nature of Apocalyptic Expectations in Antiquity

The designation "apocalyptic" is a modern invention, first used by Friedrich Lücke in 1832.[5] It is used by various scholars with greatly divergent meanings. The phenomenon itself was diverse so a definition that would encompass all of it would have to be very general. At the broadest level we are talking about a very widespread anticipation that the end of an era was approaching, that the old ways were passing, that somehow the divine world was impinging on this world to bring about basic changes, including a final judgment. Used in this general way it is possible to speak of Persian, Egyptian, Greek and Roman—as well as Jewish and Christian—apocalypticism.[6]

Apocalypticism is used to designate a social movement based on this sense of anticipation and change. Such an anticipation involves a critique of the present system, often viewed as evil. Both the critique and the nature of the anticipation vary widely among various apocalyptic movements. For our purposes I want to focus more specifically on the ideology undergirding Jewish and Christian apocalypticism and the natures of the writings that express their hopes and dreams. (See the preliminary discussion in pp. 3–5.)

So let us first distinguish between apocalyptic ideology and apocalyptic literature, and second within apocalyptic literature we can distinguish apocalypses proper and other writings that simply share in an apocalyptic worldview. Let's explore these distinctions.

THE IDEOLOGY

The origins of apocalyptic thinking are obscure, debated, and complex. It grew out of the social institution of prophecy as it declined in the period after the destruction of the monarchy in the sixth century BCE—marking the end of Israel's political significance. In addition to prophetic traditions and ancient mythic thought, apocalypticism was shaped in important ways by Babylonian dream divination and Iranian/Persian dualism. It was a slow process of adaptation and change, resulting in many and varied kinds of apocalypticism. But we can grasp something of the sea change in thinking that apocalypticism entailed in the aftermath of an event of unique importance in Jewish life: the persecution of Jews by Antiochus IV, the Greek ruler of Syria from 175–164 BCE.

In a complex political situation involving conflict with Egypt and the growing domination of Rome, Antiochus moved to enhance his power by identifying himself with Zeus-Apollo and enforcing the worship of Zeus throughout his kingdom, including Israel. When some Jews resisted, Antiochus launched a vicious program of suppression, murder, and torture to enforce compliance. Armed rebellion ensued that eventually gained a century of virtual independence for Israel, but in the meantime faithful Jews suffered greatly.

But perhaps a greater problem than the suffering was explaining the suffering. For Jews of earlier centuries were accustomed to thinking of the world as under God's direct and constant control. Thus the most common and powerful explanation for suffering was that God was punishing for some sin—either yours or that of your compatriots. This explanation still had some force, and many used it to call for repentance and change. But there was a basic flaw with this approach, a flaw that becomes obvious when we look at who is suffering and who is prospering.

Everything is backwards. Those who remain faithful to God suffer; those who abandon God prosper. How does one explain this aberration?

The explanation that eventually came together drew from many sources. The shaping force seems to have come from Persian dualism, combined with old Israelite traditions about an accuser (Hebrew: Satan) in God's heavenly court, mythic stories of rebellion among God's messengers, and the creation and fertility myths of the ancient Near East. The explanation is simple, and so widely accepted that it may seem obvious: God has an enemy and that enemy is contesting God for control of this world.[7]

In Persian (Zoroastrian) thought this enemy was sometimes thought of as an evil twin, a negative God, so the outcome of this struggle was not predetermined. If humans fought on the side of evil, evil would prevail; if they fought for good, good would prevail in this intensely ethical vision of life. In Hebrew thought the evil one could never be this autonomous or this powerful. God remained ultimately in control, with the fighting done by subordinates (see Dan 10:12–13).

Still, the suffering of the righteous was explained by the evil one having his way in this world, controlling the powers that be. He was even thought of as "the ruler of this age" (e.g. John 12:31; 2 Cor 4:4). Since Satan was in charge of this world, good people ought to expect to suffer. Conversely, people who prospered were suspect.

But Satan's rule is not permanent; this age will end and a new age begin. Between these two ages stands some world-changing divine action—often a war, though different apocalypses had different views. And one more thing: the time of the change is very near. Not all apocalypses see this as a historical change, but they all posit the change.[8]

The basic worldview of apocalypticism involves these four factors:
- The world is under the control of evil for the duration of this age. Thus the primary forces of history are not human action but supernatural forces. This is a strongly dualistic way of thinking about life.
- There are two ages and the age to come will be the complete opposite of this age: good will prevail; evil will be judged. All apocalypses posit this dualism, but some do not project it as an historical epoch of the future; rather they see it as a retribution beyond death. Again we note the strong dualism.
- God will bring about this change through some decisive act of intervention.
- We should be prepared for the change for it is near at hand.

Such a worldview seems to have been pervasive among the early Christians, who understood Jesus' life and death to have been (at least a part of) that act of intervention. The Gospel according to Mark explains Jesus' exorcisms as the result of his having overcome Satan (see Mark 3:20–27; see also Luke 10:18). Paul promised his followers that Satan's power would soon end (Rom 16:20; Gal 5:1). Jesus' resurrection was seen as the beginning of the resurrection of the righteous (1 Cor 15:20).

Clearly the Apocalypse of John assumes this worldview, with one important qualification. Although this story takes place in an evil world and good folk must expect to suffer, even die, in this world, this suffering itself is the act by which the world will be changed—just as it was changed by the suffering of Jesus. Now let us consider more closely the literary medium through which John embodies this worldview in a story.

THE GENRE

The concept of genre is used in a variety of ways and is the subject of much debate. I use it in a very pragmatic sense to mean the experience of the reader that various works of literature are alike and should be read in a similar fashion.[9] To use a modern example, everyone knows how to read a newspaper, and knows to read the various parts of a newspaper differently. We bring different expectations to the first page, the editorial page, the comics, the sports page, and so on. Each of these sections has its own conventions and techniques and an inexperienced reader would badly misconstrue their meanings to read them all alike.

We do not read our love letters with the same expectations that we bring to reading an insurance contract. We do not read a poem with the same expectations as a recipe. We do not read a novel with the same expectations as a history. When and how we learned these expectations is very complex and subtle. The problem with reading ancient literature (or literature from another culture) is that we do not know what to expect from it. Much of what has happened to the interpretation of Revelation is the result of reading it as if it were a book of magic or secret lore—both very wide of the mark.

Probably the best way to learn to read apocalypses is to read as many of them as one can.[10] To get a taste of that experience, consider the following brief extracts:

> And after <one thousand> three hundred and thirty-two days the Lord will come with his angels and with the hosts of the saints from the seventh heaven with the glory of the seventh heaven, and will drag Beliar with his hosts into Gehenna, and he will bring rest to the pious who shall be found alive in the body in this world . . . and to all who through faith in him have cursed Beliar and his kings.   *Ascension of Isaiah* 4:14–16[11]

> And these things shall come to pass in the day of judgment of those who have fallen away from faith in God and have committed sin: cataracts of fire shall be let loose; and obscurity and darkness shall come up and cover and veil the entire world, and the waters shall be changed and transformed into coals of fire . . . And the stars shall be melted by flames of fire. . . .
> *Apocalypse of Peter* 5[12]

> And it came about, when I had spoken to my sons, the men called me. And they took me up onto their wings, and carried me up to the first heaven. And they put me down there. They led before my face the elders, the rulers of the stellar orders.   *Second Enoch* 3:1–4:1[13]

> Then a great angel came forth having a golden trumpet in his hand, and he blew it three times over my head, saying, "Be courageous! O one who has triumphed. Prevail! O one who has prevailed. For you have triumphed over the accuser, and you have escaped from the abyss and Hades. You will now cross over the crossing place. For your name is written in the Book of the Living.
> *Apocalypse of Zephaniah* 9:1–3[14]

> After this I saw in the night visions, and behold, a fourth beast, terrible and dreadful and exceedingly strong; and it had great iron teeth; it devoured and broke in pieces, and stamped the residue with its feet. It was different from all the beasts that were before it; and it had ten horns. I considered the horns, and behold, there came up among them another horn, a little one, before which three of the first horns were plucked up by the roots; and behold, on this horn were eyes like the eyes of a man, and a mouth speaking great things.
> DAN 7:7–8

Clearly these all "sound like" the Apocalypse of John, both in their literary traits and their ideas, for the ideology discussed above is also evident here. Both the *Ascension of Isaiah* and the *Apocalypse of Zephaniah* show the world under the control of evil for the duration of this age but indicate that a new, opposite age of goodness is coming (and the *Apocalypse of Peter* shows the transition as a time of judgment). God will bring this about (*Ascension of Isaiah*) soon (*Apocalypse of Zephaniah*).

Literary traits evident here and in the Apocalypse include the following:

1. The most basic trait of apocalypses is their claim that a secret revelation has been given to some seer or prophet. This claim is evident in all the citations above.
2. This revelation is imparted either in a dream (Daniel), a vision, or a transportation of the seer to heaven (*Second Enoch*)—though often the three means are combined.
3. The revelation is usually mediated by some figure, such as an angel, who acts as guide and interpreter to the seer (*Second Enoch, Apocalypse of Zephaniah*).
4. The revelation is usually not self-explanatory, but consists in a variety of arcane symbols involving animals (often composites of different animals, with multiple heads), mythological figures, and numbers (especially the Daniel quotation, but also *Ascension of Isaiah*).
5. The reception of the revelation is attributed to some figure from the past, one of the ancient heroes. (None of the above works is written by the figure named in the title.) The most popular voices adopted by later apocalypse writers include Enoch and Elijah (both of whom had traditions about going to heaven without dying), Ezra, Moses, Daniel, Adam, and (for Christian writers) Peter and Paul.*

Only this last trait is not evident in the Apocalypse of John, which is clearly a secret revelation, communicated both by vision and by heavenly journey, with at least occasional angelic interpreters to explain some the arcane symbols. Why John chose to write in his own name rather than follow the otherwise universal practice of pseudonymity is a matter of conjecture (see pp. 160–64).

These traits hang together in a common pattern. The basic claim of an apocalypse is to see behind the veil of ordinary experience. It intends to transcend our common perceptions and reveal the ultimate causes of events. It is a "revelation" of the cosmic processes behind history. To communicate what is seen behind the veil, apocalypses engage in an outrageous use of symbols, for only such symbols could hope to portray the interrelatedness of historical and cosmic events.

Can we then imagine the expectations which an ancient audience might likely bring to the reading of an apocalypse? With what expectations would they approach a story that they believed to be brought back from the other

---

*This practice of writing in another's name is called pseudonymity and the major collection of such works is called the pseudepigrapha.

side? I do not suppose they would expect to understand it, not right away, not fully. They might expect it to seem mysterious, opaque, fraught with meanings not evident on the surface. A report of a trip to heaven would not be read in the same way as a travelogue. They might hope to grasp some of the symbols—or be grasped by them—finding in them some discernment of their own situation in the world.

It would be great folly to think one could translate the revelation directly into ordinary speech—or else why was there a need for the symbolism in the first place? One might understand what a symbol meant, might even be told by the revealer, but you would not thereby let go of the symbol, for it might have more to say. One would, I imagine, approach an apocalypse as a living word, never quite knowing what it might say the next time you heard it.

Such expectations are very far removed from what we moderns expect. It will require both patience and a sympathetic imagination to enter into an experience anything like that of the original audience. Let us now consider more formally what we can say about this original setting.

Implied and Actual: Literary Reflections on History

One of the first lessons we learn when we begin the study of stories is not to mistake the narrator for the author. Even children understand that the little teapot (short and stout) is not the author of the jingle it narrates. Narrators are, however, created by authors, so we might expect they will share similar points of view. In fact we can begin to deduce something about the author by studying how the narrator tells the story and asking why the author has chosen to do it this way. But just here modern critical theory has carried the discussion one stage further, for this author we deduce is not the actual author, not a living person, but only the "implied author."

The implied author is the author we can reconstruct from a text, a view of the author that the author has chosen for us to see. Perhaps the easiest way to see this is to think of Mark Twain. Mark Twain is the persona that Samuel Clemens chose to show himself to the public. Twain is a fictional creation just as surely as is Huck Finn (and both probably can tell us something about Sam Clemens). So the author we meet in a text is always created, both revealing and concealing the real author.

And the same thing can be said for the audience: the audience we meet in a text is never the actual audience but only the audience that the author imagines. An author may imagine accurately or erroneously or may even have chosen to misconstrue the audience—either to flatter them or to challenge them. Everyone we meet in a story is to some degree the creation of the storyteller. We can picture these various levels as pairs of parentheses. At the outmost level we have the actual author and audience; at the next level we have the implied author and the implied audience; and finally we have the narrator and the narratee, the person to whom the story is told by the narrator. More visually:

(author (implied author (narrator-naratee) implied audience) audience).

Another visualization, widely used, shows the pattern as follows:[15]

author → [implied author → narrator → narratee → implied audience] → audience

Everything within the square brackets is in the story; the real author and audience must have some relationship with these story-figures, but they are not identical. We can learn about the real people only from other sources. Now for modern authors we have many other sources: friends, T.V. interviews, biographies, social studies. But for ancient authors and audiences our evidence is scant. We know nothing about our author, for example, except what can be deduced from the text of the Apocalypse; thus we can never get beyond the implied author. For the audience we can do a bit more, for we know something of the inhabitants of these cities in Roman Asia Minor from other literature and from archaeology.

THE AUTHOR AND THE AUDIENCE

While the author remains hidden, this story tells us a good deal about the narrator, or rather narrators. The actual narration is quite complex, but for convenience we can speak of three levels. At the outermost level we have the one designated as "the one who reads aloud" (1:3). This narrator is without further traits: whether male or female, old or young, knowledgeable or uninformed we are not told. This is a prime difference between our reading of the text and its original situation of oral enactment, for in that setting this narrator is seen and heard. For us the person virtually disappears.

The second-level narration is told by John, who is telling what he saw. (I am conflating here John the letter writer and John the voice on Patmos, which are actually two distinct voices in the Apocalypse.) This John is on Patmos (1:9), though why is not entirely clear. Perhaps he has been banished there (as most readers seem to assume) or perhaps he has withdrawn there to produce this work. (See the discussion of Patmos in pp. 37–41.) This John is also the implied author of the work, now appearing as a character-narrator in the story.

There is also a third-level narration when a character in the story narrates. Thus the majestic human being of the opening vision then becomes the narrator of the messages to the churches (2:1; etc). But some confusion can also arise here, for John also appears as a character in the visions he narrates. He can be addressed by other characters in the visions (e.g., 5:5) and can address others (e.g., 8:14). But more important for this discussion, it is as a character in the story that he narrates these visions (e.g., 4:2, where the narrator of level two who is already in the spirit finds himself in the spirit in the vision—a vision within a vision). All three of these narrators tell us something about the author, but the narrator is not the author.

We know nothing about the author of this work except what can be implied from the writing itself. The older view that the work was written by the apostle John, one of Jesus' original disciples and also the author of the Gospel of John, is untenable for two reasons. First, it contradicts what we know about the implied author. For the implied author saw the apostles as distant and holy figures from the past, the foundations on which the heavenly city is erected (21:14). The implied author is merely a visitor to the city, not its foundation.

Second, the conceptual outlook, worldview, symbol system, and writing style of the Apocalypse are vastly different from those of the Gospel of John. While the gospel is written in very fine (not to say elegant) Greek, the Apocalypse has a rough style and makes many infelicitous and even erroneous constructions—as was already recognized in antiquity.[16] The language of the Apocalypse is built on a Semitic substructure, as if the author were thinking in Hebrew or Aramaic and translating into Greek, and thus was probably from Palestine or Babylon where these languages were common. Of course it is possible that this is, in part at least, a conscious affectation—imitating the diction of the Hebrew prophets and the imprecision of ecstatic speech (somewhat as one might adopt the diction of the King James translation in order to sound "biblical").

But even if we were to suppose that John adopted his diction deliberately or that a scribe was employed to write the gospel, still the contrast between the two works is great, for their outlooks are vastly different. Whereas the Apocalypse revels in traditional apocalyptic imagery of falling stars, angelic trumpets, and violent wars, the gospel very nearly eliminates such imagery, shifting instead toward Gnostic concepts.[17]

In fact our author makes no effort to connect himself with the apostle, which is perhaps surprising in light of the overwhelming pseudonymity of apocalypses. It has been suggested that John did not need to attribute his prophecy to some ancient worthy because Christians believed a new age of prophecy had begun. Maybe so, but all the other Christian apocalypses we have are pseudonymous.[18] More important, perhaps, is the clear indication that the implied audience knows the author (1:4, 9; 22:8). In addition, the author has chosen to cast this work that has the primary form of an apocalypse in a secondary form as letter (1:4; 22:21), addressed to an audience that must assume he knows them. This letter form, unique here amongst all surviving apocalypses, precludes pseudonymity because a letter requires a known author. There are of course pseudonymous letters, but that case is different because both the implied author and the implied audience are inventions. In this case the actual recipients of the letter must believe that the author knows them. Finally, one of the primary benefits of pseudonymity is in the literary device called the *historical review*, whereby the author "predicts" what will happen from the time of the ancient worthy who is the supposed author until the author's own time—with extraordinary accuracy of course. Since John does not use the historical review there is no need for pseudonymity. The only sense in which John's Apocalypse can be said to be pseudonymous is in its attribution of the letters to Jesus (1:19–3:22). In so far as we are expected to see Jesus as the source, and of course it is called "The Revelation of Jesus Christ . . . " (1:1), Revelation has at least some analogy to the pseudonymity of apocalypses. And we should note that John does dare to say "I Jesus" (22:16).

But Jesus is clearly not presented as the author of the work, as the rest of the opening statement makes clear. The author is John, who never actually claims to be a prophet but does call his work a prophecy (1:3; 19:10) and sees the prophets as his comrades (22:9). This John assumes he will be known in each of the seven cities to which the work is addressed, and so is probably a traveling prophet of the type we meet in works like the *Didache*.[19] These prophets moved from place to place, spending only a few days in each place but perhaps returning often. As prophets they had great authority and thus had the potential of creating a lot of trouble for the Christian leaders who lived in these places and oversaw the communities. This tension between the settled leaders (who would likely want to accommodate to their culture) and the wandering prophet (who would likely be more radical in rejecting culture) may be reflected in the hostility John manifests toward the people he calls "Jezebel" and "Balaam" (2:14–15; 20–21).

The primary fact about prophets is that they were believed to have direct contact with God and/or Jesus and to be able to speak for them. While this might on occasion bear on the future, the prophets spoke primarily to the present. Prophets were not fortune-tellers. Nor did prophets rely exclusively on trance or visionary experiences. Without discounting such experiences, we can be sure that the careful and extensive use of earlier prophetic reports in the Apocalypse clearly demonstrates that prophetic proclamation also involved the remolding of earlier words to the present need. While John never cites scripture, there are over five hundred allusions to earlier biblical works in Revelation. This is not inconsistent with the claim to prophecy, since these earlier works were believed to be directly from God.

John did not simply reinterpret scripture the way we find in Matthew (who uses the formula: this was done to fulfill x prophecy) or in the Dead Sea Scrolls (which use the formula: what was written x really means y).[20] John reused the scriptural traditions as the raw material from which he constructed new revelations.

While this may seem like a radical approach (as it does to me) our implied author is no liberal. He insists that the true community includes "those who keep the commandments of God and hold the testimony of Jesus" (12:17; see also 14:12, 1:2, 9). This is far from the "faith alone" approach of Paul, insisting on a dual allegiance to both the law and Jesus. This is in keeping with what we saw as a far more rigorous attitude than Paul's toward eating sacrificial meat. (See the discussion of John's opponents, pp. 50–51.)

A picture of our implied author begins to form. He is probably a wandering prophet, perhaps ascetic and world-denying, perhaps the head of a school of prophets. Greek is not his native tongue, for he speaks it with a strong Semitic accent—implying that he was originally from Palestine and has come to Asia Minor later in life. He is saturated with the writings of the Hebrew prophets to such an extent that he could make their words his own. He begins to look like a conservative Jewish Christian, possibly more at home with those who opposed Paul at Antioch, the so-called "people [who] came from James," than he would have been with Paul.[21] Such at least is the aspect of himself our implied author has chosen to show us in this work.

We can probably add that his activity stretched over a period of thirty or so years and that he published the final edition of his visions near the end of the first century. This would be consistent both with his attitude toward the apostles (as revered figures of the past) and with such statements as we have from ancient writers.[22] The earliest surviving comment comes from Irenaeus, a writer who originally came from this area. Writing about 180 he claims that the Apocalypse "was seen no long time ago, but almost in our own day, towards the end of Domitian's reign."[23] In addition, if the use of the code-name Babylon for Rome rests on the most obvious fact they shared (both destroyed Jerusalem) then the writing would have to be after 73, the year in which Jerusalem fell to Titus.

The basic counterevidence to dating Revelation at the end of the first century is the rather neat way 666 seems to point to Nero (see pp. 106–9).[24] At the very least it seems likely that this particular visionary segment originated during the time of Nero, who died in 68. If this is true, then we would know two further things about our implied author: that he is editing a collection of visions into a final, unified work and that these visions occured over a period of thirty years—from the late sixties to the late nineties. This seems likely, but is far from certain. I would add that the nature of the Apocalypse as an oral work means that our modern notions of writing and publication are ill-suited to explaining it. An oral work would go through countless editions and grow over time, so that it is quite possible that the Apocalypse is best understood as a work of the last third of the first century, probably reaching its present form near the end of the century.

We can also construct something of the picture of the *implied audience*, for every writing makes certain assumptions about its audience. Of course these assumptions may not correspond exactly to the actual readers, but they represent what the author thought the audience was like. For example, our author clearly thought he needed to address this audience in Greek (rather than in his native tongue) and, further, he thought they would not be overly offended by his barbarous expressions and grammatical irregularities. This implies that they were not a highly literate group—or at least that John did not choose to address his appeal to the literate segment. The latter may be the more likely, since the letters recognize (and disparage) wealthy members of the community while praising the poor (see 2:9; 3:17).

It is important to recognize this tension between what is true of the implied community and what John wishes were true. For example, we cannot assume that because John describes them as law-observant followers of Jesus (12:17) that they in fact were. This is merely the segment of the community that John is appealing to. He would exclude those less Jewish than he (by calling them followers of Jezebel, 2:20) and those more Jewish (by calling them a synagogue of Satan, 2:9). What we can be sure of is that John's audience is located at the matrix between Jewish experience and Greco-Roman life in Asia Minor.25

THE SOCIAL CONTEXT: JEWS AND CHRISTIANS IN THE ROMAN WORLD

Under the best of circumstances this matrix could be unstable, for neither of these parties fully trusted or understood the other: Jews regarded polytheists as idolaters; they in turn regarded Jews as atheists (for they failed to recognize the Gods). I am trying to avoid the pejorative term pagans, for they were hardly barbaric or primitive as the term implies. It is perhaps a sign of how little we have understood Greco-Roman religious life that we have no other term ready at hand. But Jews had for centuries been working out ways to survive in this foreign culture—both by avoidance and accommodation. We discussed the various ways religion permeated every aspect of life in the Greco-Roman world—from business to education, entertainment, and sports (see pp. 126–28). While not without tensions, Jews had developed strategies for dealing with this issue.

First, they could avoid some of the problems. Their dietary laws, for example, would facilitate the community developing their own means of food-delivery in the cities, allowing them to side-step the issue of sacrificial food. On occasion they even obtained government help in meeting their dietary laws.26 Their practice of living in Jewish communities within the cities and concentrating on a few trades would help avoid the issues of trade guilds and assistance societies. Their special dispensation to pray *for* the emperor rather than *to* the emperor would give them some protection against charges of disloyalty.27 Second, they could accommodate to and fit in with Greco-Roman culture without losing their own distinct traditions. What we can reconstruct of their social history in these cities suggests a community far more at home in the Greco-Roman environment than John was. For example, the second-century synagogue at Sardis was built right into a community building that included a Roman bath.28 While this is somewhat later than John's time, it indicates an attitude toward Rome quite at odds with that found in the Apocalypse. The Jews at Miletus even had their own seating section in the theater, while those at Aphrodisias had similiar arrangements at the Odion (music hall).29 Clearly the Jewish communities, some of which had been in these cities for centuries, had learned how to adjust to their surroundings. The community of the Apocalypse seems to have been excluded from these Jewish survival mechanisms while trying to live by standards of separation more radical than their fellow Jews. They have as yet not devised suitable alternatives that avoid what John calls "the mark of the beast" (13:16–18).

This of course would leave John's community in a very difficult position: to remain pure (unmarked) they would have to avoid the trade guilds, the free distribution of meat at festivals, mutual assistance and burial societies, holding public office and even attending public meetings. Perhaps even family gatherings would have to be avoided unless the head of the family were Christian. Various business and social gatherings would be held in temples, many of which were constructed with numerous small dining rooms.30 In addition one would have to avoid the theater, the music hall, and athletic contests—even education would be a problem. It must have seemed to some in the community that John's approach was untenable.

It is this struggle to remain free of the taint of polytheism, I think, and not persecution that is addressed by the Apocalypse. But before expanding this thesis, let us look more closely at the idea of a persecuted community. It used to be universally assumed that John's community was under intense persecution, and many commentaries still refer to a persecution by the emperor Domitian as if it were a fact. It is not. There is simply no sound evidence of imperial persecution of Christians in Asia Minor in John's time.31

There were pressures, of course. John's community is a non-conformist community with strong Jewish roots. Any distinct minority culture is bound to feel some compulsion and coercion from the dominant culture. Some would even go so far as to say that John's community *felt* oppressed even if no objective persecution can be demonstrated.32 Or, stated another way, there may have been no persecution or other crisis from the perspective of official Roman historiography, but Revelation "has adopted the 'perspective from below' and expressed the experience of those who were powerless, poor, and in constant fear of denunciation."33 There is some force in this argument, but not enough to make it the touchstone of interpretation.

The force comes from the obvious truth of these contentions—people often feel more oppressed than any objective evaluation of their situation would warrant. Even if there were no general persecution (and note that only one martyr is named in the book, Antipas at 2:13), it is worth remembering that the writing is addressed to the urban poor of subject cities under the authoritarian control of a totalitarian regime in far-off Rome. But even more, we have some good evidence that Christians in Asia Minor were soon subjected to imperial persecution, for a letter from a provincial governor, along with the emperor's response, has survived.

Around 110 the emperor Trajan dispatched Pliny the Younger to Asia Minor as a special representative in order to insure that everything was in order. A brewing conflict with Parthia would require a secure supply-line through this area. Pliny was already famous for his published letters; his official correspondence was published after his death about 112. Among these letters is one concerning Christians, which makes it clear that Pliny does not know what to make of these people or how to judge their guilt. Here is the letter:

It is a rule, Sir, which I inviolably observe, to refer myself to you in all my doubts; for who is more capable of guiding my uncertainty or informing my ignorance? Having never been present at any trials of the Christians, I am unacquainted with the method and limits to be observed either in examining or punishing them. Whether any difference is to be made on account of age, or no distinction allowed between the youngest and the adult; whether repentance admits to a pardon, or if a man has been once a Christian it avails him nothing to recant; whether the mere profession of Christianity, albeit without crimes, or only the crimes associated therewith are punishable—in all these points I am greatly doubtful.

In the meanwhile, the method I have observed towards those who have been denounced to me as Christians is this: I interrogated them whether they were Christians; if they confessed it I repeated the question twice again, adding the threat of capital punishment; if they still persevered, I ordered them to be executed. For whatever the nature of their creed might be, I could at least feel no doubt that contumacy and inflexible obstinacy deserved chastisement.

There were others also possessed with the same infatuation, but being citizens of Rome, I directed them to be carried thither.

These accusations spread (as is usually the case) from the mere fact of the matter being investigated and several forms of the mischief came to light. A placard was put up, without any signature, accusing a large number of persons by name. Those who denied they were, or ever had been, Christians, who repeated after me an invocation to the Gods, and offered adoration, with wine and frankincense, to your image, which I had ordered to be brought for that purpose, together with those of the Gods, and who finally cursed Christ—none of which acts, it is said, those who are really Christians can be forced into performing—these I thought it proper to discharge. Others who were named by that informer at first confessed themselves Christians, and then denied it; true, they had been of that persuasion but they had quitted it, some three years, others many years, and a few as much as twenty-five years ago. They all worshipped your statue and the images of the Gods, and cursed Christ.

They affirmed, however, the whole of their guilt, of their error, was that they were in the habit of meeting on a certain fixed day before it was light, when they sang in alternate verses a hymn to Christ as to a god, and bound themselves by a solemn oath, not to any wicked deeds, but never to commit any fraud, theft or adultery, never to falsify their word, nor deny a trust when they should be called upon to deliver it up; after which it was their custom to separate, and then reassemble to partake of food—but food of an ordinary and innocent kind. Even this practice, however, they abandoned after the publication of my edict, by which, according to your orders, I had forbidden political associations. I judged it so much the more necessary to extract the real truth, with the assistance of torture, from two female slaves, who were styled deaconesses: but I could discover nothing more than depraved and excessive superstition.

I therefore adjourned the proceedings, and betook myself at once to your counsel. For the matter seemed to me well worth referring to you—especially considering the numbers endangered. Persons of all ranks and ages, and of both sexes are, and will be, involved in the prosecution. For this contagious superstition is not confined to the cities only, but has spread through the villages and rural districts; it seems possible, however, to check and cure it. It is certain at least that the temples, which had been almost deserted, begin now to be frequented; and the sacred festivals, after a long intermission, are again revived; while there is a general demand for sacrificial animals, which for some time past have met with but few purchasers. From hence it is easy to imagine what multitudes may be reclaimed from this error, if a door be left open to repentance.   PLINY, *Letters* 10.96

This letter gives us some very important information, even if that information is from at least two decades after the writing of the Apocalypse. First we can be certain that there is no imperial policy aimed at rooting out Christians and there are no fixed procedures for dealing with them. Pliny would not have needed to write this letter if there were. Second, we can see that being a Christian could get one killed—though it is not clear why. Pliny is uncertain whether being a Christian is itself a crime and he is further unclear whether if being a Christian is a crime it ought to be punished even if the person stops being a Christian. He holds out hope that those who repent can be pardoned, for he thinks such leniency will rescue many from this error.

Trajan answers these questions in his reply, which was also preserved by Pliny:

The method you have pursued, my dear Pliny, in sifting the cases of those denounced to you as Christians is extremely proper. It is not possible to lay down any general rule which can be applied as the fixed standard in all cases of this nature. No search should be made for these people; when they are denounced and found guilty they must be punished; with the restriction, however, that when the party denies himself to be a Christian, and shall give proof that he is not (that is, by adoring our Gods) he shall be pardoned on the ground of repentance, even though they may have formerly incurred suspicion. Information without the accuser's name subscribed must not be admitted in evidence against anyone, as it is introducing a very dangerous precedent, and by no means agreeable to the spirit of the age.

TRAJAN'S RESPONSE TO PLINY, *Letters* 10.97

Trajan confirms that there is no standard policy and even adds that no search should be made for Christians (so that even at this date there is no active persecution). Anonymous accusations should not be given any weight. Further, he commends Pliny's methods, including the pardoning of those who repent. Still, those who are "found guilty" must be punished. We are never told why being a Christian is worthy of death, but we are given enough clues in these letters to make a reasonable guess.

First we must recognize that we are dealing with a totalitarian mindset. Pliny not only felt free to use torture to extract truth (the victims would be slowly killed to see if they could be made to change their story; if they died sticking to their original account then one knew they were telling the truth). He also felt justified in executing anyone who would disobey a direct governmental order.

Second, Pliny clearly believes there are certain (unspecified) crimes associated with being Christian. Apparently everyone knows what they are and there are enough clues in the letter to be reasonably sure what he is thinking of. Our first clue is that those who have repented say their former "guilt" consisted in innocent meetings, harmless oaths, and ordinary food. The food allegations probably stem from the Christians' own talk of eating the body and drinking the blood of Christ—certainly later sources charge them with the worst sorts of barbaric and cannibalistic behavior. The oaths and meetings can be explained by the second clue: the method by which Pliny ascertained their guilt.

To prove their innocence the accused were required to pray to the Gods, offer adoration and sacrifice to the emperor's image, and to curse Christ. Of what charges would these demonstrations acquit one? The most likely answers are atheism, treason, and insurrection. Christians were seen to be followers of an executed insurrectionist and their refusal to give the emperor due honor only confirmed their treachery, in the eyes of the Romans. We should not overstate the case, however, for neither Trajan nor Pliny is concerned very much (they will not seek Christians out). Clearly something has happened to flush them out, so to speak. That too is indicated in the letter.

Pliny has recently published a decree forbidding "political associations," namely any kind of association not under direct government control. Rome's point of view here can be seen in Trajan's reply to another letter of Pliny, wherein he requested permission to form a firefighters' guild in

Nicomedia, where a recent fire had done great damage to the city because there was no organized fire brigade. Trajan refused to grant permission, writing:

> You are of the opinion it would be proper to constitute a guild of fire-men in Nicomedia, agreeably to what has been practiced in several other places. But it is to be remembered that these sort of societies have greatly disturbed the peace of your province in general and of those cities in particular. Whatever title we give them, and whatever our object in giving it, men who are banded together for a common end will all the same become a political association before long. It will therefore be better to provide suitable means for extinguishing fires, and enjoin owners of house-property to employ these themselves, calling in the help of the populace when necessary.   *Letters* 10.34

So the bottom line seems to be obedience to imperial power, hence Pliny's easy execution of those who refused his direct order "whatever the nature of their creed might be."

But more than politics is evident here. Notice there is a class element (slaves can be tortured; Roman citizens need to be sent to Rome for examination), together with social issues (the concern for children and women and for persons of rank), and economic issues (repaired temples, revived festivals, and—note especially—sale of sacrificial meat). We should not read this situation back into John's day, but surely the defining issues are already evident in the Apocalypse.

But if anything, Pliny's letters are evidence of what has happened because of the success of the Apocalypse. They help us understand the importance of the issues John addresses. What they show us is not that there is any organized Roman persecution of Christians (quite the opposite), rather they show the attitude and mind-set of Rome that will make resistance and persecution necessary. The purpose of the Apocalypse is not so much to comfort those who suffer as it is to stiffen those soft on Rome so they might resist domination.

THE AIM OF THE APOCALYPSE: CONSISTENT RESISTANCE

John addressed his letter to seven of the most powerful cities in Asia, six of them capitals of their region.[34] The economy was flourishing and the prosperity of the cities was widely envied. While John's audience contained both poor (2:9) and wealthy (3:17), it is likely that they were all better off economically than they had been at the beginning of the century and that their prosperity was increasing.

Could Christians share in this prosperity? We know from other Christian writings that the late first century and early second century were times of social adjustment and increasing accommodation.[35] Some trajectories of the Pauline tradition seem to have adopted standards of behavior and organization quite in keeping with their cultural context.[36] Paul himself had allowed great flexibility in eating sacrificial meat (1 Corinthians 8–10), and he did not forbid his followers to hold public office (Rom 16:23)—which would have involved at least token recognition of the city's Gods. It seems quite reasonable to think that Paul's followers in Asia in the late first century would have been seeking ways to accommodate both their new faith and their cultural expectations.

Whether the characters who appear in this story as John's opponents (Jezebel, Balaam, Nicolaitans; see pp. 46–51) are cultured followers of Paul or not we cannot say. They are surely people who see the need to live in their culture and adjust to it. But John has created a story in which such action is tantamount to being in league with the Devil.

Now the implied audience of this work is not the accommodationists; they are called vile names, and the purpose of name-calling is to exclude.[37] The implied audience is the people who might be tempted to follow them. We can see this clearly if we reflect for a moment on the narratee (the person to whom the narrator directs the narration) of the three basic levels of the story. These three levels of narration are the telling of the whole work by a reader; the telling of the stories by John on Patmos; and the telling of things by characters in these stories (for example, the voice addresses the souls under the altar in 6:11). Let's consider how the narratees (hearers) are characterized on each level.

At the outermost level the narrator is the reader and the narratee is the audience gathered to hear the reading (1:3). This is the level that corresponds most closely with the implied audience but is the least defined. On the second level the narratee is the listener to whom John narrates his vision of the risen Christ, explicitly named as the seven churches and extensively characterized in the messages to the churches (chapters 2–3). These narratees are both rich and poor, both zealous and lax, both loving and cold, but they are also separate from Jezebel and Balaam. They are folk who might be tempted to follow such accommodating leaders. At the third narrative level, the narratees are the people addressed in the stories told to these second-level narratees—that is, the saints and martyrs who struggle to conquer the beast (see 6:10, 15:2, and the constant references to saints and servants). They are characterized as suffering and oppressed.

These saints and martyrs are the focal points of the story and both the second and first level narratees are encouraged to identify with them, leading one narrative critic to assert that ideal audience takes on the role of the martyr.[38] This is something of a poetical exaggeration, but it is clear that by telling the story through the point of view of those abused by Roman power, the discourse persuades the audience to resist such power.

The purpose of the Apocalypse is to remind these people of the vile things Rome has done. It was Roman power, after all, that crucified Jesus. If, as the saying goes, politics makes strange bedfellows, John wanted his audience to know just whom they were getting in bed with. John's apocalypse is a revelation of the true nature of Roman power and Roman culture.

Seeing Rome in this light could lead to despair, but it is a measure of John's achievement that he has created a story that both reveals the mistake of accommodating to Rome and provides a rationale for resistance. For the prayers, the patience, the persistent resistance of the saints overthrow the powers of evil and bring God's kingdom into reality. This will become more clear when we look at the setting of the story.

THE LITURGICAL SETTING

The primary setting for this story, as given in the opening, is a gathering of people at which someone reads this story aloud for them as if it were a letter from John (1:3–4). This at least is the implied setting of the implied audience.[39] When we combine this observation with two others, namely the extensive emphasis on worship in the story and the mode of worship Pliny describes in his letter to Trajan, an interesting hypothesis emerges. The Apocalypse can be seen as an elaborate story that explains the rite of the Eucharist.[40]

Leonard Thompson has carefully elaborated the extent to which the language of the Apocalypse is the language of worship.[41] He has shown that the kingdom of God is actualized in the liturgical materials before it is actualized in the narrative materials, so that the liturgy may be seen as the source and origin of God's rule. Not only does the Apocalypse narrate liturgical events (such as the heavenly worship in chapters four and five and the repeated hymns), it claims to have been originally received in liturgical time ("on the Lord's day," 1:10). Thus the presentation of the Apocalypse imitates both its reception and its content.[42]

This is consistent with what we know of such practices, as David Aune has shown.[43] One of the functions of the recital of such revelations was to re-actualize the original revelatory experience,[44] not just to tell but to reveal. The Apocalypse is primarily an experience, more particularly an experience of worship. Thus its consistent theme to worship God is self-actualizing: when one hears these words one is doing them.

The experience of worship is a distinctive kind of human experience. It is an altered state of consciousness in which the ordinary world no longer possesses its overwhelming reality. The closest analogy is the human capacity to play games. When one plays baseball, for example, one is no longer in a meadow; one is on a diamond. The time is no longer three o'clock; it is the third inning. The person you are with is no longer simply your friend but the shortstop, the pitcher, the batter. Times, places, and relationships all change in a game to another kind of reality. So too in worship.

Sacred time and sacred space are points at which humans believe they have access to the transcendently real.[45] Sacred space is space at which heaven and earth connect. Sacred time is a time when the worshipper enters the heavenly. It is not like ordinary time, for it is reversible; one can return to the beginning. Thus, the Lord's Supper is at the same time a present experience of the worshipping community, a re-enactment of the past supper of Jesus with the disciples, and a proleptic feasting in the messianic banquet of the end time. In worship, past, present, and future merge. In worship, one reclines at table in Ephesus, stands with John on Patmos, and enters the heavenly throne room to worship God.

The citation from Pliny above tells us a little of the actual worship practices of the churches of Asia in the late first century. From Pliny's letter to Trajan we learn that some of those who renounced Christianity informed him of the following:

> They habitually met "on a certain fixed day" [clearly the Lord's day] before sunup to sing hymns to Christ and take oaths of good behavior. They separated [Sunday was not a holiday and so they would go about their normal work.] and regathered [after sundown] to share a common meal.
>
> *Letters* 10.96

From this we can infer a practice of a brief morning service and a longer evening service that included a Eucharist. This evening Eucharist probably provided the immediate setting for the reading of the Apocalypse.[46] If so, the Apocalypse provided the story that set the context for the receiving of the Lord's Supper.

Support for the thesis that this story should be connected with the Eucharist can be drawn from the story itself, which is fascinated with the notion of blood, especially the blood of Jesus (1:5; 5:9; 7:14; 12:11; 14:20 etc.). In addition, it shares numerous themes, images, and words with other Eucharistic texts. Table 12 displays some of the parallels with one of the earliest discussions of the conducting of a Eucharist, found in the *Didache*. While there are parallels to be found throughout Revelation, the number of parallels to chapter 22 in particular is remarkable: both mention David; both say only some are worthy to participate; both compare the outsiders to "dogs;" both promise a drink of life; both invite some to come; both invite the Lord to come; both close with "Amen."[47] The language of the closing of Revelation seems to echo eucharistic language, suggesting perhaps that here is an example of a prophet "giving thanks" however he wished.

The notion that the Apocalypse represents a story that accompanied the celebration of the Eucharist is speculative, to be sure, but provocative. There is a remarkable similarity between the symbolic function of the *supper* and the *story*. The *supper* is a meal that exists simultaneously in three times: It is a meal shared in the spirit with the Risen Lord (present); it is a commemoration of the last meal Jesus had with his disciples (past); and it is a celebration of that meal to be eaten in the kingdom of God, the messianic banquet (future; see Luke 22:14–16).[48] The *story* also participates in these three times.

The story is past. Clearly chapter 12 symbolically describes a past event: the birth of the messiah. But in fact everything described in Revelation has already occurred. In all its various ways, Revelation describes the conquest of evil, the overthrow of Satan's kingdom, the triumph of God—all of

TABLE 12 *Parallels between Didache and Revelation*

Didache 9	Revelation
Concerning the Eucharist (Thanksgiving), give thanks thus: first concerning the cup—*We give you thanks*, O our Father, for the holy vine of *David*, your child, which you made known to us through your *child* Jesus; *to you be glory unto the ages*.	11:17 22:16 12:2–5 7:12, etc.
Concerning the bread—*We give you thanks*, O our Father, for the life and knowledge *which you did make known unto us through Jesus* your child; *to you be glory unto the ages*.	1:1
As this broken bread was scattered upon the mountains, but was brought together, and became one, so let your church be gathered together from the ends of the earth into your kingdom, because from you is *glory and power* through Jesus Christ *unto the ages*.	7:1–10; 21:9–10 7:12
Allow no one to eat or drink of your Eucharist, except the ones baptized in the name of the Lord. For even concerning this the Lord said: give not the holy thing to the dogs.	22:14 22:15
And after you have eaten your fill thus give thanks: *We give you thanks*, Holy Father, for your holy name, which you have made to *tabernacle* in our hearts, and for the knowledge and faith and immortality, which you have made known to us through Jesus your child; *to you be glory unto the ages*. You, *Almighty Master*, did *create all things* for your name's sake, and did give food and drink unto men for enjoyment, that they might render thanks to you; but on us you did bestow spiritual food and drink and eternal *life* through your child. Before all things *we give you thanks* that you are *powerful; to you be glory unto the ages*. Remember, Lord, your Church to deliver it from all evil and to perfect it in your love; and gather it together from the four winds—even the Church which has been sanctified—into your kingdom which you have prepared for it; for from you is the power and the glory unto the ages. May grace come and may this world pass away. Hosanna to the God of David. If anyone is holy, *let him come;* if anyone is not, let him *repent. Maran Atha. Amen.* But permit the prophets to give thanks however they wish.	21:3; 13:6 1:8; 21:22; etc. 4:11 22:17 A basic theme of Rev. A basic theme of Rev. 22:11; 22:17; chapters 2–3 22:20

which happened in the death of Christ in John's view. "The Lion of the tribe of Judah has conquered," John proclaims, but when he shows us this lion it turns out to be "a Lamb standing as though it has been slaughtered" (5:5–6). Even in the climactic scene where Jesus rides in on his white horse and slays all the wicked with his sword, we are told that it is "the sword that issues from his mouth" (19:21). It is the word of Jesus that slays the wicked, and that word is primarily the testimony of his death. There is nothing described in Revelation that Christians do not believe has already happened in the death and resurrection of Jesus.

The story is present. Evil was not only overcome when Jesus died; it must be overcome in the life of each believer. It is their testimony added to his that overthrows Satan (12:11). It is the prayers of the saints that bring judgment to the earth (8:2–5). In a real sense, the lives of Christians reduplicate the life of Jesus so that his story becomes their story.

The story is future. Talking about the future is always dangerous. At the least one can look foolish—as countless would-be prophets from antiquity to William Miller and Hal Lindsey have discovered. In addition, in John's world it could be dangerous, for Augustus had forbidden magic and divination and, although quite ineffective, charges were repeatedly brought against various diviners. Nevertheless, it would be foolhardy to suppose John did not intend to speak of the future. But given the highly symbolic way he describes the past and present, it would be equally foolhardy to take his symbols of the future at face value. While John tells a story of the ultimate and complete triumph of Christ over Satan and the elimination of evil from this world, the symbolic nature of his story gives no warrant for thinking we know any details of that triumph.[49]

Both story and ritual are part of worship, and worship by its nature transcends time. John is in the spirit "on the Lord's day," which is simultaneously the present day (Sunday) on which worshippers assembled, *the* Lord's day, Easter morning when Christ conquered death (past), and that future "day of the Lord" of which the prophets spoke: the day of God's coming justice. In an excellent article on the aspects of time in the Gospel of John, Gail O'Day both uses and critiques the literary models of flashback and flashforward. While such categories are useful they fail to capture one important aspect of John's gospel, "It does not bring the narrative present into the future, but brings the future into the present."[50] This is a crucial insight for the Revelation also. Those who experienced the reading of the Apocalypse experienced all three times: Jesus came to them in the past in his life, death, and resurrection (5:6; 12:5, 11); Jesus comes to them in the prophet and in the meal they share (2:1; 3:20; 22:17, 20); and Jesus is to come to them for final vindication (6:10–11). John serves the one "who is and who was and who is to come" (1:8; 22:13).

Seeing Revelation as embedded in worship suggests that it functions not so much to communicate information as to enable an experience. It is performative language.[51] Let me elaborate.

THE FUNCTIONS OF LANGUAGE AND THE LANGUAGE OF REVELATION[52]

Just as there are three aspects to any communications event (the speaker, what is spoken, and the one spoken to), so there are three primary purposes of communication: to express something about the speaker, to give information, and to influence the one spoken to. Think about the very simple sentence, "I would like a glass of water." Our immediate sense is that this communicates information. For example, if I were visiting in someone's home and they asked me what I would like to drink, this response would mean I wanted water (rather than some other beverage). However, this same sentence could be used to communicate something quite different.

For example, if my friend and I had been out hiking and had neglected to bring along enough water and I said this same sentence after several hours without anything to drink, I would not be communicating any information at all—at least not anything my friend did not already know. Instead, I would be expressing my growing discomfort; the sentence is equivalent to "I am very thirsty." And there is one other possibility: this sentence could be used in an effort to change someone's behavior.

For example, if I were in a restaurant and I signaled the busy waiter and said, "I would like a glass of water" it would be the equivalent of saying, "Please interrupt what you are doing and bring me a glass of water." The function of the sentence is primarily performative rather than expressive or informative. These three aspects of language can be set out visually as follows:

Process: Speaker ➡ Statement ➡ Hearer

Functions: Expressive ➡ Informative ➡ Performative

Thus, while language always seeks to communicate something from a speaker to a hearer, the nature of the "something" varies with the context and focus of the language: expressing something about the speaker, informing the hearer of some information, or calling on the hearer to perform in some way. We need to pursue these last two aspects a bit further.

The most basic function of language is to communicate information, but we need to distinguish between giving simple information and conveying complex ideas. For the informative function of the label on a cereal box is quite different from that of an essay on the causes of poverty. We might say that some information requires only that we grasp it, absorb it, while other information demands that we listen to it and interact with it. We might call the former information *descriptive* and the latter *reflective*.

Performative language is also complex, exhibiting three basic, interrelated possibilities. It may elicit action in the hearers; it may change the identity or status of the hearers; it may influence the allegiance of the hearers. When the minister at a wedding says, "I now pronounce you husband and wife," the function of such language is to change the identity and status of the couple, both in their minds and in the minds of the audience. Consider: this is not information; everyone who came the wedding knew this was to be the outcome. Nor does it express the feelings of the minister, who may or may not think this is a suitable union. This is language functioning to change the hearers' identity. In a similar way, when a group of civil rights protesters sings "We Shall Overcome" the primary function of the language is to bind the group together, though, of course, it also expresses their idealism, calls for commitment, and provides information to the guardians of the status quo who hear them. In a similar way the language of teenagers, and other cultural subgroups, functions to differentiate them from the majority culture. It establishes who is in the group.

One final consideration is necessary to complete our model of the function of language, a reflection of the functional power of the contexts of communication. We saw above that the meaning of the simple sentence, "I would like a glass of water" can shift significantly with its context (a home, a restaurant, a wilderness). There is also the context of language, for communication can fail entirely if we are not speaking the same language ("Bir su istiyorum" might fail to communicate in America, but it would get you a glass of water in Turkey). But it is also possible to "speak a different language" in other ways, as when we misunderstand the literary context of a statement.

As a crude example, consider the grouch who responds to the greeting, "Good morning" with the response, "What's good about it?" Pretending to think the person was giving an evaluation of the day (an informative function), the grouch fails to exchange pleasantries. In fact, we all recognize that this kind of language is not informational. Nor is it necessarily expressive or performative, for the expression has nothing at all to do with how one feels about the morning or what one should do as a result. No, this kind of language does something else. It guides us to hear it in a certain way, based on our past experience of such language. Thus, another aspect of language is to regulate the meanings we expect from it. This is true at the smallest level ("Good morning") and at the grandest level (genre). (See the discussion of genre, pp. 156–59.) One of the most pervasive misreadings of Revelation stems from a failure to ask how "this kind of language" expects the audience to respond to it. Now let me summarize and begin to apply this understanding of language functions to the Apocalypse.

It is likely that every significant communication event will involve all these functions—expressive, informative, and performative. Plus the kind of language used will guide the ways we ought to take it. It is no small inquiry, then, to ask how we should understand the function of the Apocalypse or what its original purpose was. Much will depend on how we read it. We can read it for its information and there is no question that there is much information given here. At the descriptive level we would be reading to decode the language, in fact this is the necessary beginning point of any understanding. Without some basic understanding of symbolic numbers and apocalyptic bestiary Revelation remains an enigma. Decoding these symbols helps us understand what was happening in the lives of these people, thus one function of Revelation is to give information about church life and Roman power. But surely the descriptive information is only preliminary, for there is also reflective information to be wrestled with: the nature of evil, the purpose of suffering, the mystery of God's rule. These are questions beyond answering, but it is a further function of Revelation to elicit reflection on such questions. Of course, how we approach both the descriptive and reflective aspects of the information will depend on how we see the kind of language used regulating our expectations.

Or we could take a quite different approach and ask what Revelation is telling us about the speaker: view the Apocalypse as an expression of Johannine sensibilities. In this case the function of Revelation is to help the audience feel what the writer feels about Roman oppression. We would seek to hear it as the cry of the oppressed, the outrage of the occupied, the anger of the pious whose piety is at odds with those in power. One function of Revelation is to express the human desire for justice.

Analyzing the informative and expressive functions of Revelation is an important task, and each analysis will lead us in some degree to reflect on the impact of this information or this expression on the audience. But Revelation was a performance, an oral recital of a story, in the special context of a community gathered for worship, and we need to ask what such a story in such a context might do to the people who heard it. What was its performative function?

As performance, this language functions to bind the hearers into a community of shared vision. Community creation is one of the most basic functions of stories, whether it be the joke told in the bar or the campfire tale reciting tribal lore. To share a story is already to share a sense of community, and the longer the story, the more esoteric, the more personal, the greater the sense of bonding. In addition, the story of the Apocalypse creates identification through the use of praise and blame. This is most obvious in the name-calling in the letters (which establishes those who are outside), but is constantly reinforced by reference to the deeds of the saints and martyrs and the contrast with those who accept the mark of the beast.[53]

By having this story repeatedly enacted in the diverse churches of Asia Minor, our author binds them both to himself and to one another. Whereas before the story there were many different communities, after the story there is one. The story creates the community. In part, this creation of community results from the power of the story to transform the hearers. We can see this as a second performative function. In fact, at least three suggestions have been made for understanding this transformative effect, each offering some insight.

First, such apocalyptic stories generally are designed to shape the imagination of the hearer, to allow one to view one's historical situation in a new way, and so allow one to act in a new way.[54] All stories teach us to see the world in certain ways, but apocalyptic stories reverse our expectations for they are revelations. What they reveal is a new way of looking at life and history, a way that shows God in control and the believer on the side of truth and justice—and ultimate victory. One function of the Apocalypse was to alter the audience's perception of the world—to transform them from victims of Roman oppression into victors over the ultimate forces of evil.

This transformation is related to the literary notion of catharsis, first elaborated by Aristotle.[55] Adela Yarbro Collins has argued that the function of the Apocalypse was to produce an emotional catharsis in the hearers.[56] Just as, in Aristotle's analysis, tragedy evokes pity and fear in the audience—arousing these emotions so that the audience experiences them in a purified way—so the Apocalypse evokes feelings of fear, resentment, and revenge. The symbolic arousing of these emotions is satisfied in the imagination, thus purging the audience of their harmful effects. This is quite at odds with my own reading of the story, as the previous commentary makes clear, but does offer some insight into the performative function of language. While critics disagree on how to define catharsis, there is general agreement that stories produce an effect in their audience—whether that effect be emotional, psychological, or intellectual—or all three at once.

My own view is that the complex psychological effect of this story is to distance the hearer from Rome and from Roman culture. To disillusion the hearer—to destroy their illusion—that they can be at home in the Roman world is the primary performative effect of this story.

Second, this transformation of the imagination can be seen more particularly in the context of myth and ritual as a kind of mythic therapy.[57] Myths are special kinds of stories, often telling what happened "in the beginning." Hearing the myth one enters again into that ideal time and so adjusts one's life to the world as it is meant to be. A marvelous example of this power of myth is told by Claude Lévi-Strauss in "The Song of the Cuna Shaman."[58] The incident concerns a woman ready to give birth but unable to do so. The midwife is baffled and goes to the shaman for assistance. The shaman visits the woman and recites a lengthy tale, beginning with her difficulty and his coming to visit her and proceeding to recount his preparation and his quest for her lost power including his descent into the inner world (here the womb) where he does battle with beasts and finally bests the one blocking the birth. His victory frees the woman to deliver her child, and the song ends with instructions to those present. Here more than the imagination is transformed, for the myth changes the physical situation in which it is spoken. It provides the woman with a kind of therapy that allows her to understand her suffering and so prevail over it. This is not unlike what happens in modern psychotherapy, where the patient is provided with hidden explanations and a new way of explaining problems. Such stories have the power to transform.

Like the shaman, John begins and ends by addressing his audience and tells of journeys to other worlds where battles are fought and victories won. One entering into the myth will be transformed. In fact it is the very performance of the story that releases its power. Its function is not to relay information or express the author's views so much as it is to create a new situation for those who hear it. Once more the performative function of the language can be seen in the power of the very enunciation of the story to effect change in the audience.

This leads us to a third, still more powerful suggestion. Building on these insights into the power of stories and myths to transform, and looking at them more specifically in their ritual setting leads us to look at Revelation as a kind of ritual text.[59] Rituals are of two kinds. Some rituals serve to confirm the world as it is, to preserve the present order. This would be the function of various rites connected with the emperor: they reaffirm the rightness of Roman rule. Other rituals serve to transform, to change the world and one's place in it. Examples of such rites would be weddings, puberty rites, and college commencement rituals. The process of ritual transformation is seen most clearly in rites of passage, which involve a three-stage process, according to anthropologists.[60]

The ritual participant moves from stage A to stage B through a transitional stage of vague and ill-defined boundaries (for example, from childhood to adulthood through a puberty ritual wherein one might be alternately taught the secrets of adulthood and terrorized with the fears of childhood). This transitional stage or state is a time-between, related to both but like neither. Anthropologists refer to it as a liminal state—a boundary crossing. It is a time when the world is reordered and the participant achieves a new place in it.

It is the dynamics of this liminal state that interest us, for here a person passes through a temporary experience and is permanently changed as a result. This model allows us to avoid undervaluing the imaginative experience of hearing the Apocalypse. Writers who interpret this experience as merely a denial of reality[61] or as a temporary, ephemeral event soon to be eclipsed by life in the real world,[62] fail to appreciate the transformative function of language. One passing through this rite, this liturgy, can be permanently altered.

We need to try to imagine the power of this story, recited in the lamp-lit darkness as Christians gather to worship God, give thanks, and celebrate the Eucharist. As they prepare to eat and drink with Jesus, they first hear of his coming to their prophet who now sends his representative to them with the story; they then hear the very voice of Jesus himself, prophetically enacted, saying, "surely, I am coming soon" (22:20).

They have been told a wonderful story in highly symbolic language, revealing a two-tiered universe and telling a story meant to reveal the true meaning of Christian existence. They have been taken on a fantastic journey into another level of existence where they have met the risen Jesus, participated in the heavenly liturgy before the throne of God, and witnessed the attack of the ancient dragon. They have seen the cosmic conflict and experienced the overthrow of the powers of evil—conquered by the death of Christ and the faithful witness of his servants. This cosmic conflict correlates with and explains the cultural and political conflict of the world they live in every day, a world that seems to coerce the worship of lesser gods.

Far from being an escapist story, far from being a fantasy about some far-off future, the Apocalypse functions to shape the understanding (informative functions), the psychology (expressive and performative functions), and the actual practices (performative function) of its audience. It transforms them into a community of a shared vision of the struggle between Roman culture and Christian conviction; it engages them as participants in a cosmic struggle of good against evil; it transforms their identity and status. They are now the army of the slaughtered lamb ready to battle with the forces of the dragon. Hearing the Apocalypse provides the means for the "consistent resistance" John so often calls for.

John exhorts his audience to hold firm, to recognize the beast behind the beauty of Greco-Roman culture, to remain faithful witnesses: to worship only God. But he does more than exhort. He enacts the story of redemption before their eyes and ears and invites them to commune with the risen Lord. As they gather around the Lord's table they experience the coming of Jesus, a coming already known from the past, a coming anticipated in the future, but also a coming that is known in the present—charging their lives with cosmic significance and enabling them to enact their consistent resistance to the forces that would dominate their lives. In this way Revelation is truly "the revelation of Jesus Christ."

APPENDIX

The following lists are provided both to give a sense of overview and perspective on the characters and scenes of the Apocalypse and to give a kind of cross-index to the action. In each case, the lists are in narrative order. The distinction between major and minor characters is not meant to be absolute. In general, major characters appear more than once and/or function to carry the action. Minor characters support or respond to the action and generally appear only in one scene.

1. *A List of Characters in the Apocalypse*

In the Frame (1:1–11 & 22:6–20)
  Major Characters:
    John (1:4, 9; 22:8)
    The one who reads (1:3; 22:18)
    Those who hear (1:3; 22:18)
  Minor Characters:
    Angel (1:1; 22:8)
    Seven churches (1:4; 20; 22:16)
    Spirit (1:4; 22:17)
    Bride (22:17)

In the First Vision on Patmos (1:9–3:22)
  Major Characters:
    One like a human being (1:13)
    John
    Each church: Ephesus, Smyrna, Pergamum, Thyatira, Sardis, Philadelphia, Laodicea (2:1, 8, 12, 18; 3:1, 7, 14)
  Minor Characters:
    Self-styled apostles (2:2)
    Nicolaitans (2:6)
    Self-styled Jews (2:9)
    Devil (2:10)

Satan (2:13)
Antipas (2:13)
Adherents of Balaam (2:14)
Jezebel, a self-styled prophet (2:20)
Jezebel's lovers (2:22)

In the Second Vision in Heaven (4:1–11:18)
  Major Characters:
    John
    One seated on the throne (4:2)
    24 elders (4:4)
    4 beings (4:6)
    Lamb (6:6)
  Minor Characters:
    Riders on horses: white, red, black, pale (6:2–8)
    Souls of martyrs (6:9)
    Kings, generals, rich, slaves, etc (6:15)
    Four angels of four directions (7:1)
    144,000 sealed (7:4)
    Innumerable host (7:9)
    Seven angels with trumpets (8:2, 6)
    Another angel at the altar (8:3)
    An eagle flying in mid-heaven (8:13)
    Star, fallen (9:1)
    Locusts (9:3)
    Abbadon/Apollyon (9:11)
    Four angels bound at Euphrates River (9:14)
    Another strong angel (10:1)
    Seven thunders (10:3)
    Two witnesses (11:3)
    Beast that ascends from the pit (11:7)

Third Vision of War on Earth (11:19–22:21)
  Major Characters:
    Woman clad with the sun (12:1)
    Huge red dragon (12:3 & 20:2, 7)
    Beast rising out of the sea (13:1)
    Beast rising from the land (13:11)
    Lamb (14:1)
    Great whore (17:1), a woman clad in purple and scarlet (17:4)
    The great city (17:18)
    The rider on white horse (19:11)
    The holy city, new Jerusalem (21:2)
    The bride of the lamb (21:2 & 10)
  Minor Characters:
    Male child (12:5)
    Michael and his angels (12:7)

Our brothers (12:10)
Earth (12:15)
Rest of her offspring (12:17)
All—rich and poor, slave and free (13:16)
144,000 sealed (14:1), celibates (14:4)
4 beings and 24 elders (& 19:4)
Another angel (14:6)
Second angel (14:8)
One resembling a human being (14:14)
Another angel (14:17)
Seven angels with seven plagues (15:1)
Those with mark of the beast (16:2)
False prophet (16:13 & 19:20)
Kings of whole world (16:14)
Seven kings (17:10)
Ten kings (17:12)
Another angel (18:1)
God's people (18:4)
Merchants of the earth (18:11)
Shipmasters and sailors (18:17)
A strong angel (18:21)
Great host in heaven (19:1)
Angel standing in the sun (19:17)
People on thrones (20:4)
Rest of the dead (20:5)
One on a great white throne (20:11)
Sea, Death, and hades (20:13)

2. *A List of Places in the Apocalypse*

In the Opening and the Patmos Vision (1:1–3:22)
Asia (1:4)
Patmos (1:9)
Cities (1:11)

In the Vision of Heavenly Worship (4:1–11:18)
Heaven (4:1)
Throne (4:2)
(Earth 6:2)
Altar (6:9)
(Earth 6:12)
Earth (7:1)
Temple (7:15)
(Earth 8:7)
Sea (8:8)
Rivers (8:10)
Sun (8:12)

Abyss (9:2)
Golden altar (9:13)
Euphrates River (9:14)

In the Vision of Cosmic War (11:19–22:21)
Temple (11:1)
Great city (11:8)
Heaven (11:15)
Sky (12:1)
Heaven (12:7)
Earth (12:13)
Sea (13:1)
Earth (13:11)
Mount Zion (14:1)
Mid-heaven (14:6)
White cloud (14:14)
Temple in heaven (14:17)
Sky (15:1)
Temple in heaven (15:5)
Earth (16:2)
  Earth (16:2)
  Sea (16:3)
  Rivers (16:4)
  Sun (16:8)
  Throne of beast (16:10)
  Euphrates: war (16:12)
(Air; Temple 16:17)
Armageddon (16:16)
Babylon (16:19)
Wilderness (17:3)
Heaven (19:11)
Sun (19:17)
Earth (19:19)
Lake of fire (19:20)
Abyss (20:1)
Earth (20:8)
Throne (20:11)
Lake of fire (20:14)
New heaven, new earth, new Jerusalem (21:1–2)
Mountain (21:10)
Jerusalem (21:10)

NOTES

Preface

1. Page 48. My thanks to Pamela Thimmes for pointing me to this story.

Prologue

1. From *Black Elk Speaks*, as told through John G. Neihardt, 250.
2. See the extended discussion of Leitch, *What Stories Are*.
3. See Conacher, *Aeschylus' Oresteia*, 3–6.
4. Chatman, *Story and Discourse*.
5. D. H. Lawrence, *Apocalypse*.
6. For a discussion of patronage see Elliott, "Patronage and Clientism in Early Christian Society"; Eisenstadt and Roniger, *Patrons, Clients and Friends*; Wallace-Hadrill, *Patronage in Ancient Society*; and Gellner and Waterbury, *Patrons and Clients in Mediterranean Societies*.
7. This is no place to debate the question of valid interpretations versus erroneous ones, but the reader is entitled to know my position. I can give it facetiously in the way I often tell my classes how I grade their essays: there is no correct answer to this question, but there are wrong answers. By that, I mean there are any number of correct answers to a question (at least to any important question), though some will be more persuasive than others. But there are also many ways to fail to answer a question. In the same way, any narrative is capable of numerous interpretations, as well as an even greater number of misinterpretations.

    A reasonable guide to the issues is Armstrong, *Conflicting Readings*. One could profitably compare the contrasting views of Hirsch, *Validity in Interpretation* and Fish, *Is There a Text in This Class?* My own approach, which I will sketch at the end of this introduction, is closer to that of Iser, *The Act of Reading*.
8. See Albanese, *Corresponding Motion*.
9. Consider the use of witness in Rev 6:9; 11:7; 12:11; 19:10; 20:4; etc.
10. The conventions of the genre apocalypse are more fully discussed in the Epilogue. The most important works to date on the notion of the genre of the

apocalypse are John J. Collins, ed., *Semeia 14* and Adela Yarbro Collins, ed., *Semeia 36,* especially the article by David E. Aune.

11. There is now a fine collection of twenty or so apocalypses in a handy paperback edition edited by Reddish, *Apocalyptic Literature: A Reader.* The standard scholarly collections are Hennecke and Schneemelcher, *New Testament Apocrypha,* vol. 2, and Charlesworth, *Old Testament Pseudepigrapha,* vol. 1.

12. See the extended discussion of this dynamic in Sweet, *Revelation,* 125–32. See also Ong's important distinction between the visual and the oral, *The Presence of the Word.* Ong generalizes that things seen remain external to us whereas things heard penetrate us (117).

13. See Matthew chapters 1 and 2, which make repeated use of the fulfillment formula. See Stendahl, *The School of St. Matthew.*

14. Aristotle, *On the Heavens* 268a 10–17.

15. For a study of the significance of numbers and numerology, see Menninger, *Number Words and Number Symbols* and Schimmel, *The Mystery of Numbers.*

16. See chapter 1 of Adela Yarbro Collins, *The Combat Myth in the Book of Revelation;* Farrer, *The Revelation of St. John the Divine.*

17. See Sweet, *Revelation,* 44–54.

18. For an analysis of Revelation as a chiasm see Schüssler Fiorenza, *Revelation: Vision of a Just World,* 35–36. See also her more extended discussion in "Composition and Structure," 344–66. Also see Lambrecht, "A Structuration of Revelation 4:1–22:5," in *L'Apocalypse johannique,* 77–104.

19. *Poetics* 1450a 51.

20. Forster, *Aspects of the Novel,* 87.

21. The terms are Chatman's, *Story and Discourse,* 53–54. According to Chatman, "Kernels are narrative moments that give rise to cruxes in the direction taken by events." "Kernels cannot be deleted without destroying the narrative logic."

22. See the vivid story of the shaman's descent into the womb/underworld in Lévi-Strauss, "The Effectiveness of Symbols."

23. Aune, "The Influence of Roman Imperial Court Ceremonial."

24. I first encountered the O. Henry story in Leitch's *What Stories Are,* 47–48. Leitch makes the point that what changes in such a story is the audience's, not the hero's, understanding of the world.

25. For a discussion of the history of the view that Revelation contains extensive recapitulations of the same action rather than a linear development narrating separate actions see Wainwright, *Mysterious Apocalypse,* 29, 35, 53–55, 69.

26. For an orientation to reader response criticism see Booth, *The Rhetoric of Fiction,* 88–116. For a range of approaches see Suleiman and Crosman, eds., *The Reader in the Text;* for an excellent formulation of the issues in terms that apply to ancient literature see Iser, *The Act of Reading;* for an analysis of reader response theory for biblical studies see Fowler, "Who Is 'the Reader' in Reader Response Criticism?"

27. For a complete translation of the oldest version known to us, probably from the early second millennium BCE, see Pritchard, ed., *Ancient Near Eastern Texts,* 60–72. For recent research on the myth see, Adela Yarbro Collins, *The Combat Myth in the Book of Revelation;* Day, *God's Conflict with the Dragon and the Sea;* Hooke, "The Myth and Ritual Pattern in Jewish and Christian Apocalyptic";

Kang, *Divine War in the Old Testament and in the Ancient Near East;* Miller, *The Divine Warrior in Early Israel;* von Rad, *Holy War in Ancient Israel.*

28. For a fuller exposition of this myth, complete with bibliography, see the discussion on pp. 103–5.

29. For further discussion see the commentary on 1:13, p. 39.

30. For other references to the lamb in this third movement see 12:11, 13:8, 11; 14:1, 4, 10; 15:3; 17:14 (as a warrior!); 19:7; 21:9, 14, 22; 22:1, 3.

31. See Hemer, *Letters to the Seven Churches of Asia;* I note some of the correlation in the commentary on each church.

32. Jones, *The Cities of the Eastern Roman Provinces,* 73–83. Only Philadelphia, the easternmost city, was not a capitol, being included in the Coventus of Sardis. Nevertheless, Philadelphia was the dominant city of its area, ruling an extensive territory in the Cogamus valley.

33. Broughton, *Roman Asia.*

34. Based on information in Ekrem Akurgal, *Ancient Civilizations and Ruins of Turkey.*

35. The commentary will discuss the evidence in detail. For a full presentation of this view see Thompson, *The Book of Revelation.*

36. From the *Collected Poems of Archibald MacLeish,* 50–51.

37. For a sophisticated presentation of this viewpoint see Fish, *Is There a Text in This Class?*

38. For a sophisticated presentation of this viewpoint see Hirsch, *The Aims of Interpretation.*

39. Iser, *The Implied Reader,* 282. Iser is a good representative of this third perspective.

40. Boesak, *Comfort and Protest.*

41. See Iser, *Implied Reader,* 10.

42. For the notion of the boundary between oral and written text see Kelber, *The Oral and the Written Gospel.* The most influential work on primary orality is that of Ong, see especially his *The Presence of the Word* and *Interfaces of the Word.* For an overview of orality studies and biblical criticism see *Semeia 39* edited by Silberman and titled *Orality, Aurality and Biblical Narrative.* For a general discussion of orality and literacy in antiquity see Harris, *Ancient Literacy.* Stock traces the shift in interpretive models in *The Implications of Literacy.* For a preliminary application to Revelation see Barr, "The Apocalypse of John as Oral Enactment."

The Letter Scroll

1. Page 48.

2. For a discussion of the technology of writing see Roberts and Skeat, *The Birth of the Codex* and Gamble, *Books and Readers.* For a broader discussion of the history of publishing see Boorstin, *The Discoverers;* see also Reynolds, *Scribes and Scholars.*

3. Petronius discusses this ability in *Satyricon* 75.

4. For a general discussion of reading in antiquity see Kenyon, *Books and Readers in Ancient Greece and Rome.* For implications of reading practices for New

Testament studies see Achtemeier's SBL presidential address, "Omne Verbum Sonat."

5. Boorstin, *Discoverers*, 530.
6. For a fine introduction see John J. Collins, *Apocalyptic Imagination*.
7. See Hellholm, *Apocalypticism in the Mediterranean World* and the follow-up study, Collins and Charlesworth, *Mysteries and Revelations*.
8. For the writings outside the New Testament see the second volume of Hennecke and Schneemelcher, *New Testament Apocrypha*.
9. See Doty, *Letters in Primitive Christianity* or White, *Light from Ancient Letters*.
10. See the early list of acceptable works known as the Muratorian Canon. An English translation can be found in Hennecke and Schneemelcher, *New Testament Apocrypha*, I.42–45.
11. It is impossible to translate this into English with the same force and jarring impact of the Greek. Since Greek declines its nouns, attaching various endings depending on how they are used in a sentence, the first expression should have been *tou ontos*. This would be something like saying "from he who is" in English rather than "from him who is." One thing that makes it different, however, is that *ho ōn* had become a technical expression for God. The author could have preserved both the form and the grammar by writing: *apo tou ho ōn* (as English: from the one who is). The second member is more awkward still. There is no past participle for *to be* in Greek, so the author resorts to the simple past tense, prefaced by the definite article, *ho ēn*, literally, the was. This is the first of several grammatical mistakes in this writing, leading many to conclude that the author was not a native Greek speaker.

   For a discussion of the likely Hebraic background of this expression, see Charles, *Critical and Exegetical Commentary*, I.10. Charles see the expression not so much as evidence that John writes poor Greek as indicating that he would rather violate the rules of grammar than violate a form of the Divine Name.
12. Compare "Zeus was, Zeus is, Zeus will be." Pausanius 10.12.5.
13. See 1:7, 3:11, 16:15, 21:2, 22:7, 22:1, 22:20.
14. See the strong case for astrological influence made by Malina, *On the Genre and Message of Revelation*.
15. Vanni, "Liturgical Dialogue."
16. See the provocative discussion of the difference between the "paramount reality" of everyday life and the "finite provinces of meaning" that function in enclaves within the paramount reality in Berger and Luckmann, *The Social Construction of Reality*.
17. David Aune, in "Form and Function," has pointed out that these are not formally letters, that is, they do not have the form of letters. Ancient letters always follow the pattern: sender to receiver, greeting, message, benediction. Here we have receiver, sender, revelation, praise/warning, admonition, promise. Aune suggests that this is closer in form to an imperial decree than a letter, and he is surely right. However, it is not unimportant that readers of Revelation from time immemorial think of them as letters. They function as letters even if they lack the form of letters. We might think of them as letters with the authority of decrees.
18. Also 2:4, 9, 13; 3:4, 9, 15.

19. Prince, *A Dictionary of Narratology*, 46. See also Culler, *The Pursuit of Signs*; Savran, *Telling and Retelling*; Aune, "Intertextuality and the Genre."
20. For a popular overview see Snyder, *Models of the Kingdom*. Two powerful statements of the symbolic dimension of the kingdom are Perrin, *Jesus and the Language of the Kingdom* and Scott, *Jesus, Symbol-Maker for the Kingdom*.
21. *Revelation: Vision of a Just World*, 51; also by this author, *The Book of Revelation*.
22. For a discussion of the issues see Adela Yarbro Collins, *Crisis and Catharsis*, 102–4.
23. Sweet, *Revelation*, 74.
24. See the specialized study of Davidson, *Angels at Qumran* and the more general interpretive work of Wink, *Naming the Powers*.
25. For a description of the early divisions of the text see Metzger, *The Text of the New Testament*, 21–23.
26. See the important study by Petersen, *Rediscovering Paul*. The introduction addresses the theoretical issues treated here.
27. Chatman, *Story and Discourse*, 31–34.
28. Petersen, *Rediscovering Paul*, 9.
29. The most recent comprehensive study of the cities is Hemer's *The Letters to the Seven Churches*. He provides extensive historical and archaeological data on the cities and relates them to these letters, though with little sense of the literary nature of the Apocalypse. These issues are now being addressed by Friesen; see his "Revelation, Realia, and Religion" and *Twice Neokoros*.
30. See Friesen, *Twice Neokoros*.
31. For archaeological information on this region see Akurgal, *Ancient Civilizations and Ruins of Turkey*. For specific information on the seven cities see Finegan, *The Archaeology of the New Testament*, 155–82.
32. Apuleius, *The Golden Ass*, 251. For a general discussion of religions with secret rites, see Burkert, *Ancient Mystery Cults*. For recent discussion of the worship of Isis, see Takács, *Isis and Sarapis in the Roman World*.
33. *The Twelve Caesars*, "Augustus" 100.
34. And the climactic vision of the warrior from heaven (19:16) will also reuse some of these characterizing traits; see pp. 109–11.
35. For a careful discussion of possible relations with the Pauline tradition see Schüssler Fiorenza, "Apokalypsis and Propheteia," 105–27.
36. This is an enormously complicated subject which I have greatly oversimplified. For further clarification see Sanders, *Schismatics, Sectarians, Dissidents, Deviants*. See also Siker, *Disinheriting the Jews*. Our best contemporary evidence for such synagogal exclusion is the Gospel of John, which in some way is related to the community addressed by the Apocalypse; for a summary see Brown, *The Community of the Beloved Disciple*.
37. Vv. 9, 13, and 24.
38. See Prince, "Notes Toward a Categorization of Fictional 'Narratees'," and the explanation of Chatman, *Story and Discourse*, 146–51.
39. Schüssler Fiorenza was the first to argue this case; see her "Visionary Rhetoric and the Social-Political Situation" in *The Book of Revelation*, 181–203; and "The Followers of the Lamb," 123–46. She is perhaps not quite as conscious of the inventiveness of the author as I would want.

40. See Willis, *Idol Meat in Corinth.*
41. Bonsirven, *Palestinian Judaism,* 132; see Schoeps, *The Jewish-Christian Argument,* 39 and the critical evaluation of Kimelman, "Birkat Ha-Minim and the Lack of Evidence for an Anti-Christian Jewish Prayer in Late Antiquity") with extensive notes.
42. For similar ideas see Gartner, *The Temple and the Community* and Juel, *Messiah and Temple.*

The Worship Scroll

1. Page 20.
2. See the list in John J. Collins, *Semeia 14,* 15, 36ff, 64ff. For a discussion see Segal, "Heavenly Ascent."
3. For example, Exod 24:9–18; I Kgs 22:19–22; and especially Isa 6:1–13, Ezek 1:1–28; 10:1–22; and Dan 7:9–10.
4. Scholem, *Major Trends in Jewish Mysticism;* Gruenwald, *Apocalyptic and Merkavah Mysticism.*
5. See Chatman's rudimentary discussion, *Story and Discourse,* 143.
6. Aune, "The Influence of Roman Imperial Court Ceremonial."
7. See White, *Building God's House in the Roman World.*
8. And there is the further echo of the law court, where a central figure sits on a throne (see Dan 7:9–10 and Rev 20:11–12).
9. For an imaginative trip to hell long before Dante see the *Apocalypse of Peter* 7–13, which can be found in Hennecke and Schneemelcher, *New Testament Apocrypha,* 2.668ff; or James, *The Apocryphal New Testament,* 505ff. For a study see Himmelfarb, *Tours of Hell.*
10. Such a notion seems to stand behind both the Gospel of Mark and the writings known as the Dead Sea Scrolls. John alluded earlier to such a spiritualized notion of temple when he showed the risen Christ promising the victorious at Philadelphia that they would be made a pillar in the temple of God (3:12). Compare Gartner, *Temple and Community* and Juel, *Messiah and Temple.*
11. See Eliade, *The Sacred and the Profane,* 20–65.
12. For an introductory overview see Rollins, *The Gospels;* for a more detailed study see Kee, *Jesus in History* or Nickle, *The Synoptic Gospels.* For my own views see *New Testament Story.*
13. In fact the lamb begins to look suspiciously like a ram, one of the dominant images of the sun God Mithras. Often John's imagery challenges that of Mithras, even as his vision of life contrasts so sharply with the ideology of power characteristic of the Mithras mythology.
14. On the other hand, two of the other gospels, and even Paul, associate Jesus with the Paschal Lamb; see Mark 14:12; Luke 22:7; and 1 Cor 5:7.
15. See Hurtado, "Revelation 4–5 in the Light of Jewish Apocalyptic Analogies," 112.
16. *Midrash Shemoth R.* 23; quoted from Sweet, *Revelation,* 120.
17. See Matt 16:14 for evidence that some included Jeremiah in this expectation. More commonly Moses and Elijah were expected, the former based on Deut

18:15, and the latter on Mal 4:5. For gospel traditions that show these two returning to advise Jesus see Mark 9:4, Matt 17:3, and Luke 9:30.

18. See the excellent study of John J. Collins, *The Scepter and the Star* and the collections of Neusner, Green and Smith *Judaisms and Their Messiahs* and Charlesworth, *The Messiah*. The older works of Klausner, *The Messianic Idea in Israel* and Mowinckel, *He That Cometh* are also valuable. See also Higgins, "Jewish Messianic Belief in Justin Martyr's Dialogue with Trypho."

19. See the careful study of Ulfgard, *Feast and Future*.

20. See Boring, *Revelation*, 100.

21. See the brief discussion on pp. 10–16 of the Prologue and the discussion in Chatman, *Story and Discourse*, 53ff.

22. Two alternative types of plot would include the plot of maturing (coming of age) and the plot of deciding (figuring out life). These have been called plots of action, character, and thought. See Crane, "The Concept of Plot," 233–43.

23. Compare Havelock's discussion of the meaning of the Muse's concern with the future "not as a novelty to be prophesied but a tradition which will continue and remain predictable." *The Muse Learns to Write*, 80.

24. Genette, *Narrative Discourse*, 93–94.

25. For an excellent and provocative literary analysis of the hymns of the Apocalypse, with extensive bibliography, see Harris, "The Literary Function of the Hymns."

26. Quoted from Charlesworth, *The Old Testament Pseudepigrapha*, 1.789.

27. Apuleius, *The Golden Ass*, chapter 11.

28. They are most commonly called interludes (e.g., Boring, *Revelation;* Schüssler Fiorenza, *Revelation*. Michaels questions the term, *Interpreting the Book of Revelation*, 55. Aune calls them digressions ("Revelation," in *Harper's Bible Commentary*, ed. Mays.

29. See similar scenes in Joel 2:10; Isa 13:10; Matt 24:29; Mark 13:8, 24; Luke 21:11, 25; Rev 8:5; 11:13, 19; 16:18; the scene here is perhaps built on that in Ezek 38:17–23. See also Luke 23:28–31.

30. Quoted from Boring, *Revelation*, 133–34.

31. See Caird, *Commentary on Revelation*, 122.

32. Schüssler Fiorenza suggests this apt metaphor; see *Revelation: Vision of a Just World*, 33.

33. See Genette, *Narrative Discourse*, 33–160.

34. See the careful study by Schüssler Fiorenza, *The Book of Revelation*.

The War Scroll

1. Page 88.

2. Compare the convention in the stories of Jesus' crucifixion that remark on the splitting of the Temple curtain; Mark 15:38; Matt 27:51; Luke 23:45.

3. Schüssler Fiorenza was the first to make clear the radical shift in the action at this point in the story; see her structuralist analysis in "Composition and Structure."

4. The idea that the Gods control human destiny in war is pervasive throughout the *Iliad* (Book 5, for example) but reaches a climax with direct warfare between the Gods (21.342–610).

5. See John J. Collins, "Mythology of Holy War."

6. For an extensive and nuanced discussion of these ideas see Adela Yarbro Collins, *The Combat Myth*. See also Hanson, *The Dawn of Apocalyptic*. For a specific version of the myth see Pritchard, *Ancient Near Eastern Texts*, 60–72; for a more recent translation and introduction to Akkadian literature see Foster, *Before the Muses* or Foster, *From Distant Days*.

7. Though the word translated "deep" in Gen 1:2 is a cognate word to Tiamat and the process of creation is seen as one of overcoming chaos.

8. See Russell, *The Devil* and Russell, *Satan: The Early Christian Tradition*.

9. Many commentators connect this slain head with the supposed belief in *Nero redivivus*, that the dead Nero would return to rule Rome, but this is unconvincing both because the legends about Nero's return did not involve his death and because what is restored here is not the head. See Adela Yarbro Collins' review of the Nero legend in her *Combat Myth*, 176–83.

10. See *Sibylline Oracles* 1.324ff.

11. Job 40–41; 2 Esdr 6:49ff; 1 Enoch 40:7ff; 2 Bar 29:4.

12. See chapter two of Day, *God's Conflict with the Dragon*.

13. See the provocative, if unconvincing, treatment by Pippin, *Death and Desire*.

14. The *Ascension of Isaiah* can be found in Hennecke and Schneemelcher, *New Testament Apocrypha*, 2.642–63 and the *Testament of Dan* in Charlesworth, *Old Testament Pseudepigrapha*, 2.808–10.

15. Compare 1:14–16, 2:16–18 and 19:12, 15, 21.

16. Compare 7:17; 12:5; 19:15; also 2:27.

17. The pseudonymous author of 2 Esdras (4 Ezra) actually shows the woman transformed into a city, see 2 Esdr 10:27.

18. For a general overview of women and religion see Kraemer, *Her Share of the Blessings*. On a broader level see Pomeroy, *Women's History*. For an excellent collection of primary sources see Lefkowitz and Fant *Women's Life in Greece and Rome*.

19. The Temple Scroll requires that women be excluded from the whole city "when they are in their menstrual impurity and in their birth impurity, so that they do not cause impurity in their midst." 48:16; quoted from Maier, *Temple Scroll*, 43.

20. See Lev 15 and the story of David in 1 Sam 21:1–6.

21. Suggested in the older work of Farrer, *Rebirth of Images* and elaborated in the new work by Malina, *On the Genre and Message of Revelation*. The suggestion takes on added significance when we remember the analogy between stars and angels (1:20) and the reference here to stars (12:3).

22. See the discussion in chapter five of Adela Yarbro Collins, *The Combat Myth*. Also Hooke, "The Myth and Ritual Pattern in Jewish and Christian Apocalyptic."

23. See the suggestive remarks of Farrer, *Rebirth of Images*.

24. There is even a version of the story for Rome. Romulus and Remus are born of a union of the God Mars with the daughter of a deposed king. Discovered, the usurper throws them into the flooded Tiber river, but they survive. Rescued and

nursed by a wolf, they are raised by shepherds till they grow strong and eventually overthrow the usurper and restore the rightful king. See Livy, *Hist.* 1.3.10ff; Plutarch *Romulus* 3ff.

25. See Witt, *Isis;* Takács, *Isis and Sarapis;* and Heyob, *The Cult of Isis among Women.* For a summary of the increasing veneration of Mary at Ephesus, see Koester, ed., *Ephesos,* 321–27. See also Limberis, *Divine Heiress.*

26. Jewish tradition too will see mythic parallels between Eve and Isis; see *Avodah Zara* in Neusner, trans., *Abodah Zarah.*

27. A translation can be found in Charlesworth, *Old Testament Pseudepigrapha,* 2.262.

28. See the discussion in Pilch and Malina, *Biblical Social Values.*

29. See the nuanced discussion in Thompson, *The Book of Revelation.*

30. See 13:4, 12; 19:10; 20:4; 22:8–9.

31. See Sebesta and Bonfante, *The World of Roman Costume.*

32. Many have attempted to use this statement to date the revelation, but without real success. There are two insurmountable problems. We do not know whether John would have begun the series of emperors with Julius Caesar or with Augustus, and we do not know whether he would have counted all or any of the three would-be emperors who each ruled a few months after Nero's suicide until Vespasian managed to establish a new imperial line. An even more basic problem is the likelihood that John intends the statement symbolically rather than numerically. The present emperor is always a six (or 666) and never a seven; that is, the emperor may claim divine titles but he is only human.

33. Consider the rhetoric of 4 Maccabees that, rather like Stoicism, praised the martyrs who "by despising sufferings that bring death, demonstrated that reason controls the emotions. . . . Even their torturers marveled at their courage and endurance, and they became the cause of the downfall of tyranny over their nation. By their endurance they conquered the tyrant, and thus their native land was purified through them" (1:9, 11). Note that their deaths are said to cause the downfall of the tyrant.

34. Quoted from Wise, Abegg, and Cook, *Dead Sea Scrolls,* 152. The final battle is described in great detail in *War Scroll* (1QM) 15–19.

35. See, for example Vermes, *Dead Sea Scrolls,* 51.

36. See Ps 74:13–14; 2 Bar 29:1–2; 2 Esdr 6:49–52.

37. In some traditions, one thousand years was the intended human lifespan. Adam lived only to 930 because of disobedience, and succeeding generations continued to decline until we reach the present pathetic life expectancy. There may also be some echo of the scheme in which the days of creation are identified with periods of one thousand years (based on a creative reading of Ps 90:4), thus the period here is like a Sabbath day ending one week (age) and preparing for a new one.

38. On the Greek idea see Bernstein, *The Formation of Hell.*

39. For a full discussion of the development of beliefs in the afterlife in this period see Nickelsburg, *Resurrection, Immortality, and Eternal Life,* and Cullmann, *Immortality of the Soul or Resurrection of the Dead?*

40. Detailed in Caird, *A Commentary on Revelation.* 275ff.

41. Lawrence, *Apocalypse,* 103.

42. Peirce, "Evolutionary Love."
43. Pippin, *Death and Desire*, 105.
44. Pippin, *Death and Desire*, 86.
45. Rabinowitz, *Before Reading*, 161.
46. 14:7; 19:10; 20:9; see also 4:10; 5:14; 7:11; 11:16; 19:4; contrast 13:4; 13:8–15; 14:9f; 19:20.
47. Goodspeed, *The Apostolic Fathers*, 211.
48. 2:7, 17, 26, 28; 3:5, 12, 21.

Epilogue

1. *A Paraphrase and Notes on the Revelation of St. John*, 2d ed. (London: John Noon, 1745:xxxiii), quoted in Wainwright, *Mysterious Apocalypse*, 78.
2. Bedell, Sandon, and Wellborn, *Religion in America*, 193.
3. Gaustad, *Religious History of America*, 152.
4. As quoted by Castelli, "The Environmental Gospel According to James Watt," B2. See the discussion in O'Leary, *Arguing the Apocalypse*.
5. See the excellent discussion and review of the history of scholarship in John J. Collins, *Apocalyptic Imagination*.
6. See the broad collection of papers in Hellholm, *Apocalypticism*.
7. See Russell, *The Devil*.
8. My approach tries to mediate the work of Klaus Koch, *The Rediscovery of Apocalyptic*, 28–33, and John J. Collins, *Apocalyptic Imagination*, 2–11. Koch seems right to identify these kinds of ideas as typically apocalyptic, but Collins seems right to insist that they do not always apply to history. Some apocalypses are more mystically and individually oriented.
9. This is in contrast to the prescriptive approach of John J. Collins, *Semeia 14*, who wants to identify the characteristics that are true of all apocalypses.
10. For a good cross-section, see Reddish, *Apocalyptic Literature: A Reader;* Christian apocalypses can be found in Hennecke and Schneemelcher, *New Testament Apocrypha*, vol. 2; and Jewish apocalypses in Charlesworth, *Old Testament Pseudepigrapha*, vol. 1.
11. Quoted from Hennecke and Schneemelcher, *New Testament Apocrypha*, 2.649.
12. Quoted from Hennecke and Schneemelcher, *New Testament Apocrypha*, 2.761.
13. Quoted from Charlesworth, *Old Testament Pseudepigrapha*, 1.111.
14. Quoted from Charlesworth, *Old Testament Pseudepigrapha*, 1.514.
15. See the discussion and chart in Chatman, *Story and Discourse*, 146–51.
16. Eusebius quotes extensive material from the third-century writer Dionysius of Alexandria who argued that the author of the Revelation cannot be the same person who wrote the Gospel of John, for while the Gospel is written "with remarkable skill" the Revelation "uses barbarous idioms." See *Church History* 7.25.24–27. For a brief treatment see Georgi, "Who Is the True Prophet?"; for a thorough examination of John's Greek see Mussies, *Morphology* and Thompson, *Apocalypse and Semitic Syntax*.
17. The other gospels continue to use such images, for example, Mark 13 and parallels. For an analysis of John's unique view, see Countryman, *The Mystical Way*. Smalley, "John's Revelation and John's Community," sees both works from the

same community by different authors at different times. For a fine study of what is known about the apostle John see Culpepper, *John, the Son of Zebedee.*

18. See the long list in Reddish, *Apocalyptic Literature,* 32.
19. See the translation in Goodspeed, *The Apostolic Fathers;* wandering prophets are discussed in chapters 11–13. See the discussion of prophetic lifestyles in Horsley, "Like One of the Prophets of Old."
20. On Matthew see Stendahl, *School of St. Matthew.* On Qumran see Gartner, "The Habakkuk Commentary." More generally see Brewer, *Techniques and Assumptions.*
21. The story is narrated in Gal 2:1–14. For a discussion see Gunther, *St. Paul's Opponents* and the recent commentary of Dunn, *Epistle to the Galatians.*
22. We have seen that attempts to date the book based on cryptic references to the Roman emperors in the story (such as 17:8–14) are doomed to failure because of the highly symbolic nature of these references and the uncertainty about who should be counted in such a list. See the discussion in pp. 133–36 and 106–9.
23. *Against the Heretics,* 5.30.3; Domitian reigned from 81–96. Of course we do not know whether this claim rests on knowledge, hearsay, or inference and so should not give it too much weight. By his own statement it would be an event some 85 years before his time.
24. The vast majority of interpreters date the Apocalypse about 95, but for a strong argument for an earlier date see Wilson, "The Problem of the Domitianic Date."
25. The confusion about angels evident in this story may spring from this same mixture of Jewish and Greco-Roman values. It was not uncommon for Jews to regard the Gods as really angels (or demons). The easy identification of Jesus and Michael in (12:7–12) and John's repeated attempts to worship the angel may indicate some degree of controversy in the community over the proper piety toward angels.
26. See the interesting story in Josephus (*Antiquities* 16.171) about how the Jews of Sardis warded off an attempt of the city to confiscate some of the money they sent yearly to Jerusalem (the so-called Temple Tax). Not only did Caesar side with the Jews but they also managed "to secure an official plot of land for the Synagogue and special consideration of Jewish dietary needs from city officials" (Hanfmann and Waldbaum, "New Excavations at Sardis," 319).
27. Of course many tensions remained and things that would work in theory did not always work in practice. For good overviews of a very complex topic see Smallwood, *The Jews Under Roman Rule;* Trebilco, *Jewish Communities in Asia Minor;* and Grabbe, *Judaism from Cyrus to Hadrian.*
28. Kraabel, "Paganism and Judaism."
29. For a discussion of how theaters worked, including a description of the theater at Miletus, see Akurgal, *Ancient Civilizations,* 196–209. For the inscription from Miletus see Frey, *Corpus Inscriptionum Judaicarum,* II:748. Rouché, *Performers and Partisans* discusses inscriptions that show Jews had reserved seating in the Odion (music hall).
30. Stambaugh, "The Functions of Roman Temples."
31. There was an intense persecution of Christians in Rome in the last four years of Nero's reign (64–68). While this persecution was localized in both time and place, and there is no evidence that it spread to Asia, it may well have colored

the thinking of leaders like John. See the careful work of Thompson, "A Sociological Analysis of Tribulation," and especially, *The Book of Revelation: Apocalypse and Empire.*

32. Adela Yarbro Collins, *Crisis and Catharsis,* 84.
33. Schüssler Fiorenza, *The Book of Revelation,* 8–9.
34. Jones, *The Cities of the Eastern Roman Provinces,* 73–83.
35. See, for example, Dunn, *Unity and Diversity.*
36. Evident, for example, in the treatment of women in the Pastoral Letters, especially I Timothy; see the interesting analysis of MacDonald, *The Legend and the Apostle.*
37. Adela Yarbro Collins, "Vilification and Self-Definition."
38. See the excellent, if technical, discussion of the reader as martyr in chapter four of Harris, "The Literary Function of the Hymns," 227–301.
39. And the temporal setting of the work is "the Lord's day" (1:10), the day Christians celebrate Jesus' resurrection.
40. The discipline of religion studies has developed the categories myth and ritual to represent the dynamic interaction between word and rite, wherein rite enacts the word and word explains the rite. See Fontenrose, *The Ritual Theory of Myth.* Also see the works of Eliade, perhaps beginning with his *Rites and Symbols of Initiation; Cosmos and History;* or *The Sacred and the Profane.*
41. Thompson, *The Book of Revelation: Apocalypse and Empire,* 69–73; also see his "Cult and Eschatology."
42. For a careful and provocative discussion of the Apocalypse as liturgical see Ruiz, "Betwixt and Between on the Lord's Day."
43. Aune, *The Cultic Setting;* see also his classic study *Prophecy in Early Christianity.*
44. Aune, "The Apocalypse of John and the Problem of Genre," 89.
45. The concepts were profoundly shaped by Eliade, *The Sacred and the Profane* but are used widely in the study of religion. For a recent treatment see Bell, *Ritual Theory.*
46. For a fuller discussion of this thesis see Barr, "The Apocalypse of John as Oral Enactment." While the elaborate thesis of Cabannis that the Apocalypse is liturgically organized does not seem tenable, he presents some interesting data, especially on nocturnal worship, see *Liturgy and Literature.*
47. Although the Amen at Rev 22:21 may be an addition to the text by a scribe who perhaps sensed the eucharistic language.
48. See Wainwright, *Eucharist and Eschatology.*
49. See the surprisingly similar conclusions, on quite other grounds, of the English evangelical scholar James D. G. Dunn, "He Will Come Again."
50. O'Day, "I Have Overcome the World," 162.
51. See the seminal discussion of Caird, *Language and Imagery* and the general theory of speech-acts: Austin, *How To Do Things with Words* and Searle, *Expression and Meaning.* Thompson has applied speech-act theory to Revelation in his "Mooring the Revelation in the Mediterranean."
52. For a more technical discussion of the relation of linguistic functions to the social setting of the Apocalypse see, Barr, "Blessed Are Those Who Hear," 95–101.

53. For an overview of naming as a means of social formation see Malina and Neyrey *Calling Jesus Names*, 35–42. For specific reflections on Revelation see Adela Yarbro Collins, "Vilification and Self-Definition," and "Insiders and Outsiders."
54. John J. Collins, *Apocalyptic Imagination*, 32.
55. See Aristotle's *Poetics*, 2.11; Leon Golden elaborates a rational explanation of the concept in "Catharsis," and in "The Clarification Theory of Katharsis." For a general overview see Abdulla, *Catharsis in Literature*.
56. See *Crisis and Catharsis*, 141–60.
57. Gager, *Kingdom and Community*, 49–57.
58. Lévi-Strauss, "The Effectiveness of Symbols."
59. Ruiz, "Betwixt and Between."
60. See Van Gennep, *The Rites of Passage* and Turner, *The Ritual Process.*
61. So Adela Yarbro Collins, *Crisis and Catharsis*, 155.
62. So Gager, *Kingdom and Community*, 56.

SUGGESTED READINGS

The bibliography that follows is modestly comprehensive, including all the works cited in the notes and a few more. Its size makes it a little daunting, so I have decided to recommend a few outstanding works. These are the works I return to again and again—works I have found invaluable in my own quest to understand the Apocalypse. I have limited myself to ten.

Among the dozens of very fine commentaries, I recommend three:

J. P. M. Sweet, *Revelation*. Philadelphia: Westminster Press, 1979; Philadelphia: Trinity Press International, 1990.

G. B. Caird, *A Commentary on the Revelation of St. John the Divine*. Harper's New Testament Commentaries. New York: Harper and Row, 1966.

M. Eugene Boring, *Revelation*. Interpretation: A Bible Commentary for Teaching and Preaching. Atlanta: John Knox, 1989.

To understand the phenomenon of apocalypticism there is nothing better than:

John J. Collins, *The Apocalyptic Imagination: An Introduction to the Jewish Matrix of Christianity*. Los Angeles: Crossroad, 1984.

On the genre of Revelation, the most helpful work is:

David Aune, "The Apocalypse of John and the Problem of Genre." In *Semeia 36: Early Christian Apocalypticism: Genre and Social Setting*, edited by Adela Yarbro Collins, 65–96. Decatur: Scholars Press, 1986.

Technically a commentary, but really a fine example of an ethical, political, and feminist reading of the Apocalypse, is the provocative work of:

Elisabeth Schüssler Fiorenza, *Revelation: Vision of a Just World*. Minneapolis: Fortress Press, 1991.

Two works that have been seminal for the current understanding of John's social situation are:

Adela Yarbro Collins, *Crisis and Catharsis: The Power of the Apocalypse.*
   Philadelphia: Westminster Press, 1984.
Leonard L. Thompson, *The Book of Revelation: Apocalypse and Empire.* Oxford:
   Oxford University Press, 1990.

For a good example of a modern Christian finding the Apocalypse relevant to modern life without indulging in fanciful speculations, read:

Allan A. Boesak, *Comfort and Protest: Reflections on the Apocalypse of John of
   Patmos.* Philadelphia: Westminster Press, 1987.

Finally, for a really fine overview of the history of the reading of the Apocalypse, both ancient and modern, I recommend:

Arthur W. Wainwright, *Mysterious Apocalypse: Interpreting the Book of
   Revelation.* Nashville: Abingdon Press, 1993.

WORKS CONSULTED

Abdulla, Adnan K. *Catharsis in Literature*. Bloomington: Indiana University Press, 1985.

Achtemeier, Paul J., ed. "Special Issue on Revelation." *Interpretation* 40/3 (1986).

——————. "Omne Verbum Sonat: The New Testament and the Oral Environment of Late Western Antiquity." *Journal of Biblical Literature* 109 (1990): 3–27.

Adas, Michael. *Prophets of Rebellion: Millenarian Protest Movements Against the European Colonial Order*. Chapel Hill: University of North Carolina Press, 1979.

Akurgal, Ekrem. *Ancient Civilizations and the Ruins of Turkey: From Prehistoric Times until the End of the Roman Empire*. Istanbul: Haset Kitabevi, 1985.

Albanese, Catherine. *Corresponding Motion: Transcendental Religion and the New America*. Philadelphia: Temple University Press, 1977.

Allison, Dale C. *The End of the Ages Has Come: An Early Interpretation of the Passion and Resurrection of Jesus*. Philadelphia: Fortress Press, 1985.

Apuleius. *The Golden Ass*. Trans. Jack Lindsay. Bloomington: Indiana University Press, 1960.

Armstrong, Paul B. *Conflicting Readings: Variety and Validity in Interpretation*. Chapel Hill and London: University of North Carolina Press, 1990.

Arvin, Leila. *Scribes, Script and Book: The Book Arts from Antiquity to the Renaissance*. Chicago: American Library Association, 1991.

Aune, David E. "St. John's Portrait of the Church in the Apocalypse." *Evangelical Quarterly* 38 (1966): 131–49.

——————. *The Cultic Setting of Realized Eschatology in Early Christianity*. Leiden: E. J. Brill, 1972.

——————. "The Social Matrix of the Apocalypse of John." *Biblical Research* 26 (1981): 16–32.

——————. "The Influence of Roman Imperial Court Ceremonial on the Apocalypse of John." *Biblical Research* 28 (1983): 5–26.

——————. *Prophecy in Early Christianity and the Ancient Mediterranean World*. Grand Rapids: Eerdmans, 1983.

—————. "The Apocalypse of John and the Problem of Genre." In *Semeia 36: Early Christian Apocalypticism: Genre and Social Setting*, edited by Adela Yarbro Collins, 65–96. Decatur: Scholars Press, 1986.

—————. "The Apocalypse of John and Graeco-Roman Revelatory Magic." *New Testament Studies* 33, no. 4 (1987): 481–501.

—————. *The New Testament in Its Literary Environment*. Library of Early Christianity, 8. Philadelphia: Westminster Press, 1987.

—————. "The Prophetic Circle of the John of Patmos and the Exegesis of Revelation 22:16." *Journal for the Study of the New Testament* 37 (October 1989): 103–16.

—————. "The Form and Function of the Proclamations to the Seven Churches (Revelation 2–3)." *New Testament Studies* 36 (1990): 182–204.

—————. "Intertextuality and the Genre of the Apocalypse." In *Society of Biblical Literature 1991 Seminar Papers*, 142–60. Atlanta: Scholars Press, 1991.

Austin, Jane L. *How to Do Things with Words*. 2d ed., edited by J. O. Urmson and M. Sbisa. Cambridge: Harvard University Press, 1975.

Babcock, Barbara A. *The Reversible World: Symbolic Inversion in Art and Society*. Ithaca: Cornell University Press, 1978.

Baird, William. "Visions, Revelation, and Ministry: Reflections in 2 Corinthians 12:1–5 and Galatians 1:11–17." *Journal of Biblical Literature* 104, no. 4 (1985): 651–62.

Barnes, Timothy D. "Legislation Against the Christians." *Journal of Roman Studies* 58 (1968): 49.

Barr, David L. "The Apocalypse as a Symbolic Transformation of the World: A Literary Analysis." *Interpretation* 38 (1984): 39–50.

—————. "The Apocalypse of John as Oral Enactment." *Interpretation* 40 (1986): 243–56.

—————. "Elephants and Holograms: From Metaphor to Methodology in the Study of John's Apocalypse." In *Society of Biblical Literature 1986 Seminar Papers*, 400–11. Atlanta: Scholars Press, 1986.

—————. "Metaphors and Methodologies: The Holographic Model as a Guide for Research." *Proceedings of the Eastern Great Lakes and Midwest Biblical Societies* 6 (1986): 1–17.

—————. "The Reader of/in the Apocalypse: Exploring a Method." *Proceedings of the Eastern Great Lakes and Midwest Biblical Societies* 10 (1990): 79–91.

—————. *New Testament Story: An Introduction*. 2d ed. Belmont, CA: Wadsworth, 1995.

—————. "Using Plot to Discern Structure in John's Apocalypse." *Proceedings of the Eastern Great Lakes and Midwest Biblical Societies* 15 (1995): 23–33.

—————. "Blessed Are Those Who Hear: John's Apocalypse as Present Experience." In *Biblical and Humane: A Festschrift for John Priest*, edited by Linda Bennett Elder, David L. Barr, and Elizabeth Struthers Malbon, 87–103. Atlanta: Scholars Press, 1996.

Bartlett, David L. "John G. Gager's *Kingdom and Community:* A Summary and Response." *Zygon* 13 (1978): 109–22.

Batto, Bernard, F. *Slaying the Dragon: Mythmaking in the Biblical Tradition*. Louisville: Westminster/John Knox Press, 1992.

Bauckham, Richard J. "Eschatological Earthquake in the Apocalypse of John." *Novum Testamentum* 19 (July 1977): 224–33.

—————. "The Role of the Spirit in the Apocalypse." *Evangelical Quarterly* 52 (1980): 66–83.

—————. "The Book of Revelation as a Christian War Scroll." *Neotestamentica* 22 (1988): 17–40.

—————. "Resurrection as Giving Back the Dead: A Traditional Image of Resurrection in the Pseudepigrapha and the Apocalypse of John." In *The Pseudepigrapha and Early Biblical Interpretation,* edited by James H. Charlesworth and Craig Evans, 269–91. Sheffield: JSOT Press, 1993.

—————. *The Theology of the Book of Revelation.* Cambridge: Cambridge University Press, 1993.

Bauer, Walter. *Orthodoxy and Heresy in Earliest Christianity.* Edited by Robert Kraft and Gerhard Krodel. Minneapolis: Fortress Press, 1971.

Bean, George. *Aegean Turkey: An Archeological Guide.* New York: Praeger, 1966.

Becker, Udo. *The Continuum Encyclopedia of Symbols.* Trans. Lance W. Garmer. New York: Continuum, 1994.

Bedell, George, Leo Sandon, and Charles J. Wellborn. *Religion in America.* New York: Macmillan, 1975.

Bell, Albert A. "Date of John's Apocalypse: The Evidence of Some Roman Historians Reconsidered." *New Testament Studies* 25 (October 1978): 93–102.

Bell, Catherine. *Ritual Theory, Ritual Practice.* Oxford: Oxford University Press, 1992.

Benko, Stephen. *Pagan Rome and the Early Christians.* Bloomington: Indiana University Press, 1985.

Berger, Peter L., and Thomas Luckmann. *The Social Construction of Reality: A Treatise in the Sociology of Knowledge.* Garden City, NY: Anchor/Doubleday, 1966.

Bernstein, Alan E. *The Formation of Hell: Death and Retribution in the Ancient and Early Christian Worlds.* Ithaca: Cornell University Press, 1993.

Blasi, Anthony J. *A Sociology of Johannine Christianity.* Lewiston, NY: Mellen Press, 1996.

Blevins, James L. "The Genre of Revelation." *Review and Expositer* 77 (1980): 393–408.

—————. *Revelation.* Atlanta: John Knox, 1988.

Bloom, Harold. *Revelation of St. John the Divine.* New York: Chelsea House, 1988.

Boesak, Allan A. *Comfort and Protest: Reflections on the Apocalypse of John of Patmos.* Philadelphia: Westminster Press, 1987.

—————. "The Woman and the Dragon: Struggle and Victory in Revelation 12." *Sojourners* 16 (1987): 27–31.

Bonsirven, Joseph. *Palestinian Judaism in the Time of Jesus Christ.* Trans. W. Wolf. New York: Holt, Rinehart, and Winston, 1964.

Boorstin, Daniel J. *The Discoverers: A History of Man's Search to Know His World and Himself.* New York: Random House, 1983.

Booth, Wayne C. *A Rhetoric of Irony.* Chicago: University of Chicago Press, 1974.

—————. *The Rhetoric of Fiction.* 2d ed. Chicago: University of Chicago Press, 1983.

Boring, M. Eugene. "The Theology of Revelation: 'The Lord Our God Almighty Reigns.'" *Interpretation* 40 (1986): 257–69.

——————. *Revelation*. Interpretation: A Bible Commentary for Teaching and Preaching. Atlanta: John Knox, 1989.

——————. "The Voice of Jesus in the Apocalypse of John." *Novum Testamentum* 34 (October 1992): 334–59.

Botha, Pieter J. J. "God, Emperor Worship and Society: Contemporary Experiences and the Book of Revelation." *Neotestamentica* 22 (1988): 87–102.

Bowman, John W. "The Revelation to John: Its Dramatic Structure and Message." *Interpretation* 9 (1955): 436–53.

Boyer, J. L. "Are the Seven Letters of Revelation 2–3 Prophetic?" *Grace Theological Journal* 6 (1985): 67–273.

Brady, David. *The Contribution of British Writers Between 1560 and 1830 to the Interpretation of Revelation 13:16–18 (The Number of the Beast)*. Tübingen: Mohr (Siebeck), 1983.

Bratcher, Robert. *A Translator's Guide to the Revelation to John*. Helps for Translators Series. New York: United Bible Society, 1984.

Brewer, David Instone. *Techniques and Assumptions in Jewish Exegesis Before 70 CE*. Tübingen: J. C. B. Mohr (Paul Siebeck), 1991.

Brewer, Raymond R. "Revelation 4:6 and Translations Thereof." *Journal of Biblical Literature* 71, no. 4 (1952): 227–31.

Broughton, T. R. S. *Roman Asia*. An Economic Survey of Ancient Rome, no. 4. New York: Octagon Books, 1975.

Brown, Raymond E. *The Community of the Beloved Disciple: The Life, Loves, and Hates of an Individual Church in the New Testament*. Ramsey, NJ: Paulist Press, 1979.

Burkert, Walter. *Ancient Mystery Cults*. The Jackson Lectures. Cambridge, MA: Harvard University Press, 1987.

Cabannis, Allen. *Liturgy and Literature*. Tuscaloosa: University of Alabama Press, 1970.

Caird, G. B. *A Commentary on the Revelation of St. John the Divine*. Harper's New Testament Commentaries. New York: Harper and Row, 1966.

——————. *The Language and Imagery of the Bible*. Philadelphia: Westminster Press, 1979.

Calder, William M., Ernst Herzfeld and Samuel Guyer, eds. *Monumenta Asiae Minoris Antiqua*. 3 vols. London: Longmans, Green, and Co., 1928.

Campbell, J. B. *The Emperor and the Roman Army*. Oxford: Clarendon Press, 1984.

Castelli, Jim. "The Environmental Gospel According to James Watt." *Chicago Tribune*, October 25, 1981, B2.

Charles, R. H. *A Critical and Exegetical Commentary on the Revelation of St. John*. Edinburgh: T & T Clark, 1920.

Charlesworth, James H., ed. *The Old Testament Pseudepigrapha*. 2 vols. Garden City, NY: Doubleday, 1983–1985.

——————, ed. *The Messiah: Developments in Earliest Judaism and Christianity*. Minneapolis: Fortress Press, 1992.

Chatman, Seymour. *Story and Discourse: Narrative Structure in Fiction and Film.* Ithaca: Cornell University Press, 1978.

Collins, Adela Yarbro. *The Combat Myth in the Book of Revelation.* Chico, CA: Scholars Press, 1976.

——. *The Apocalypse.* New Testament Message, no. 22. Wilmington, DE: Michael Glazier, 1979.

——. "Dating the Apocalypse of John." *Biblical Research* 26 (1981): 33–45.

——. *Crisis and Catharsis: The Power of the Apocalypse.* Philadelphia: Westminster Press, 1984.

——. "Insiders and Outsiders in the Book of Revelation." In *To See Ourselves As Others See Us: Christians, Jews, "Others" in Late Antiquity,* edited by Jacob Neusner and Ernest S. Frerichs, 187–218. Atlanta: Scholars Press, 1985.

——. "Vilification and Self-Definition in the Book of Revelation." *Harvard Theological Review* 79 (1986): 308–20.

——. "Women's History and the Book of Revelation." In *Society of Biblical Literature 1987 Seminar Papers,* edited by Kent H. Richard, 80–91. Atlanta: Scholars Press, 1987.

——, ed. *Semeia 36: Early Christian Apocalypticism: Genre and Social Setting.* Decatur: Scholars Press, 1986.

Collins, John J. "Mythology of Holy War in Daniel and the Qumran War Scroll: A Point of Transition in Jewish Apocalyptic." *Vetus Testamentum* 25, no. 3 (1975): 596–612.

——. "Cosmos and Salvation: Jewish Wisdom and Apocalyptic in the Hellenistic Age." *History of Religions* 17 (1977): 122–42.

——. "Pseudonymity, Historical Reviews and the Genre of the Revelation of John." *Catholic Biblical Quarterly* 39 (1977): 329–43.

——. *The Apocalyptic Imagination: An Introduction to the Jewish Matrix of Christianity.* Los Angeles: Crossroad, 1984.

——. *Daniel: With an Introduction to Apocalyptic Literature.* Forms of the Old Testament Literature, 20. Grand Rapids: Eerdmans, 1984.

——. *The Scepter and the Star: The Messiahs of the Dead Sea Scrolls and Other Ancient Literature.* New York: Doubleday, 1995.

——, ed. *Semeia 14: Apocalypse: The Morphology of a Genre.* Chico, CA: Scholars Press, 1979.

Collins, John J., and James H. Charlesworth, eds. *Mysteries and Revelations: Apocalyptic Studies Since the Uppsala Colloquium.* JSP Sup Series, no. 9. Sheffield: Sheffield Academic Press, 1991.

Conacher, D. J. *Aeschylus' Oresteia: A Literary Commentary.* Toronto: University of Toronto Press, 1987.

Corsini, Eugenio. *The Apocalypse: The Perennial Revelation of Jesus Christ.* Good News Studies 5. Wilmington, DE: Michael Glazier, 1983.

Countryman, L. William. *The Mystical Way in the Fourth Gospel: Crossing Over Into God.* Philadelphia: Fortress Press, 1985.

Court, John M. *Myth and History in the Book of Revelation.* Atlanta: John Knox, 1979.

Crane, R. S. "The Concept of Plot." In *Approaches to the Novel*, edited by Robert Scholes 233–43. Revised ed. San Francisco: Chandler Publishing Co, 1966.

Culler, Jonathan. *The Pursuit of Signs: Semiotics, Literature, Deconstruction*. Ithaca: Cornell University Press, 1981.

Cullmann, Oscar. *Immortality of the Soul or Resurrection of the Dead? The Witness of the New Testament*. London: Epworth, 1958.

Culpepper, R. Alan. *John, the Son of Zebedee: The Life of a Legend*. Columbia: University of South Carolina Press, 1994.

van Daalen, D. H. *A Guide to the Revelation*. Theological Education Fund Study Guide. London: SPCK, 1986.

Davidson, Maxwell J. *Angels at Qumran: A Comparative Study of I Enoch 1–36, 72–108 and Sectarian Writings from Qumran*. Sheffield: Sheffield Press, 1992.

Day, John. *God's Conflict with the Dragon and the Sea in the Old Testament*. Cambridge: Cambridge University Press, 1985.

Dean-Otting, Mary. *Heavenly Journeys: A Study of the Motif in Hellenistic Jewish Literature*. Judentum und Umwelt, no. 8. Frankfurt am Main: Peter Lang, 1984.

Detweiler, Robert, ed. *Semeia 23: Derrida and Biblical Studies*. Atlanta: Scholars Press, 1982.

Dillistone, F. W. *The Power of Symbols in Religion and Culture*. New York: Crossroad, 1986.

Doty, William G. *Letters in Primitive Christianity*. Guides to Biblical Scholarship. Philadelphia: Fortress Press, 1973.

Draper, Jonathan A. "The Heavenly Feast of Tabernacles: Revelation 7:1–17." *Journal for the Study of the New Testament* 19 (1983): 133–47.

Du Rand, J. A. "The Imagery of the Heavenly Jerusalem (Revelation 21:9–22:5)." *Neotestamentica* 22 (1988): 65–86.

──────. "A Socio-Psychological View of the Effect of the Language (Parole) of the Apocalypse of John." *Neotestamentica* 24/2 (1990): 351–65.

Dunn, James D. G. *Unity and Diversity in the New Testament: An Inquiry Into the Character of Earliest Christianity*. 2d ed. Philadelphia: Trinity Press International, 1990.

──────. *The Epistle to the Galatians*. Black's New Testament Commentary. Peabody, MA: Hendrickson, 1993.

──────. "He Will Come Again." *Interpretation* 51, no. 1 (January 1997): 42–56.

Eisenstadt, S. N. and L. Roniger. *Patrons, Clients and Friends: Interpersonal Relations and the Structure of Trust in Society*. Cambridge: Cambridge University Press, 1984.

Eliade, Mircea. *The Sacred and the Profane: The Nature of Religion*. New York: Harper Torchbooks, 1957.

──────. *Cosmos and History: The Myth of the Eternal Return*. New York: Harper and Row, 1959.

──────. *Rites and Symbols of Initiation*. New York: Harper and Row, 1965.

Elliott, J. K. *The Apocryphal New Testament: A Collection of Apocryphal Christian Literature in an English Translation*. Oxford: Oxford University Press, 1994.

Elliott, John H. "Patronage and Clientism in Early Christian Society: A Reading Guide." *Forum* 3, no. 4 (1987): 39–48.

Ellul, Jacques. *Apocalypse: The Book of Revelation*. Trans. George Schreiner. New York: Seabury Press, 1977.

Erim, Kenan T. *Aphrodisias: City of Venus Aphrodite*. New York: Facts on File, 1986.

Farmer, Ron. "Divine Power in the Apocalypse to John: Revelation 4–5 in Process Hermeneutic." In *Society of Biblical Literature 1993 Seminar Papers*, 70–103. Atlanta: Scholars Press, 1993.

Farrer, Austin. *The Revelation of St. John the Divine*. Oxford: Oxford University Press, 1964.

——————. *A Rebirth of Images: The Making of St. John's Apocalypse*. Gloucester: Peter Smith, 1970, 1949.

Feen, Richard Harrow. "Nekyia as Apocalypse: A Study of Cicero's Dream of Scipio." *Journal of Religious Studies* 9 (1981): 28–34.

Fekkes, Jan III. "'His Bride Has Prepared Herself': Revelation 12–21 and Isaian Nuptial Imagery." *Journal of Biblical Literature* 109 (1990): 269–87.

Finegan, Jack. *The Archaeology of the New Testament: The Mediterranean World of the Early Christian Apostles*. Boulder, CO: Westview Press, 1981.

Fish, Stanley E. *Is There a Text in This Class?* Cambridge, MA: Harvard University Press, 1980.

Fishbane, Michael. *Judaism: Revelation and Traditions*. Religious Traditions of the World. San Francisco: Harper and Row, 1987.

Fontenrose, Joseph. *The Ritual Theory of Myth*. Folklore Studies, no. 18. Berkeley: University of California Press, 1966.

Ford, J. Massynbaerde. "Persecution and Martyrdom in the Book of Revelation." *Bible Today* 28 (1990): 141–6.

——————. "BTB Readers' Guide: Prostitution in the Ancient Mediterranean World." *Biblical Theology Bulletin* 23, no. 3 (1993): 128–34.

Forster, E. M. *Aspects of the Novel*. New York: Penguin Books, 1962.

Foster, Benjamin R. *From Distant Days: Myths, Tales, and Poetry of Ancient Mesopotamia*. Bethesda, MD: CDL Press, 1995.

——————. *Before the Muses: An Anthology of Akkadian Literature*. Bethesda, MD: CDL Press, 1996.

Fowler, Robert M. "Who Is 'the Reader' in Reader Response Criticism?" *Semeia* 31 (1985): 5–23.

Frey, J. B. *Corpus Inscriptionum Iudaicarum*. Roma: Pontifico Ins. di Archeologia, 1952.

Friesen, Steven J. *Twice Neokoros: Ephesus, Asia and the Cult of the Flavian Emperors*. Religions of the Greco-Roman World. Leiden: E. J. Brill, 1993.

——————. "Revelation, Realia, and Religion: Archaeology in the Interpretation of the Apocalypse." *Harvard Theological Review* 88 (1995): 291–314.

Gager, John G. *Kingdom and Community: The Social World of Early Christianity*. Prentice-Hall Studies in Religion Series. Englewood Cliffs: Prentice-Hall, 1975.

Galambush, Julie. *Jerusalem in the Book of Ezekiel: The City as Yahweh's Wife*. Atlanta: Scholars Press, 1992.

Gamble, Harry. *Books and Readers in the Early Church: A History of Early Christian Texts.* New Haven: Yale University Press, 1995.

Gartner, Bertil. "The Habakkuk Commentary (DSH) and the Gospel of Matthew." *Studia Theologica* 8 (1954): 1–24.

——————. *The Temple and the Community in Qumran and the New Testament.* SNTS Monograph Series 1. Cambridge: Cambridge University Press, 1965.

Gaustad, Edwin Scott. *A Religious History of America.* New York: Harper and Row, 1966.

Gellner, Ernest, and John Waterbury, eds. *Patrons and Clients in Mediterranean Societies.* London: Duckworth, 1977.

Genette, Gerard. *Narrative Discourse: An Essay in Method.* Trans. Jane Lewin. Ithaca: Cornell University Press, 1980.

Gennep, Arnold Van. *The Rites of Passage.* Chicago: University of Chicago Press, 1960.

Georgi, Dieter. "Who Is the True Prophet?" *Harvard Theological Review* 79 (1986): 100–26.

Georgues, Michael. "The Thousand-Year Reign (Revelation 20:1–6): Terrestrial or Celestial." *Catholic Biblical Quarterly* 47 (1985): 676–81.

Giblin, Charles Homer. "Recapitulation and the Literary Coherence of John's Apocalypse." *Catholic Biblical Quarterly,* 56 (January 1994): 81–95.

Golden, Leon. "Catharsis." *Transactions of the American Philological Association* xciii (1962): 51–60.

——————, "The Clarification Theory of Katharsis," *Hermes* 104/Band 4 (1976): 437–52.

Goldsworthy, G. *The Lamb and the Lion: The Gospel in Revelation.* Nashville: Thomas Nelson, 1985.

Good, E. M. "Apocalyptic as Comedy: The Book of Daniel." *Semeia* 32 (1984): 41–70.

Goodman, Felicitas D. *Where the Spirits Ride the Wind: Trance Journeys and Other Ecstatic Experiences.* Bloomington: Indiana University Press, 1990.

Goodspeed, Edgar J. *The Apostolic Fathers: An American Translation.* New York: Harper and Brothers, 1950.

Grabbe, Lester L. *Judaism from Cyrus to Hadrian. Volume Two: The Roman Period.* Minneapolis: Fortress Press, 1992.

Grimal, Pierre. *Roman Cities: Les villes romaines.* Trans. G. M. Woloch. Madison: University of Wisconsin Press, 1983.

Gruenwald, Ithamar. *Apocalyptic and Merkavah Mysticism.* Leiden: E. J. Brill, 1980.

Gunther, John J. *St. Paul's Opponents and Their Background. A Study of Apocalyptic and Jewish Sectarian Teachings.* Leiden: E. J. Brill, 1973.

Guthrie, Donald. "The Lamb in the Structure of the Book of Revelation." *Vox Evangelica* 12 (1981): 64–71.

——————. *The Relevance of John's Apocalypse.* Grand Rapids: Eerdmans, 1987.

Halperin, David J. *Faces of the Chariot: Early Jewish Responses to Ezekiel's Vision.* Tübingen: Mohr (Siebeck), 1988.

Hanfmann, George M. A. *Letters from Sardis.* Cambridge, MA: Harvard University Press, 1972.

Hanfmann, George M. A., and Jane C. Waldbaum. "New Excavations at Sardis and Some Problems of Western Anatolian Archaeology." In *Near Eastern Archaeology in the Twentieth Century*, edited by James A. Sanders, 307–26. Garden City, NY: Doubleday, 1970.

Hanson, Paul D. *The Dawn of Apocalyptic: The Historical and Sociological Roots of Jewish Apocalyptic Eschatology*. Revised ed. Philadelphia: Fortress Press, 1979.

———. *Visionaries and Their Apocalypses*. Issues in Religion and Theology 2. Philadelphia: Fortress Press, 1983.

Harding, Thomas. "Take Back the Apocalypse." *Touchstone* 3, no. 1 (January 1985): 29–35.

Harrington, Wilfrid. *Drama of Christ's Coming*. Wilmington, DE: Michael Glazier, 1987.

Harrington, Wilfrid J. *Revelation*. Collegeville, MN: Liturgical Press, 1993.

Harris, Michael. "The Literary Function of the Hymns in the Apocalypse." Ph.D. diss., Southern Baptist Theological Seminary, 1989.

Harris, William V. *Ancient Literacy*. Cambridge, MA: Harvard University Press, 1989.

Havelock, Eric A. *The Muse Learns to Write: Reflections on Orality and Literacy from Antiquity to the Present*. New Haven: Yale University Press, 1986.

Hellholm, David. "The Problem of Apocalyptic Genre and the Apocalypse of John." In *Society of Biblical Literature 1982 Seminar Papers*, 157–98. Atlanta: Scholars Press, 1982.

———. *Apocalypticism in the Mediterranean World and Near East: Proceedings of the International Colloquium on Apocalypticism, Uppsala, August 12–17, 1979*. 2d ed. Tübingen: Mohr-Siebeck, 1989.

Hemer, Colin. *Letters to the Seven Churches of Asia in Their Local Setting*. Journal for the Study of the New Testament Supplemental Series 11. Sheffield: JSOT/Sheffield Academic Press, 1986.

Hennecke, Edgar, and Wilhelm Schneemelcher. *New Testament Apocrypha*. Revised ed. 2. vols. Trans. R. McL. Wilson. Louisville: Westminster Press, 1991–1992.

van Henten, Jan Willem. "Dragon Myth and Imperial Ideology in Revelation 12–13." In *Society of Biblical Literature 1994 Seminar Papers*, 496–515. Atlanta: Scholars Press, 1994.

Heyob, Sharon Kelly. *The Cult of Isis among Women in the Greco-Roman World*. Leiden: E. J. Brill, 1973.

Higgins, A. J. B. "Jewish Messianic Belief in Justin Martyr's Dialogue with Trypho." *Novum Testamentum* 9 (1967): 298–305.

Hill, David. "Prophecy and Prophets in the Revelation of St. John." *New Testament Studies* 18 (1972): 402–18.

———. *New Testament Prophecy*. Atlanta: John Knox, 1979.

Himmelfarb, Martha. *Tours of Hell: An Apocalyptic Form in Jewish and Christian Literature*. Philadelphia: University of Pennsylvania Press, 1983.

———. *Ascent to Heaven in Jewish and Christian Apocalypses*. Oxford: Oxford University Press, 1993.

Hirsch, E. D. *Validity in Interpretation*. New Haven: Yale University Press, 1967.

———. *The Aims of Interpretation*. Chicago: University Chicago Press, 1976.

Hooke, S. H. "The Myth and Ritual Pattern in Jewish and Christian Apocalyptic."

In *The Labyrinth: Further Studies on the Relationship Between Myth and Ritual in the Ancient World*, 213–33. New York: Macmillan, 1935.

Horsley, Richard A. "Like One of the Prophets of Old: Two Types of Popular Prophets at the Time of Jesus." *Catholic Biblical Quarterly* 47 (1985): 435–63.

Humphrey, Edith M. "The Ladies and the Cities: Transformation and Identity in Four Apocalypses." Ph.D. thesis, McGill University, 1991.

————. "The Sweet and the Sour: Epics of Wrath and Return in the Apocalypse: The Apocalypse As Macro-Genre." In *Society of Biblical Literature 1991 Seminar Papers*, 451–60. Atlanta: Scholars Press, 1991.

Hurtado, Larry W. "Revelation 4–5 in the Light of Jewish Apocalyptic Analogies: A Distinctively Christian View of Heaven." *Journal for the Study of the New Testament* 25 (1985): 105–24.

Iser, Wolfgang. *The Implied Reader: Patterns of Communication in Prose Fiction from Bunyan to Beckett*. Baltimore: Johns Hopkins University Press, 1974.

————. *The Act of Reading: A Theory of Aesthetic Response*. Baltimore: Johns Hopkins University Press, 1978.

————. *Prospecting: From Reader Response to Literary Anthropology*. Baltimore: Johns Hopkins University Press, 1989.

Jacobson, Roman. "Closing Statement: Linguistics and Poetics." In *Style in Language*, edited by Thomas Sebeok, 350–77. Cambridge, MA: M.I.T. Press, 1960.

James, Montague Rhodes. *The Apocryphal New Testament: Being the Apocryphal Gospels, Acts, Epistles, and Apocalypses*. Oxford: Clarendon Press, 1924.

Jeske, Richard. *Revelation for Today: Images of Hope*. Philadelphia: Fortress Press, 1983.

————. "Spirit and Community in the Johannine Apocalypse." *New Testament Studies* 31, no. 3 (1985): 452–66.

Johnson, Sherman E. "Early Christianity in Asia Minor." *Journal of Biblical Literature* 77 (1958): 1–17.

Jones, A. H. M. *The Cities of the Eastern Roman Provinces*. Oxford: Clarendon Press, 1971, 1937.

Jones, Brian W. *The Emperor Titus*. London: Croom Helm, 1984.

Judge, E. A. *Rank and Status in the World of the Caesars and St. Paul*. The Broadhead Memorial Lecture 1981. Canterbury: University of Canterbury Press, 1982.

————. "The Reaction Against Classical Education in the New Testament." *Evangelical Review of Theology* 9, no. 2 (1985): 166–74.

————. "The Mark of the Beast, Revelation 13:16." *Tyndale Bulletin* 42/1 (1991): 158–60.

Juel, Donald H. *Messiah and Temple: The Trial of Jesus in the Gospel of Mark*. Society of Biblical Literature Dissertation Series, no. 31. Atlanta: Scholars Press, 1977.

Kang, Sa-Moon. *Divine War in the Old Testament and in the Ancient Near East*. Berlin: de Gruyter, 1989.

Kealy, Sean P. *Apocalypse of John*. Message of Biblical Spirituality Series, 15. Wilmington, DE: Michael Glazier, 1987.

Kee, Howard Clark. *Jesus in History: An Approach to the Study of the Gospels*. New York: Harcourt, Brace, Jovanovich, 1977.

Keel, Othmar. *The Symbolism of the Biblical World: Ancient Near Eastern Iconography and the Book of Psalms.* Trans. Timothy J. Hallett. New York: Seabury Press, 1978.

Kelber, Werner H. *The Oral and the Written Gospel: The Hermeneutics of Speaking and Writing in the Synoptic Tradition, Mark, Paul, and Q.* Philadelphia: Fortress Press, 1983.

Kenyon, Fredric G. *Books and Readers in Ancient Greece and Rome.* Oxford: Clarendon Press, 1932.

Keresztes, P. "The Jews, the Christians, and the Emperor Domitian." *Vigiliae Christianae* 27 (1973): 1–28.

Kermode, Frank. *The Sense of an Ending: Studies in the Theory of Fiction.* New York: Oxford University Press, 1967.

Kimelman, R. "Birkat Ha-Minim and the Lack of Evidence for an Anti-Christian Jewish Prayer in Antiquity." In *Jewish and Christian Self-Definition*, edited by E. P. Sanders, 2.226–44. Philadelphia: Fortress Press, 1981.

Kio, Stephen H. "Exodus as the Central Symbol of Liberation in the Book of Revelation." *Bible Translator* 40/1 (1989): 120–35.

Kirby, John. "The Rhetorical Situations of Revelation 1–3." *New Testament Studies* 34 (1988): 197–207.

Klassen, William. "Vengeance in the Apocalypse of John." *Catholic Biblical Quarterly* 28 (July 1966): 300–11.

Klausner, Joseph. *The Messianic Idea in Israel from the Beginning to the Completion of the Mishnah.* Trans. W. Stinespring. New York: Macmillan, 1955.

Koch, Klaus. *The Rediscovery of Apocalyptic.* Studies in Biblical Theology, Second Series, 22. London: SCM, 1972.

Koester, Craig R. *The Dwelling of God in the Old Testament, Intertestamental Jewish Literature, and the New Testament.* Washington, DC: Catholic Biblical Association, 1989.

Koester, Helmut, ed. *Ephesos: Metropolis of Asia.* Valley Forge, PA: Trinity Press International, 1995.

Kraabel, Alf Thomas. "Paganism and Judaism: The Sardis Evidence." In *Paganisme, Judaisme, Christianisme: Influences et affrontements dans le monde antique*, edited by André Benoit, M. Philonenko, and C. Vogel, 13–33. Paris: Boccard, 1978.

Kraybill, J. Nelson. *Imperial Cult and Commerce in John's Apocalypse.* Sheffield: Sheffield Press, 1996.

Kraemer, Ross S. *Her Share of the Blessings: Women's Religions among Pagans, Jews, and Christians in the Greco-Roman World.* New York and Oxford: Oxford University Press, 1992.

Kreitzer, Larry. "Hadrian and the Nero Redivivus Myth." *Zeitschrift für die Neutestamentliche Wissenschaft* 79 (1988): 92–95.

————. "Sibylline Oracles 8, the Roman Imperial Adventus Coinage of Hadrian and the Apocalypse of John." *Journal for the Study of the Pseudepigrapha* 4 (April 1989): 69–85.

Krodel, Gerhard A. *Revelation.* Augsburg Commentary on the New Testament. Minneapolis: Augsburg Publishing House, 1989.

Lambrecht, Jan. *L'Apocalypse johannique et l'apocalyptique dans le Nouveau Testament.* BETL 53. Louvain: University Press, 1980.

Lawrence, D. H. *Apocalypse*. New York: Viking Press, 1982, 1931.

Laws, Sophie. *In the Light of the Lamb: Imagery, Parody, and Theology in the Apocalypse of John*. Good News Studies, 31. Wilmington, DE: Michael Glazier, 1989.

Lefkowitz, Mary R., and Maureen B. Fant. *Women's Life in Greece and Rome: A Source Book in Translation*. 2d ed. Baltimore: Johns Hopkins University Press, 1992.

Leitch, Thomas M. *What Stories Are: Narrative Theory and Interpretation*. University Park: Pennsylvania State University Press, 1986.

Lévi-Strauss, Claude. "The Effectiveness of Symbols." In *Structural Anthropology*, 181–202. New York: Anchor/Doubleday, 1967.

Limberis, Vasiliki. *Divine Heiress: The Virgin Mary and the Creation of Christian Constantinople*. London: Routledge, 1994.

Lindsey, Hal, with C. C. Carlson. *The Late Great Planet Earth*. New York: Bantam Books, 1970.

Linton, Gregory. "Reading the Apocalypse as Apocalypse." In *Society of Biblical Literature 1991 Seminar Papers*, 161–86. Atlanta: Scholars Press, 1991.

Lopez, Barry. *Crow and Weasel*. San Francisco: North Point Press, 1990.

MacDonald, Dennis Ronald. *The Legend and the Apostle: The Battle for Paul in Story and Canon*. Philadelphia: Westminster Press, 1983.

MacKay, W. M. "Another Look at the Nicolaitans." *Evangelical Quarterly* 45 (1973): 111–15.

MacKenzie, Robert K. *The Author of the Apocalypse: A Review of the Prevailing Hypothesis of Jewish-Christian Authorship*. Lewiston NY: Mellen Press, 1997.

MacLeish, Archibald. *Collected Poems of Archibald MacLeish*. Boston: Houghton, Mifflin Co., 1962.

MacMullen, Ramsay. *Enemies of the Roman Order: Treason, Unrest, and Alienation in the Empire*. Cambridge, MA: Harvard University Press, 1966.

Magie, David. *Roman Rule in Asia Minor to the End of the Third Century after Christ*. 2 vols. Princeton: Princeton University Press, 1950.

Maier, Johann. *The Temple Scroll: An Introduction, Translation and Commentary*. JSOT Supplemental Series 34. Trans. R. T. White. Munich: Ernst Reinhardt Verlag, 1978 = Sheffield: Sheffield Academic Press, 1985.

Malina, Bruce J. *On the Genre and Message of Revelation: Star Visions and Sky Journeys*. Peabody, MA: Hendrickson, 1995.

Malina, Bruce J., and Jerome H. Neyrey. *Calling Jesus Names: The Social Value of Labels in Matthew*. Sonoma, CA: Polebridge Press, 1988.

Mays, James L. *Harper's Bible Commentary*. San Francisco: Harper and Row, 1988.

Mazzaferri, Frederick David. *The Genre of the Book of Revelation from a Source-Critical Perspective*. BZNW 54. Berlin/New York: de Gruyter, 1969.

McGinn, Bernard. *Antichrist: Two Thousand Years of the Human Fascination with Evil*. San Francisco: HarperSanFrancisco, 1994.

Meeks, Wayne A. *The Moral World of the First Christians*. Library of Early Christianity 6. Philadelphia: Westminster Press, 1986.

Menninger, Karl. *Number Words and Number Symbols: A Cultural History of Numbers*. Edited by Paul Broneer. Cambridge, MA: M.I.T. Press, 1969.

Metzger, Bruce M. *The Text of the New Testament: Its Transmission, Corruption and Restoration.* 3d ed. Oxford: Oxford University Press, 1992.
————. *Breaking the Code: Understanding the Book of Revelation.* Nashville: Abingdon, 1993.
Michaels, J. Ramsey. "Revelation 1.19 and the Narrative Voices of the Apocalypse." *New Testament Studies* 37, no. 4 (1991): 604–20.
————. *Interpreting the Book of Revelation.* Grand Rapids: Baker Book House, 1992.
Millar, Fergus. *The Emperor in the Roman World.* Ithaca: Cornell University Press, 1977.
Miller, Patrick D. *The Divine Warrior in Early Israel.* Harvard Semitic Monographs, 5. Cambridge, MA: Harvard University Press, 1973.
Minear, Paul S. *New Testament Apocalyptic.* Interpreting Biblical Texts. Nashville: Abingdon, 1981.
————. "Far as the Curse Is Found: The Point of Revelation 12:15–16." *Novum Testamentum* 33 (1991): 71–7.
Mommsen, Theodor. *The Provinces of the Roman Empire from Caesar to Diocletian.* Trans. with additions by William P. Dickson. London: Macmillan, 1909 = Chicago: Ares Publishers 1974 .
Moore, Michael S. *The Balaam Traditions: Their Character and Development.* Atlanta: Scholars Press, 1990.
Morris, Leon. *The Revelation of St. John.* 2d ed. Grand Rapids: Eerdmans, 1987.
Mounce, Robert H. *The Book of Revelation.* New International Commentary. Grand Rapids: Eerdmans, 1977.
Mowinckel, Sigmund. *He That Cometh.* Oxford: Blackwell, 1956.
Mussies, G. *The Morphology of Koine Greek as Used in the Apocalypse of St. John: A Study in Bilingualism.* Suppl NT, 27. Leiden: E. J. Brill, 1971.
Neihardt, John. *Black Elk Speaks: Being the Life Story of a Holy Man of the Oglala Sioux.* Lincoln: University of Nebraska Press, 1979.
Neusner, Jacob, trans. *Abodah Zarah: A Preliminary Translation and Explanation.* Chicago: University of Chicago Press, 1982.
Neusner, Jacob, William S. Green, and Jonathan Smith. *Judaisms and Their Messiahs at the Turn of the Christian Era.* Cambridge: Cambridge University Press, 1987.
Nickelsburg, George W. E. *Resurrection, Immortality, and Eternal Life in Intertestamental Judaism.* Harvard Theological Studies XXVI. Cambridge, MA: Harvard University Press, 1972.
Nickle, Keith F. *The Synoptic Gospels: Conflict and Consensus.* Atlanta: John Knox, 1980.
O'Brien, Tim. *The Things They Carried: A Work of Fiction.* Boston: Houghton Mifflin, 1990.
O'Day, Gail R. "I Have Overcome the World (John 16:33): Narrative Time in John 13–17." *Semeia* 53 (1991): 153–66.
O'Donovan, O. "The Political Thought of the Book of Revelation." *Tyndale Bulletin* 37 (1986): 61–94.
O'Leary, Stephen D. *Arguing the Apocalypse: A Theory of Millennial Rhetoric.* Oxford: Oxford University Press, 1994.

Ong, Walter J. *The Presence of the Word: Some Prolegomena for Cultural and Religious History*. New Haven: Yale University Press, 1967.

——. *Interfaces of the Word: Studies in the Evolution of Consciousness and Culture*. Ithaca: Cornell University Press, 1977.

——. *Orality and Literacy: The Technologizing of the Word*. New York: Methuen, 1982.

Oster, Richard E. "The Ephesian Artemis as an Opponent of Early Christianity." *Jahrbuch für Antike und Christentum* 19 (1976): 24–44.

——. *A Bibliography of Ancient Ephesus*. ATLA Bibliography Series, 19. Metuchen, NJ: Scarecrow Press, 1987.

Ozanne, C. G. "The Language of the Apocalypse." *Tyndale House Bulletin* 16 (1965): 3–9.

Parker, Harold M. "The Scriptures of the Author of the Revelation of John." *Iliff Review* 37 (1980): 35–51.

Patrides, C. A., and Joseph Wittreich. *The Apocalypse in English Renaissance Thought and Literature*. Ithaca: Cornell University Press, 1984.

Pearcy, L. T. "Galen's Pergamum." *Archaeology* 38 (1985): 33–9.

Peirce, Charles S. "Evolutionary Love." In *The Essential Peirce: Selected Philosophical Writings,* edited by Nathan Houser and Christian Klossel, 365–66. Bloomington: Indiana University Press, 1992.

Perkins, Pheme. *Resurrection: New Testament Witness and Contemporary Reflection*. Garden City, NY: Doubleday, 1984.

——. *Gnosticism and the New Testament*. Minneapolis: Fortress Press, 1993.

Perrin, Norman. *Jesus and the Language of the Kingdom: Symbol and Metaphor in New Testament Interpretation*. Philadelphia: Fortress Press, 1976.

Petersen, Norman R. *Rediscovering Paul: Philemon and the Sociology of Paul's Narrative World*. Philadelphia: Fortress Press, 1985.

Peterson, Eugene H. *Reversed Thunder: The Revelation of John and the Praying Imagination*. San Francisco: Harper and Row, 1988.

Pietersma, Albert. *Apocalypse of Elijah Based on P. Chester Beatty (2018)*. Society of Biblical Literature Texts and Translations 19. Chico, CA: Scholars Press, 1981.

Pilch, John J. *What Are They Saying about the Book of Revelation?* New York: Paulist Press, 1978.

Pilch, John J., and Bruce J. Malina. *Biblical Social Values and Their Meaning: A Handbook*. Peabody, MA: Hendrickson, 1993.

Piper, Otto A. "The Apocalypse of John and the Liturgy of the Ancient Church." *Church History* 20 (March 1951): 10–22.

Pippin, Tina. *Death and Desire: The Rhetoric of Gender in the Apocalypse of John*. Louisville: Westminster/John Knox, 1992.

——. "Eros and the End: Reading for Gender in the Apocalypse of John." *Semeia* 59 (1992): 193–210.

——. "The Heroine and the Whore: Fantasy and the Female in the Apocalypse of John." *Semeia* 60 (1992): 67–82.

——. "Wisdom and Apocalyptic in the Apocalypse of John: Desiring Sophia." In *In Search of Wisdom*, edited by L. Perdue et al., 285–95. Louisville: Westminster John Knox, 1993.

Pleket, H. W. "Domitian, the Senate and the Provinces." *Mnemosyne* 14 (1961): 296–315.

Pomeroy, Sarah B. *Women's History and Ancient History*. Chapel Hill: University of North Carolina Press, 1991.

Prevost, Jean-Pierre. *How to Read the Apocalypse*. New York: Crossroad, 1993.

Price, S. R. F. "Gods and Emperors: The Greek Language of the Roman Imperial Cult." *Journal of Hellenic Studies* 104 (1984): 79–95.

—————. *Rituals and Power: The Roman Imperial Cult in Asia Minor*. Cambridge: Cambridge University Press, 1984.

Prigent, Pierre. *Apocalypse et liturgie*. Neuchâtel, Suisse: Delachaux et Niestlé, 1964.

—————. "Au temps de l'Apocalypse, I: Domitien." *Revue d'Histoire et de Philosophie Religieuse* 54 (1974): 455–83.

Prince, Gerald. "Notes Toward a Categorization of Fictional 'Narratees'." *Genre* 4 (1971): 100–105.

—————. *A Dictionary of Narratology*. Lincoln: University of Nebraska Press, 1987.

Pritchard, James, ed. *Ancient Near Eastern Texts Relating to the Old Testament*. Princeton: Princeton University Press, 1955.

Rabinowitz, Peter J. *Before Reading: Narrative Conventions and the Politics of Interpretation*. Ithaca: Cornell University Press, 1987.

Rad, Gerhard von. *Holy War in Ancient Israel*. Grand Rapids: Eerdmans, 1991.

Ramsay, William M. *The Letters to the Seven Churches of Asia and Their Place in the Plan of the Apocalypse*. New York: Hodder and Stoughton, 1906.

—————. *The Social Basis of Roman Power in Asia Minor*. Aberdeen: Aberdeen University Press, 1941.

Ramsey, James B. *Book of Revelation: An Exposition of the First Eleven Chapters*. With an Introduction by Charles Hodge. Originally published as *The Spiritual Kingdom*. Carlisle, PA: Banner of Truth Trust, 1977.

Ratte, C., T. N. Howe, and C. Foss. "An Early Imperial Pseudodipteral Temple at Sardis." *American Journal of Archaeology* 90 (1986): 45–68.

Reddish, Mitchell. *Apocalyptic Literature: A Reader*. Nashville: Abingdon Press, 1990.

Reicke, Bo. "Die judische Apokalyptik und die johanneische Tiervision." In *Judéo-Christianisme*, edited by Birger Gerhardsson, 173–92. Paris: Éditions, 1972.

Reumann, John. *Supper of the Lord: The New Testament, Ecumenical Dialogues, and Faith and Order on Eucharist*. Philadelphia: Fortress Press, 1985.

Reynolds, Leighton Durham. *Scribes and Scholars: A Guide to the Transmission of Greek and Latin Literature*. Oxford: Clarendon Press, 1974.

Roberts, Colin H., and T. C. Skeat. *The Birth of the Codex*. Oxford: Oxford University Press, 1984.

Rollins, Wayne G. *The Gospels: Portraits of Christ*. Philadelphia: Westminster, 1963.

Roloff, Jürgen. *The Revelation of John: A Continental Commentary*. Trans. John E. Alsup. Minneapolis: Fortress Press, 1993.

Rouché, Charlotte. *Performers and Partisans at Aphrodisias in the Roman and Late*

Roman Periods. JRS Monograph, no. 6. London: Society for the Promotion of Roman Studies, 1993.

Rowley, H. H. *The Relevance of Apocalyptic: A Study of Jewish and Christian Apocalypses from Daniel to the Revelation.* 3d ed. New York: Association Press, 1963.

Ruiz, Jean-Pierre. *Ezekiel in the Apocalypse: The Transformation of Prophetic Language in Revelation 16:17–19:10.* European University Studies, no. 23. New York: Peter Lang, 1989.

—————. "Betwixt and Between on the Lord's Day: Liturgy and the Apocalypse." In *Society of Biblical Literature 1992 Seminar Papers,* 654–72. Atlanta: Scholars Press, 1992.

—————. "Hearing and Seeing But Not Saying: A Look at Revelation 10:4 and 2 Corinthians 12:4." In *Society of Biblical Literature 1994 Seminar Papers,* 182–202. Atlanta: Scholars Press, 1994.

—————. "The Apocalypse of John and Contemporary Roman Catholic Liturgy." *Worship* 68 (November 1994): 482–504.

Russell, Jeffrey Burton. *The Devil—Perceptions of Evil from Antiquity to Primitive Christianity.* Ithaca: Cornell University Press, 1977.

—————. *Satan: The Early Christian Tradition.* Ithaca: Cornell University Press, 1982.

Sanders, Jack T. *Schismatics, Sectarians, Dissidents, Deviants: The First 100 Years of Jewish Christian Relations.* Valley Forge, PA: Trinity International, 1993.

Savran, George W. *Telling and Retelling: Quotation in Biblical Narrative.* Bloomington: Indiana University Press, 1988.

Schick, Edwin A. *Revelation: The Last Book of the Bible.* Philadelphia: Fortress Press, 1977.

Schimmel, Annemarie. *The Mystery of Numbers.* New York: Oxford University Press, 1993.

Schoeps, Hans Joachim. *The Jewish-Christian Argument: A History of Theologies in Conflict.* Trans. David E. Green. New York: Holt, Rinehart and Winston, 1963.

Scholem, Gershom G. *Major Trends in Jewish Mysticism.* New York: Schocken, 1954.

Schowalter, Daniel N. *The Emperor and the Gods: Images from the Time of Trajan.* Minneapolis: Fortress Press, 1993.

Schüssler Fiorenza, Elisabeth. "Composition and Structure of the Book of Revelation." *Catholic Biblical Quarterly* 39 (1977): 344–66.

—————. "Apokalypsis and Propheteia: The Book of Revelation in the Context of Early Christian Prophecy." In *L'Apocalypse johannique et l'apocalyptique dans le Nouveau Testament,* edited by Jan Lambrecht, 105–27. Louvain: University Press, 1980.

—————. *Invitation to the Book of Revelation.* Garden City, NY: Image Doubleday, 1981.

—————. *The Book of Revelation: Justice and Judgment.* Philadelphia: Fortress Press, 1985.

—————. "The Followers of the Lamb: Visionary Rhetoric and Socio-Political Situation." *Semeia* 36 (1986): 123–46.

—————. "The Ethics of Interpretation: De-Centering Biblical Scholarship." *Journal of Biblical Literature* 107 (1988): 3–17.

—————. *Revelation: Vision of a Just World*. Minneapolis: Fortress Press, 1991.

Scott, Bernard Brandon. *Jesus, Symbol-Maker for the Kingdom*. Philadelphia: Fortress Press, 1981.

Searle, John. *Expression and Meaning: Studies in the Theory of Speech Acts*. Cambridge: Cambridge University Press, 1979.

Sebesta, Judith Lynn, and Larissa Bonfante. *The World of Roman Costume*. Wisconsin Studies in Classics. Madison: University of Wisconsin Press, 1993.

Segal, Alan F. "Heavenly Ascent in Hellenistic Judaism, Early Christianity, and Their Environment." *Aufstieg und Niedergang der römischen Welt* 23, no. 2 (1980): 1333–94.

Segal, Robert A. "The Application of Symbolic Anthropology to Religions of Greco-Roman World [Review Article]." *Religious Studies Review* 10 (July 1984): 216–23.

Shepherd, Massey H., Jr. *The Paschal Liturgy and the Apocalypse*. Ecumenical Studies in Worship 6. Atlanta: John Knox, 1960.

Sherwin-White, A. N. *The Letters of Pliny: A Historical and Social Commentary*. Oxford: Clarendon Press, 1966.

Siker, Jeffrey S. *Disinheriting the Jews: Abraham in Early Christian Controversy*. Louisville: Westminster/John Knox, 1991.

Silberman, Lou H., ed. *Semeia 39: Orality, Aurality and Biblical Narrative*. Atlanta: Scholars Press, 1987.

Simcox, William Henry. *The Revelation of St. John the Divine*. Revised by G. A. Simcox. Cambridge: Cambridge University Press, 1909.

Sleeper, C. Freeman. *The Victorious Christ: A Study of the Book of Revelation*. Louisville: Westminster/John Knox, 1996.

Smalley, Stephen S. "John's Revelation and John's Community." *Bulletin of the John Rylands Library* 69 (1987): 549–71.

Smallwood, E. Mary. *The Jews Under Roman Rule: From Pompey to Diocletian: A Study in Political Relations*. Leiden: E. J. Brill, 1976.

Smith, David. *The Disciple's Commentary on the New Testament*. Vol. 5. New York: Harper and Bros., 1932.

Smith, Robert H. "Why John Wrote the Apocalypse (Rev 1:9)." *Currents in Theology and Mission*, 22 (October 1995): 356–61.

Snyder, Howard. *Models of the Kingdom: Some Say God Rules the Heart. Some Say the Church. Some Say the Cosmos. Some Say.* Nashville: Abingdon Press, 1991.

Spanos, William V. "Breaking the Circle: Hermeneutics as Disclosure." *Boundary* 2, no. 5 (1977): 421–57.

Spinks, Leroy C. "Critical Examination of J. W. Bowman's Proposed Structure of the Revelation." *Evangelical Quarterly* 50 (1978): 211–22.

Stambaugh, John E. "The Functions of Roman Temples." *Aufstieg und Niedergang der römischen Welt II* 16, no. 1 (1978): 554–608.

Stendahl, Krister. *The School of St. Matthew and Its Use of the Old Testament*. Philadelphia: Fortress Press, 1968 = Uppsala, 1954.

Stevenson, Gregory M. "Conceptual Background to Golden Crown Imagery in the Apocalypse of John (4:4,10; 14:14)." *Journal of Biblical Literature* 114 (1995): 257–72.

Stock, Brian. *The Implications of Literacy: Written Language and Models of*

Interpretation in the Eleventh and Twelfth Centuries. Princeton: Princeton University Press, 1983.

Stone, Michael E. *Scriptures, Sects and Visions: A Profile of Judaism from Ezra to the Jewish Revolts.* Philadelphia: Fortress Press, 1980.

——. "Coherence and Inconsistency in the Apocalypses: The Case of 'the End' in 4 Ezra." *Journal of Biblical Literature* 102, no. 2 (1983): 229–43.

——. *Jewish Writings of the Second Temple: Apocrypha, Pseudepigrapha, Qumran Sectarian Writings, Philo, Josephus.* CRINT Section 2.2. Philadelphia: Fortress Press, 1984.

Stuckenbruck, Loren T. *Angel Veneration and Christology: A Study in Early Judaism and in the Christology of the Apocalypse of John.* WUNT 2/70. Tübingen: Mohr, 1995.

Suleiman, Susan R., and Inge Crosman, eds. *The Reader in the Text: Essays on Audience and Interpretation.* Princeton: Princeton University Press, 1980.

Sweet, J. P. M. *Revelation.* Philadelphia: Westminster Press, 1979; Philadelphia: Trinity Press International, 1990.

Swete, Henry B. *The Apocalypse of St. John.* 3d ed. London: Macmillan, 1909.

Takács, Sarolta. *Isis and Sarapis in the Roman World.* Leiden: E. J. Brill, 1995.

Talbert, Charles H. *The Apocalypse: A Reading of the Revelation of John.* Louisville: Westminster John Knox, 1994.

Thompson, Leonard L. "Cult and Eschatology in the Apocalypse of John." *Journal of Religion* 49 (1969): 330–50.

——. "Hymns in Early Christian Worship." *Anglican Theological Review* 55 (1973): 458–72.

——. "Domitianus Dominus: A Gloss on Statius Silvae 1.6.84." *American Journal of Philology* 105 (1984): 469–75.

——. "A Sociological Analysis of Tribulation in the Apocalypse of John." *Semeia* 36 (1986): 147–74.

——. "The Literary Unity of the Book of Revelation." *Bucknell Review* 33 (1989): 347–63.

——. *The Book of Revelation: Apocalypse and Empire.* Oxford: Oxford University Press, 1990.

——. "Mooring the Revelation in the Mediterranean." In *Society of Biblical Literature 1992 Seminar Papers,* 635–53. Atlanta: Scholars Press, 1992.

Thompson, Steven. *Apocalypse and Semitic Syntax.* Society for New Testament Studies Monograph Series 52. Cambridge: Cambridge University Press, 1985.

Thrupp, Sylvia. *Millennial Dreams in Action: Essays in Comparative Studies.* The Hague: Mouton, 1962.

Trebilco, Paul R. *Jewish Communities in Asia Minor.* Society for New Testament Studies Monograph Series 69. Cambridge: Cambridge University Press, 1991.

Trevett, Christine. "The Other Letters to the Churches of Asia: Apocalypse and Ignatius of Antioch." *Journal for the Study of the Old Testament* 37 (1989): 117–35.

Trompf, G. W., ed. *Cargo Cults and Millenarian Movements.* Berlin and New York: Mouton de Gruyter, 1990.

Trudinger, Paul. "The 'Nero Redivivus' Rumour and the Date of the Apocalypse of John." *St. Mark's Review* 131 (September 1987): 43–4.

Turner, Victor W. *The Ritual Process: Structure and Anti-Structure.* Ithaca: Cornell University Press, 1969.

Ulfgard, Haken. *Feast and Future: Revelation 7:9–17 and the Feast of Tabernacles.* Coniectanea Biblica. New Testament Series 22. Stockholm: Almqvist and Wiksell, 1989.

Vanni, Ugo. "The Ecclesial Assembly: 'Interpreting Subject' of the Apocalypse." *Religious Studies Bulletin* 4, no. 2 (May 1984): 79–85.

————. "Liturgical Dialogue as a Literary Form in the Book of Revelation." *New Testament Studies* 37 (1991): 348–72.

Vermes, Geza. *The Dead Sea Scrolls in English.* New York: Penguin, 1995.

De Villiers, P. G. R. "The Lord Was Crucified in Sodom and Egypt: Symbols in the Apocalypse of John." *Neotestamentica* 22 (1988): 125–38.

Vorster, W.S. "'Genre' and the Revelation of John: A Study in Text, Context and Intertext." *Neotestamentica* 22 (1988): 103–23.

Wagnar, Warren M. *Terminal Visions: The Literature of Last Things.* Bloomington: Indiana University Press, 1982.

Wainwright, Arthur. *Mysterious Apocalypse: Interpreting the Book of Revelation.* Nashville: Abingdon Press, 1993.

Wainwright, Geoffrey. *Eucharist and Eschatology.* Oxford: Oxford University Press, 1981.

Walker, William O. "The Son of Man: Some Recent Developments." *Catholic Biblical Quarterly* 45 (1983): 584–607.

Wall, Robert W. *Revelation.* New International Biblical Commentary 18. Peabody, MA: Hendrikson, 1991. .

Wallace-Hadrill, Andrew. *Patronage in Ancient Society.* London: Routledge, 1989.

Wenham, David. *The Jesus Tradition Outside the Gospels.* Sheffield: JSOT/Sheffield Academic Press, 1985.

White, John L. *Light from Ancient Letters.* Foundations and Facets: New Testament. Philadelphia: Fortress Press, 1986.

White, L. M. *Building God's House in the Roman World: Architectural Adaptation Among Pagans, Jews, and Christians.* Baltimore: Johns Hopkins University Press, 1990.

Wilder, Amos N. *Early Christian Rhetoric: The Language of the Gospel.* Cambridge, MA: Harvard University Press, 1971.

Willis, Wendell Lee. *Idol Meat in Corinth: The Pauline Argument in I Corinthians 8 and 10.* Society of Biblical Literature Dissertation Series 68. Atlanta: Scholars Press, 1985.

Wilson, J. Christian. "The Problem of the Domitianic Date of Revelation." *New Testament Studies* 39 (1993): 586–605.

Wilson, Robert R. "From Prophecy to Apocalyptic: Reflections on the Shape of Israelite Religion." *Semeia* 21 (1982): 79–95.

Wink, Walter. *Naming the Powers: The Language of Power in the New Testament.* Philadelphia: Fortress Press, 1984.

————. *Unmasking the Powers: The Invisible Forces That Determine Human Existence.* Minneapolis: Fortress Press, 1986.

————. *Engaging the Powers: Discernment and Resistance in a World of Domination.* Minneapolis: Fortress Press, 1992.

Wise, Michael, Martin Abegg, Jr., and Edward Cook. *The Dead Sea Scrolls: A New Translation*. San Francisco: HarperSanFrancisco, 1996.

Witt, R. E. *Isis in the Graeco-Roman World*. Ithaca: Cornell University Press, 1971.

Worsley, Peter. *The Trumpet Shall Sound: A Study of "Cargo" Cults in Melanesia*. 2d ed. New York: Schocken Books, 1968.

Yamauchi, Edwin M. *New Testament Cities in Western Asia Minor*. Grand Rapids: Baker Book House, 1987.

Zamora, Lois Parkinson, ed. *The Apocalyptic Vision in America: Interdisciplinary Essays on Myth and Culture*. Bowling Green, OH: Bowling Green University Popular Press, 1982.

INDEX

144,000, 74, 87
666, 107, 128
  as humanity, 108
  as Nero, 108

Abdulla, Adnan K., 197n55
Abegg, Martin, 193n34
abyss, 64, 139, 141
Achtemeier, Paul J., 187n4
Akurgal, Ekrem, 187n34, 189n31, 195n29
Albanese, Catherine, 185n8
altars, types of, 86
ambiguity, 67
angels, 129, 141
  meaning of, 40, 55
  work of, 88
animals, meaning of, 9
Antiochus IV, 154
aorist tense, 129
Apocalypse
  as story, 1
  ethics of, 131
  meaning of term, 27
  traits of, 5, 27, 155–58
apocalyptic expectations, 154
apocalyptic ideology, 154–56
Apollo, 112, 123
Apuleius, 47, 81
Aristotle, 8n14, 178
Armagedon
  (see Harmagedon)
Armstrong, Paul B., 185n7
Artemis, Temple of, 43
Asclepias, 43
astrology, 32, 44, 46, 123, 131
audience, 51
  implied, 16, 35, 51, 159
  of Revelation, 16

Augustine, 61, 79
Augustus, 47, 174
  Temple of, 43
Aune, David E., 185n10, 186n23, 188n17,
    190n6, 191n28, 196n43
Austin, Jane L., 196n51
author, 28, 34, 159–63
  implied, 52, 159

Babylon, 17, 133
  as commercial center, 135
  as whore, 133
  fall of, 119, 129, 133–35
  stories from, 32
Babylonian creation myth, 104
Balaam, 45, 50, 57, 162
Barr, David L., 187n42, 190n12, 196n46,
    196n52
beast, 18, 39, 64, 75, 94, 107, 109, 118,
    127, 180
  and lamb, 107
  actions of, 119, 126
  as false prophet, 132
  as humanity, 108
  characterization of, 107
  destroyed, 137, 138
  interpretation of, 133
  mark of, 127, 139, 165
  slain head, 127
  time of, 118
  unexplained appearance, 75
Bedell, George, 194n2
Behemoth, 108
Bell, Catherine, 196n45
Berger, Peter, 188n16
birth pangs, 102, 126
Boesak, Allan A., 187n40
Bonfante, Larissa, 193n31